In accordance with the latest syllabus prescribed by the Central Board of Secondary Education, New Delhi, for Class XI Examination.

CBSE

A TEXT BOOK OF

LEGAL STUDIES

For Class XI

By

Gurmeet Kaur

LLB (Gold Medalist), LLM, Ph.D (Law)

Asstt. Professor, School of Law

Indira Gandhi National Open University (IGNOU)

Edited by

Souvik Chatterji

LLM (Warwick University, UK), Ph.D (Law)

Asstt. Professor, National Law University, Jodhpur

OSWAL PUBLISHERS

1/12, Sahitya Kunj, M. G. Road, AGRA-282 002

Edition : 2020

Price : 321 /-

ISBN : 978-93-88623-95-7

OSWAL PUBLISHERS

Head office	:	1/12, Sahitya Kunj, M.G. Road, Agra-282 002
Phone	:	(0562) 2527771– 4, +91 75340 77222
E-mail	:	contact@oswalpublishers.com, sales@oswalpublishers.com
Website	:	www.oswalpublishers.com
Facebook link	:	https://www.facebook.com/oswalpublishersindia
Available at	:	amazon.in, Flipkart, snapdeal, PayTM

Preface

Law is socially significant and manifests itself in all realms of life. The law as a legal order distributes and defines the powers of organs of government, regulates the business, raises revenue and protects the public and private interests through various redressal mechanisms. The legal system of any nation is based on legal sources such as customs, precedents, codification, Case Laws and legislation, principles of statutory interpretation and is reflected by analysis of legal concepts such as property, contract, torts, fundamental rights etc.

The legal studies is an academic endeavor that focuses on learning meaning, purpose and application of law and its interrelation with political science, morality and justice. This book on An Introduction to the law, legal and justice system in India has been written with the principle mission to serve as a text for the undergraduate course on legal studies. The present book is designed to stimulate critical understanding of and inquiry about the theoretical frameworks of concept of state/nation, organs of government and separation of powers between them, the constitutional frame work of India, Civil and Criminal Courts and Process in India. This book is a modest attempt to examine nature and sources of Law, how law shapes a legal system and is shaped by political, economic, and cultural forces that lead to law reforms and the institutional framework in India for the civil, criminal and family justice system in a simple and understandable language.

The suggested readings and the references cited has also made the text valuable and informative for the law students, teachers, researchers and anyone interested in knowing the concept and various systems of law, features of constitution of India, basic fundamental and legal rights, structure of civil and criminal courts and its process, concepts of Family law : marriage and divorce, marital rights and obligations of spouses, child rights and the institutional and legal Framework for family justice system in India.

I owe my debt to all the writers, books and websites which I have consulted in coming out with this book especially, the authors like Salmond, Holland, Thomas Hobbes, J.W. Garner, Steven Vago and Muhammad Basheer Ahmad to name a few. I am also thankful to have Dr. Souvik Chatterji, who deserve a special mention for his unconditional and uninterrupted support and the editorial team of oswal publications for their advice, assistance and active support throughout this project.

My special thanks and gratitude goes to my father and husband who have always been an inspirational source, friend and guide.

Author

SYLLABUS

Legal Studies (Code 074)

One Paper   Times : 3 hours   Marks : 100

Units	Periods	Marks
1. Theory and Nature of Political Institutions	40	15
2. Nature and Sources of Law	45	15
3. Historical Evolution of Indian Legal System	45	10
4. Judiciary : Constitutional, Civil and Criminal Courts and Process	45	20
5. Family Justice System	45	20
6. Project on Unit 2		20
Total	220	100

Course Contents :	Periods
1. Theory and Nature of Political Institutions Concept of State/Nation Organs of Government – Legislative, Executive and Judiciary Separation of Powers – Parliamentary Sovereignty and Judicial Independence Basic Features of Constitution of India	40
2. Nature and Sources of Law Nature, Meaning and School of law Classification of Law–International and Municipal law Source of Law–Custom, Legislation and Precedent Law Reform	45
3. Historical Evolution of Indian Legal System Ancient Indian Law Administration of Justice in British India Marking of the Indian Constitution	45
4. Judiciary : Constitutional, Civil and Criminal Courts and Process Constitution–Roles and Impartiality Hierarchy of Courts The Civil Court Structure Structure and Functioning of Criminal Courts in India Other Courts in India	45
5. Family Justice System Introduction to Family Laws Institutional Framework Marriage and Divorce Children Domestic Violence Property, Succession and Inheritance	45
6. Project on Unit 2 In Class XI, differentiate between ratio decidendi and obiter dicta of any 5 case laws related to the curriculum The project should speak of the facts, issue and the decision of the case clearly differentiating between the obiter and ratio A viva along with the file will be assessed in the following format Presentation and preparation of file–5 marks Research–5 marks Application of the understanding of legal context–5 marks Viva–5 marks	

CONTENTS

★★★★

1. Theory and Nature of Political Institutions

Concept of State

The concept of state has emerged out of society which is governed by certain legal norms and sets of rules and regulations. For natural law philosopher, Aristotle (384-322 BCE) : city-state and political rule are natural. The state is defined by Aristotle as "a body of citizens sufficing for the purposes of life." (Pol. 1275b 20-21). Every state is a community and every community is established with a view to some good. The state itself is made up of many communities (*Politics* book I. 1252a 25-30). To him, the state is a union of families and villages having for its end, a perfect and self-sufficient life.

Although there is no accepted definition of the state, it has been defined by various philosophers and Jurists in their own way. The state has been looked upon as the highest moral and ethical institution. (See Plato, Aristotle, Rousseau, Hegel, Kant and Green). The state, for *Rousseau*, was the collective moral person formed by the whole body of citizens; the government was merely an executive organ by which the state-will could be carried into effect. ("Contract Social," Bk. III, Ch. 1). *Bodin*, defines state as "an association of families and their common affairs is governed by supreme power and reason." (De Republica).

Holland defines a state as an assemblage of human beings, generally occupying certain territory, among whom the will of the majority or of an ascertainable class of persons is by the strength of such a majority or class made to prevail against any of their number who opposes it.

Grotius defined the state, as "a perfect society of free men united for the sake of enjoying the advantages of right and the common utility." Savigny- "The state is the bodily form of the spiritual community of the nation" (Savigny, "System des romischenRechts," vol. I, p. 22).

Let us see below the definition of state by various jurists and philosophers in brief :

Concept of State	Philosophers
A body of citizens sufficing for the purposes of life.	Aristotle
Collective moral person formed by the whole body of citizens.	Rousseau
An association of families.	Bodin
An assemblage of human beings, generally occupying certain territory.	Hobbes
Bodily form of the spiritual community of the nation	Savigny
Society of free men united for the sake of enjoying the advantages of right and the common utility.	Grotious
System of relations, men establish among themselves as means of securing certain objects and to carry out activities within system of order.	J. l. Brierly
Regulates the outstanding external relationships of men in society.	R.N. Maciver
Is politically organised people of a definite territory.	Bluntschli
A particular portion of mankind viewed as an organised unit.	Burgess
A human community that (successfully) claims the monopoly of the legitimate use of physical force within a given territory.	Weber
Geographically delimited segment of human society united by common obedience to a single sovereign.	Frederick M. Watkins
As a territorial area in which a population is governed by a set of political authorities, and which successfully claims the compliance of the citizenry for its laws, and it is able to secure such compliance by its monopolistic control of legitimate force.	Geoffrey K. Roberts

Nature and Role of State

Over the period of times, different writers have attempted to describe the nature of state through different notions. Plato and Aristotle propounded the ethical notion of the nature of the state and considered state as natural institution representing the highest morality. This view was supported by writers like Rousseau, Kant, Hegel and T. H. Green.

The writers like Bodin, Hobbes, Bentham, Beccaria and Austin propounded legal notion of state having distinctive personality and will of its own, regulating human behaviour. They asserted that the state is the result of social contract or an agreement between the people and the sovereigns.

The philosophers like Adam Smith, Jeremy Bentham and Herbert Spencer considered that the state is necessary to maintain law and order in the society. On the other hand, anarchist viewed that the political authority in all its form, and especially in the form of the state, is both evil and unnecessary. The state is a compulsory and coercive authority. With the development in human personality, the need for state as an agency for regulating human conduct became less necessary.

According to the Pluralist view, the state is a mechanism through which the interests of every member of the state are represented, pluralism believes in the vitality and the legitimacy of self-governing associations as a means of organising social life. The political representation by associations like trade unions, churches, and voluntary bodies implies that group access to government to ensure broad democratic responsiveness. The important advocates of this view are MacIver and Laski.

As per the totalitarian view of the state, the state has absolute powers and unlimited control over the individuals but there are no rights of individuals against the state. Philosophers like Hegel and Nietzsche, writers like Bernhardi and Treitschke and dictators like Mussolini and Hitler supported the totalitarian notion of the state.

The *Classical* liberals believed in a 'minimal' state, whose function is limited to the maintenance of domestic order and personal security. They think that human beings are essentially self-interested and largely self-sufficient and as far as possible, people should be responsible for their own lives and circumstances. According to Locke, the legitimate role of government is limited to the protection of 'life, liberty and property'. Therefore, the functions of governments should not extend beyond the 'minimal' functions of preserving public order and protecting property, providing defence against external attack and ensuring that contracts are enforced. The view was also supported by political thinkers Robert Nozick, Ayn Rand (1905–82), Murray Rothbard (1926–95) and David Friedman.

The Modern liberalism or welfare liberalism has linked freedom to personal development and self-realisation and believe that state intervention can enlarge liberty by safeguarding individuals from the social evils that blight their existence. The concept of state as a welfare was supported by J. S. Mill, T. H. Green, MacIver and Laski. According to this view, the state is not merely an agency for the maintenance of law and order but also plays a key role in the protection and promotion of the economic and social welfare of its citizens. This notion of state as welfare state was criticized by the classical liberals and free-market economists as the state intervention in social and economic affairs in the nineteenth century but the function of state as welfare state has been widely recognised in modern times. The function of modern welfare state implies an efficient administration, maintenance of law and order, health services and providing education to the masses, speedy justice for the people, social and legal services and eradication of social evils.

> **Do you know?**
>
> India is a welfare state, the Constitution of India aims to establish political, social and economic justice to the people and the Directive Principles of State Policy incorporated in Part IV (Article 36-51) of the Constitution of India promote the idea of a welfare state.

Theories on the Origin of the State

There are different theories on origin of state and are discussed below :

Theory of Kinship

♦ In this theory, the state is considered to be based on relationship in the family. The head of the family had the command over other member of the family.

♦ Then the group of families formed into clans and the group of clans formed into tribes. The families, clans and tribes together formed a society.

♦ Memberships were based on blood relationship.

♦ As per this theory, the first element of social unity was the blood relationship.

♦ The council of elders of the tribe used to make rules for the tribe which all tribe members had to follow. There used to be a chief of the tribe as a political head.

♦ R.M. MacIver was the supporter of this theory.

Divine Right Theory–According to Plato, state cannot be established without faith in God. The theory purports that state is established and governed by God. The king is appointed by the god as his agent and king is responsible to God for his actions. It is the duty of all people to obey the ruler as they would obey God and any opposition to the divine right of kings is subject of punishment for sin. "God is King, let the Earth rejoice," saith the Psalmist. (Psal. 96. 1) and again, "God is King though the Nations be angry; and he that sitteth on the Cherubins, though the earth be moved." (Psal. 98. 1) (See Thomas Hobbes, *Leviathan*). The divine theory was supported by James, Roberfilmers and Bossuet.

Bossuet in his "Politics as derived from the Scriptures," had asserted that God established kings as his ministers through whom he ruled over his people, like a father over his children, and who were accountable only to him for their acts.

The theory has religious sanctity among Jew, Christians, Muslims and Hindus. The text of Manu Smriti, Arthshastra provides for rule of divine law to be followed by the king as the incarnation of God having divine rights. The Mahabharata also contains many passages which suggest the divine origin of the state. In several earlier civilisations such as the Aztec and Mayan, and those of Egypt, China, and Japan widely believed that the People should obey their ruler as they obeyed God. In the sixteenth and seventeenth centuries in England, the theory of the Divine Right of king prevailed but this theory was considered as unprogressive and only as a religious explanation of state. Later in seventeen and eighteenth century, the social contract theory of origin of state was advanced.

Social Contract Theory–According to this theory, man originally lived in a state of nature, where every-one was equal in the sense that all had everything required for their life. The theory was advocated by various writers like:

◆ Richard Hooker - Treatise on *Ecclesiastical Polity,* 1594;

◆ Grotius- Treatise on the *Law of War and of Peace,* 1625;

◆ Thomas Hobbes - *Leviathan,* 1651;

◆ John Locke - Two Treatises of Government,1690;

◆ J. J. Rousseau - Le Contrat social ("The Social Contract" 1762)

The main components of social contract theory are :

◆ Men lived in a 'state of nature'.

◆ The people agreed with one another by a social contract to create a state.

◆ State arose out of a voluntary act of free people and is not the divine institution.

◆ The people are the sole source of political power.

◆ The state came in to existence only to serve the will of the people.

◆ They are free to give or to withhold that power as they choose.

The origin of the term social contract can be found in the writings of *Plato*. However, English philosopher *Thomas Hobbes* expanded on the idea when he wrote *Leviathan* in response to the English Civil War (Martin Kelly).

◆ *Hobbes* opined that society came into being as a means for the protection of men against the consequences of their own nature.

◆ A State of Nature was anarchy that makes life "poor, nasty, brutish and short", because of four features of the human condition *viz.* equality of need; scarcity; the essential equality of human power and limited altruism.

◆ In a "state of nature", there are no social good, no farming, industry, education, housing, technology etc. It is due to the fact that the social cooperation needed to produce these things doesn't exist.

◆ In order to avoid this fate, there must be guarantees that people will not harm one another, and the people must be able to rely on one another to keep their agreements and thus arose the need for government as the provider of the guarantees.

◆ In establishing a government, people give up some of their personal freedom (the freedom of anarchy, such as it is) and give the government the authority to enforce laws and agreements.

◆ Those living under a government are parties to a social contract. Each person agrees to follow the laws of the state on the condition that everyone else does the same.

◆ That way, we are all relatively safe from each other and we all benefit from the other social goods that will result.

◆ According to *Locke,* the law of nature regulates the life of the people in the state of nature. It ensures that the individual enjoy the right to life, liberty and property.

◆ The life of the people in the state of nature was happy, peaceful but inconvenient as there was no agency to interpret natural law and enforce the natural rights of people in the state of nature.

◆ Therefore, according to Locke, people entered into two contracts such as :

1. **Social contract :** Contract was among the people and led to formation of civil society.

2. **Governmental :** It took place between the people and the government/ruler to establish state for the development of system of law. The ruler as per Locke can be changed by revolt of the people in case of abuse of power.

Locke's conception of the state of nature thus differs from that of Hobbes. According to Locke, the liberty of the individual is not limited by human law, yet it is limited by the law of nature and the dictates of reason; and hence the "natural" man has a right, not to everything he is physically capable of appropriating, but only to such things as he can use without depriving others of a similar advantage.

- As per Rousseau, the man in the state of nature used the life of Novel Savage.
- But with the passage of time and emergence of the institution of private property, the peaceful life of the state was disturbed.
- Because of such disturbance, there were mutual conflict between human beings.
- To avoid such conflict, human beings entered into a social contract among themselves.
- By such social contract, the individual surrendered all his rights to the collective will.
- This collective will was known as General Will of the people *i.e.*, Sovereign. This transform the state of nature into civil state.

But during the nineteenth century, the social contract theory had to face criticism and was rejected by many scholars like Ludwig von Haller, Jeremy Bentham, Sir Henry Maine, Thomas Hill Green, Edmund Burke, Professor Bluntschli, and Sir Frederick Pollock to name a few.

- The theory was criticised to be unhistorical, without any proof.
- The theory was also rejected upon grounds of philosophy and reason.
- The theory was criticised on logical grounds. According to Lieber, "If we mean (by the contract theory), an actual agreement at some definite time between human beings running wild, who enter after mature deliberation into a solemn covenant, and that a contract of this sort with a particular government or dynasty is binding forever, the idea is radically wrong and leads to dangerous conclusions, favoring tyranny or licentiousness." ("Political Ethics," vol. I, pp. 283-294.).
- According to McKechnie, all men ought to have a share in moulding the form of the constitution of a state from a logical and intelligible position; but to hold that, the individual atoms vote the state itself into existence as the result of an unanimous plebiscite is absurd.

The Patriarchal and Matriarchal Theories–In the nineteenth century, Sir Henry Maine, was the main exponent of the Patriarchal theory. In his "Ancient Law", *Maine* asserts that the patriarchal theory is defined as the theory of the origin of society in separate families, held together by the authority and protection of the eldest male descendant. Regarding the genesis of society, he says: "The elementary group is the family connected by common subjection to the highest male descendant. The aggregation of families forms the gens or house. The aggregation of houses makes the tribe. The aggregation of tribes constitutes the commonwealth. The other supporters of the patriarchal theory are the English writer Donisthorpe and the French writer Duguit.

One of the chief weaknesses of the Patriarchal society is its simplicity. The considerable number of writers hold that not the patriarchal but the matriarchal family theory exist and the chief exponents of matriarchal family theory: McLennan, in his Patriarchal Theory, Jenks, in his History of Politics and Morgan, in his Ancient Society has opined that there is considerable evidence to show that the primitive family had no common male head, but that kinship was traced through females. Before the patriarchal family, there was the matriarchal family. The patriarchal family is possible where either monogamy or polygamy exists, but the earliest form of marriage relation was polyandry, according to which one woman had several husbands. Descent in such a state could only be through the female. The prevalence of queens in Malabar and the power of princesses among the Marathas may be cited as evidence in favour of the matriarchal theory. (R. N. Gilchrist, 1921)

The Force Theory–The theory of Force states that civil society originated in the subjugation of the weaker by the stronger. It was advocated by writers of the individualist school to prove that it is in tribe nature of society that the stronger should prevail against the weaker. Force and compulsion have played an important part in the consolidation of states and in the erection of new state forms as the state, unlike all other associations of mankind, possesses the power to compel obedience from its members and no objection could be made to it and this tends to correct the false impression that was created by the contract theory that political authority always rests upon the voluntary consent of those who are subjected to it (see Bluntschli, Allgemeine Staatslehre, Bk. IV). However the writers like Leacock, has pointed out that the force can be only be one element of origin of state and not the sole factor; Mussolini has criticised the theory as supportive of war; and T. H. Green has stated that it did not take in to account moral basis of origin of state.

Types of state systems evolved in World Polity

The various types of states existed at different times in the world as a result of several factors such as kinship, religion, property, war, technical development and political consciousness and the modern nation-states has evolved over a period of time. The same is represented below in chart :

The Tribal State–The tribal states were actually not state or had attributes of the state in any sense of the term. It was a state formed by sized tribe with tribal chief as head, who was really the first among the equals, who dictated terms and the members of the tribe obeyed him. The tribal states did not have permanent territory and people kept on moving. The membership of the tribal state was determined by birth, the tribes were based on the kinship; they were integrated together by common religion, cultural and trade practices based on social equality.

The Oriental Empire–In due course, Nomadic tribes settled in places where their basic needs of food to eat, water to drink and pastures for their cattle and other necessities were fulfilled. The oriental empires were land empires based on conquest and force. It was characterised with the existence of social rigidity, caste system, inequality of the rich and the poor, the free and the slave, the warrior nobles and the servile peasants, the priestly class and the ignorant masses. The oriental king or emperor was the master of but the autocracy of the oriental kings was limited by custom, religion and tradition.

The Greek City-State–Several city states emerged due to local patriotism in ancient Greece with a variety of political institution. Athens and Sparta were two such city-states which attained a higher level of political development and individual liberty. The other city states were Orinth, Argos, Thebes and Attica.

The Roman Empire (27 BC - 476 AD)–After the downfall of the Greek city-states, the Roman state emerged which passed through several periods. The first period was that of the monarchical state, the king was the head of the state and also the chief priest of the community. The king was required to consult the Council of Elders and follow their advice. During this period, the nobles known as the Patricians shared political power with a monarch but the Plebians that included average working citizens of Rome like farmers, bakers, builders or craftsmen enjoyed no political rights. Gradually, Monarchy was succeeded by a Republic and both Patricians and Plebians got equal political and civil rights. During this period Rome started annexing the neighbouring territories and consequently, the Republic gave way to the Roman Empire which extended over Austria, Germany, France, Spain, England, the Balkans, Greece, Asia Minor and the whole of the Mediterranean coast and its hinterland. In due courses of time, the Roman Empire began to decay as institutions of democracy and local self-government disappeared.

Feudal State–After the fall of the Roman Empire, feudalism emerged as the consequence and central authority was eroded and its vast territories fell into the hands of powerful feudal chiefs, *i.e.*, the landlords holding big estates. Each of these nobles created a community of his own based on ownership of big estates. These feudal chiefs began to exercise powers in fifth century A.D. Each feudal lord, Nobels let their land to tenants-in-chief for cultivation, who in turn gave the same to tenants and tenants in turn to the vassals and serfs. This led to a hierarchical community based on the land ownership, with the king as the supreme lord at the top and serfs and the landless peasants at the bottom. However, the erosion of the authority of kings, led to the emergence of the Christian church as another symbol of authority. By the beginning of the fourteenth century, when Popes were using their authority arbitrarily, the authority of the church was challenged and power of monarchy restored. Further, there was industrial revolutions leading to demand for workers and renaissance that gave rise to the concept of new state system.

The Modern Nation-State–Feudalism was succeeded by nation-states in England, France, Spain, Portugal, Switzerland, the Netherlands, Russia, Germany and Italy based on the bonds of culture, nationality, language, religion strengthened by territorial boundaries. Initially, the nation-states were mostly monarchies. However, since the middle of the eighteenth century, there has been a slow transition from the absolute monarchy to the constitutional monarchy and expansion of democracy, the principles of liberty, equality, and popular sovereignty in large parts of Europe.

In 17th and 18th centuries, the nation state emerged only in Europe and the United States where the American Revolution brought forth the concept of a state. French revolution in 1789 and declaration of rights brought change in political set up of nation state. The growth of the Modern Nation State picked up pace after the war and during the 1960s when many African states became independent from their colonial rulers. Bruce and Voas (2004) defend the view that nation-states are about politics and religions.

International Law and Entities—After the fall of the Roman Empire, emergence of independent kingdoms and nation-states, the need for rules of international trade and conduct between different states arose. Barry E. Carter et al., 2007, has noted that the traditional concept of 'International law was generally one of law between nation states'. The traditional international law scholars located international law in the acts of official governmental bureaucratic entities, such as the treaties and agreements entered into by nation-states, the declarations and protocols of the United Nations...or other affiliated bodies, and the rulings of international courts and tribunals" (see Barry E. Carter & Philip R. Trimble, 1999). However today on the contrary, it is a complex web of treaties, regulations, customary norms, and codes of conduct that shapes relationships among state as well as non-state actors along horizontal and vertical axes of power (Berman, 2007).

The United Nations was established to coordinate and aid States in an efforts to achieve common goals under the founding principles of sovereignty and non-intervention, it gives states the tools to resolve disputes themselves

Essential Elements of the State

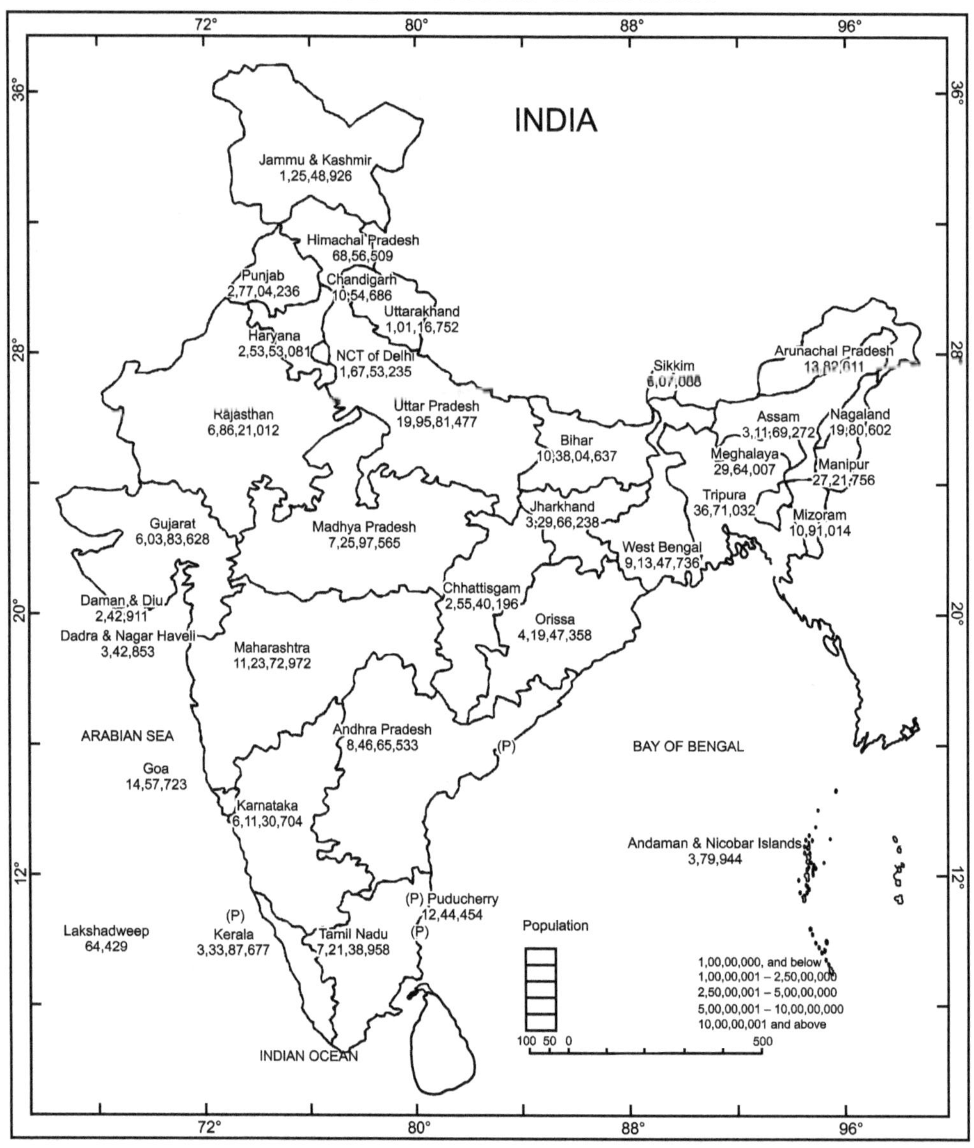

Indian population per states

A *state* can be said to be a legal and political entity that is comprised of the following essential elements:

(a) A number of people or a permanent population; (b) a definite territory; (c) a government; and (d) sovereignty (independence of external control)

(a) Population–It is obvious that to have a state, which is a human institution, a population of some kind which is beyond a single family is necessary for its existence. Family may be a centre, around which the state grows, but till there is a series of families there can be no state.

In earlier times, the city-state was the working ideal for Greeks with small size of the population.The necessity of population as an essential element of state has been recognised but there is no unanimity with regard to its size. Plato, Aristotle and Rousseau, all the philosophers had opined that small numbers for a population in a state is essential to good government.

The population in the modern states may vary from few thousands to the many millions and it is not possible to fix a definite number of people in a state. The state of Monaco (independent off-and-on since the 13th century), lies along the French Riviera on the French Mediterranean coast near Nice has a small population of 32,000 people; San Marino located on Mt. Titano in north central Italy has 29,000 residents only and is the oldest state in Europe, having been founded in the fourth century. On the other hand, China and India are highly populated.

(b) Territory–The second essential constituent of a state is territory; it is the physical basis of the state. There cannot be a state in absence of any definite territory for the residence of the people who continue to move from one place to another. Bluntschli, has opined "a people does not become a permanent state till it has acquired a territory."

The geographical situation and the shape and conformation of the territory, as well as extent of domain, have an important bearing upon the institutions and national life of the state. The territorial jurisdiction of a state extends not only over the land but also over rivers, lakes, mountains, marginal sea, subsoil and aerial space above it.

(c) Government–Population and territory alone cannot form a state; the third essential constituent of the state is the government and the people of a territory are subjected to the control of government, which is the political machinery or an organisation through which the collective will of the state is formulated, expressed and executed. Locke has held that government was simply a trust, an agent entrusted with respecting the natural rights of the people. Rousseau has defined government as "an intermediate body established between the subjects and the sovereign for their mutual communication, and charged with the execution of the laws and the preservation of liberty, both civil and political.

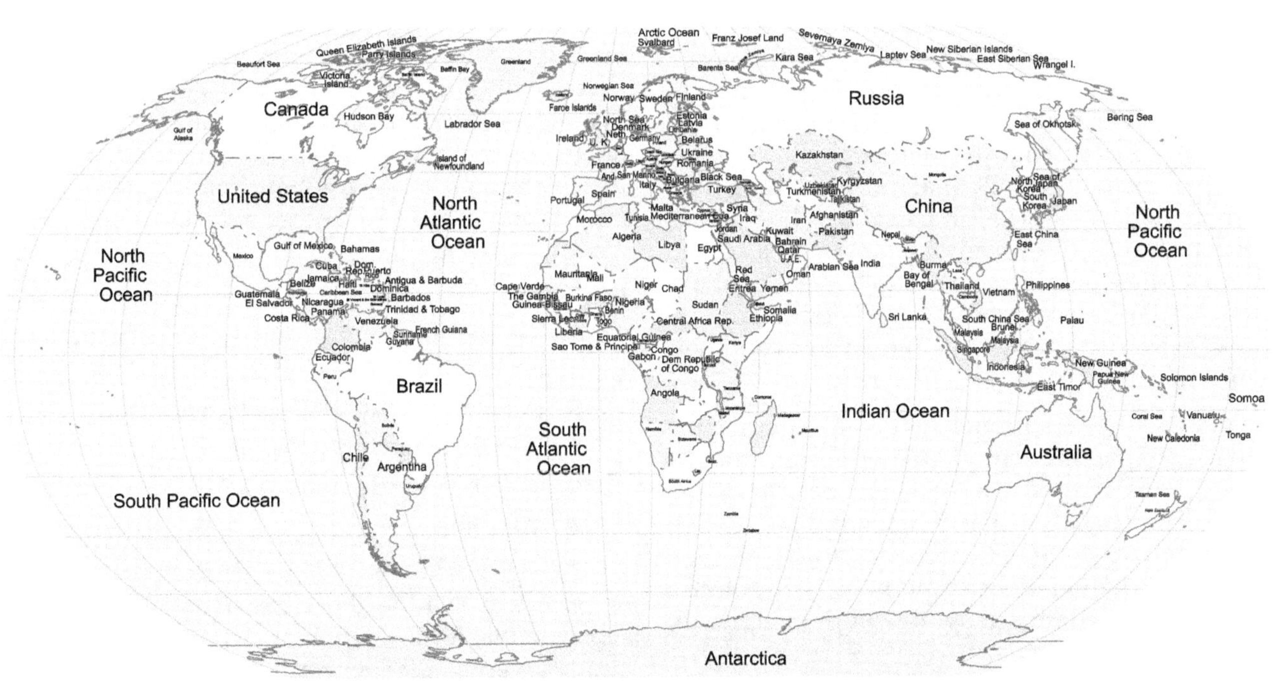

World Map on Globe showing territories of different nations

It can be said that in modern state, government is the agency, distinct from the people but intermediate between them through which society is politically organised; common policies determined, common affairs are regulated and common interests are promoted. The government is responsible for the maintenance of law and order and for the provision of common services like defence, issue of currency, foreign relations, roads, bridges, transport and communications, water, electricity, health and education, etc.

(d) Sovereignty–Sovereignty is the most important characteristic of the state. It is what distinguishes a state from other forms of human organisations. There can be no state in the absence of sovereignty. Broadly speaking, sovereignty means the original, supreme, and unlimited power of the state to impose its will upon all persons, associations, and things within its jurisdiction, it means supremacy of the state. Sovereignty is of two types-internal sovereignty and external sovereignty. Internal sovereignty means that the state is supreme in all internal matters. It exercises its supremacy over all the institutions and the people of the state

Indian flag held by Indians

and the latter have to obey its commands. It commands and enforces obedience to the exclusion of all other wills. External sovereignty implies that a state must be free from foreign control. It has right to live its life and pursue its ends independently of the will of other states.If a state is controlled by another state, the former will no longer be regarded as a sovereign state and it will become a part of the state which exercises control over it.

Concept of Nation–The term Nation is very near in meaning to the term state and they are often used interchangeably but the 'Nation' is broader in significance, it is the state plus something else. T. H. Green, the modern english political thinkers in his "Principles of Political Obligation, has stated that Nation, underlies the state, and, again, he has characterised the state as "the nation organised in a certain way." He also points out that the members of a nation "in their corporate or associated action are animated by certain passions arising out of their organization."

Nationality is a spiritual sentiment or principle arising among a number of people usually of the same race, resident on the same territory, sharing a common language, the same religion, similar history and traditions, common interests, with common political association, and common ideals of political unity but Nationality may develop in spite of difference of sect, religion.

Seton Watson (1977) had noted that a 'scientific' definition of nation had never been achieved and probably never will be. Each nation is unique in the way its elements are combined, let alone how successfully they have jelled into a durable identity. The most significant elements in nation-building are language, religion, and historical experience, but there are also more unquantifiable ones such as custom and usage or the sense of togetherness.

A nation therefore may be described as comprising of:

- people sharing the same historical experience, traditions,
- religious, cultural and linguistic unity,
- common territory/residence,
- common ideals, interests,
- common race,
- common political associations and aspirations.

However, all the above elements are not absolutely essential for formation of a Nation. For example: India gives a good example of different culture, religion, language and race. In modern times, diversity can be seen across the globe.

Forms of Government

Many writers of Political Science have attempted to classify forms of government based on the number of people in whom the supreme power resides, and on the form of the state organisation or government. Plato and Aristotle classified forms of states and powers of governments. But in those, days no distinction was made between state and government. In modern times the term classification of government is more appropriately used, however it is difficult to find a satisfactory basis for the classification of modern governments.

Let us see the following table that will give us an idea of traditional classification of government by Socrates, Plato and Aristotle.

Forms of Government							
Thinkers	**Socrates**		**Plato**			**Aristotle**	
Criteria to rule	Knowledge		Perfect Knowledge	Imperfect knowledge	Lack of knowledge/ ignorance		
Ruled by	State	Contrasted with	Best state	(Law obeyed)	Lack of knowledge/ ignorance	Normal (welfare of all)	Perverted (common welfare ignored)
one	Monarchy (Respect for law)	Tyranny	No Such state exist	Monarchy (best form)	Tyranny (worst form)	Monarchy (king)	Tyranny
Few	Aristocray (capacity to rule is recognized)	Plutocracy (wealth is the test of rule)		Aristocracy (Intermediate form)	Oligarchy (Intermediate Form)	Aristocracy (political power shared by other persons of virtue and merit)	Oligarchy
Many	Democracy (is rule of ignorance)			Moderate democracy	Extreme democracy	Polity	Democracy

Let us now discuss in brief the various forms of government:

Monarchy

It is the oldest type of government. The monarch (individual) in earlier societies has sovereign power of lawmaking and the rest only have to obey. Jean Bodin has further classified monarchy, into three categories:

Monarchy -

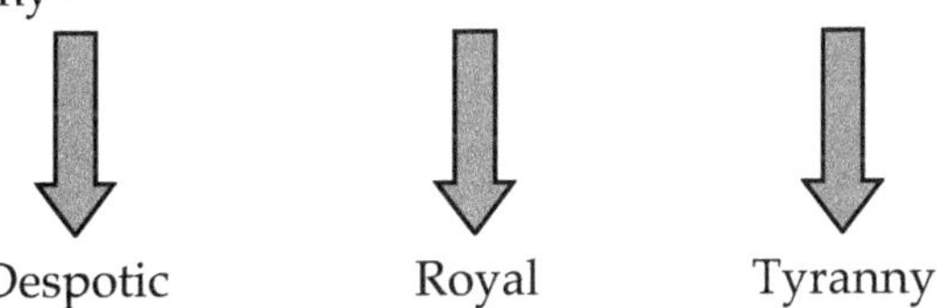

1. **Despotic,** in which the monarch (prince) is lord and master of both the possessions and the persons of his subjects by right of conquest in a just war and like the ancient patriarch, rules his subjects as the master rules his slaves.

2. **Royal or Pure Monarchy,** is one in which the subjects are secure in their natural liberty and natural rights of person and property, while the monarch (prince) obeying the laws of God and of nature, receives willing obedience of the subjects, to the law he himself establishes.

3. **Tyranny,** in which the prince, spurning the laws of nature, abuses the natural liberty of his subject's as if they were slaves and their property is invaded as if it belonged to the tyrant.

Bodin has regarded Royal Monarchy if the matter of succession is firmly fixed on the principle of heredity, primogeniture and the exclusion of the female line as the best form of state or government.

Woolsey, in "Political Science," vol. I, pp. 485 have classified monarchies as: city states, absolute monarchies, theocratic monarchies, limited, elective, mixed, and constitutional monarchies.

This monarchy may also be classified as Absolute Monarchy, Limited or Constitutional Monarchy, Hereditary Monarchy and Elective Monarchy.

Aristocracy

The word aristocracy has originated from Greek word 'aristos' which means the best and Greek word kartein which means to rule. In aristocratic state, a minority collectively enjoys sovereign power and imposes law on the rest, generally and severally. Rousseau in Contract social, bk. Ill, ch. 5, had classified aristocracies as natural (suited only to simple people), hereditary, and elective. The second is the best and is the aristocracy properly so-called while the third is the worst of any government. Roscher in Politik had classified them as noble or landed, priestly, and plutocracies and oligarchies. The ancient writers Aristotle considered an oligarchy as a perversion of aristocracy, where power is concentrated in hands of wealthy minority in their own interest. Thus in an aristocratic state, the political power is vested in few numbers of people on different basis such as wealth (Land owners), education (Nobles), religious positions (Priests), family succession, physical force etc.

Democracy

The term Democracy is derived from combination of Greek words "demos" means the people or popular government and *Kratos,* which means 'Rule of strength'. In democracy, all the people, or a majority among them, exercise sovereign power collectively, people are free to express their views and rule themselves by consensus. It is the government of the people (equal distribution of political powers and influence among the citizens in forming a government), it is government by the people and government for the people (*i.e.,* the rule of government is for the promotion of public welfare). Bryce has defined democracy as a form of government as one where ruling power of state was vested not in particular class or classes but in the community as a whole.

Democracy is of two kinds: (1) Pure or direct democracy, and (2) Representative or indirect democracy.

However, the classification of governments as monarchies, aristocracies, has lost its former importance with the development of republic and democratic form of government and necessitated the need for finding other principles of classification of governmental forms which is more satisfactory, consistent and scientific. Let us see below the classification of governments by modern writers on various basis:

Dictatorship

The dictatorship form of government is an autocratic or authoritarian government ruled by either an individual (a dictator) or by a small group of an authoritarian party like in an oligarchy form of government with an extra ordinary power to govern without the consent of those being governed. The basic civil liberties and many other rights of the people are suppressed by the government by the use of intimidation and terror. The totalitarian states can be an example of modern dictatorship.

According to Alfred Cobban: The Dictator :

◆ Possesses absolute sovereignty (is not subject to any other authority) and all the political power emanates from his will.

◆ Powers are unlimited in scope and in duration.

◆ Exercise power in arbitrary manner by Decree rather than by law.

◆ Is not answerable to citizens and occupies the position by force invasion, intervention and militarism.

Classification of Forms of Governments				
On Basis of	**By Burgess**		**By Stephen Leacock**	
Identity or non-identity of state with its government	Primary	Representative		
Tenure of executive	Hereditary	Elective		
Relation between executive and legislature	Parliamentary	Presidential	Parliamentary (as a form of democratic government)	Presidential (as a form of democratic government)
Concentration and distribution of power	Unitary	Federal	Unitary	Federal
Location of sovereign power			Dictatorship	Democracy
Method of acquiring power by head of the state in democratic government			Constitutional monarchy	Republic

Sources: Stephen Leacock.*Elements of Political Science.*Houghton Mifflin Company.1906

John W. Burgess. *Political Science and Comparative Constitutional Law.*Ginn& Co. Publications. Boston. 1891.

Unitary system

In unitary system of governance, only one government rules the whole country, all of the governing power resides and is concentrated in a centralised government and all the local governments are sub-ordinates for better administration and are subject to a central authority in all respects.

Salient Features of Unitary Government:

◆ There is no constitutional division of powers, though there may be the delegation of authority by the central government to the local authority.

◆ The central government/legislature which is the supreme over the local governments or administrative units.

◆ There may be unwritten and flexible constitution which can be changed by the supreme authority.

◆ The judiciaries do not possess independent powers in administration.

◆ The countries like United Kingdom, Republic of France has unitary system.

A Federal System (Federalism)

The term *federalism* is derived from the Latin root *foedus*, which means "formal agreement or covenant." A federal system of government is one that divides or distributes the powers, decisions and functions of government between the centre at national level and its constituents at regional, state and local level. under federalism, each level of government has sovereignty (power) in some areas and the centre and state may share powers in other areas. For example, central government can only declare war but both the state and centre have power to impose taxes.

Salient Features of Federal Government :

◆ There is a constitutional division of powers between the central and state governments.

◆ There are separate legislatures, both at the central and state levels.

◆ There may be a written and rigid constitution, difficult to amend as both, the Union and the State legislatures take part in the amendment of the Constitution with respect to all matters.

◆ Constitution is supreme and lays down the powers of the two sets of government.

◆ There maybe separate constitutions for the union and the States.

◆ Bi-cameral legislature where the upper house of the legislature has equal representation from the constituting units or the states.

◆ The federal states can be constitutional democracies or non-democratic.

◆ There is an independent judiciary that decides the disputes that arise between the centre and the states' governments or between one state and the other. It interprets the constitution and may declare an act of government as ultra vires.

Australia and the United States of America are federal countries. Germany is a federal republic and has constitutional democracy; the Republic of Sudan is non-democratic federal state.

The Constitution of India has not described India as a federation but as a "Union of States" (Article 1 of the Constitution)[1]. In India, some of the features of a federal form of government like Division of Power; Written Constitution; Supremacy of the Constitution; Judiciary; Bi-cameral legislation has been followed but it also consists of some unitary or non-federal features which makes it a Quasi federal country. The Constitution is not rigid and can be amended by the Indian Parliament and on many subjects, the Parliament does not need the approval of the State legislatures to amend the Constitution. In India, there is no separate constitution for the Union and the States and the Central exercise control over the States. The upper house, Rajya Sabha, of the Indian Parliament does not have equal representation from states; India has system of unified or integrated judicial system. Further, in times of emergency, the government of states lose their autonomy and come under the full control of the union or central governments. Thus, it can be said that India has adopted federal form of government but there are various features of our Constitution which are non-federal or unitary.

Presidential System

It is a system of government where an executive branch exists and presides separately from the legislature; executive is chosen by the citizens whether directly or indirectly, for a fixed period and is not responsible to the legislature. The legislature cannot dismiss it in normal circumstances. The President formulates the national policy, has power to mobilise military troops and declare state emergency.

The Salient Features of Presidential System :

◆ The President as the Chief Executive, is independent of the legislature and all the powers are vested in him. He is the head of government and the head of state.

---

1 Article 1 in the Constitution states that India, that is Bharat, shall be a Union of States. *The territory of India shall consist of : The territories of the states, The Union territories* and *any territory that may be acquired.*

♦ The President (executive) and the legislature (legislative functions of the government) are separate.

♦ Both, President and members of legislatures are elected separately by the people for a fixed term as per the strict schedule of elections.

♦ There is possibility that the President may be from one political party and the legislature is controlled by a different political party.

♦ It is difficult to remove President from his or her position except only in extreme cases and can only be removed by impeachment by the legislature as per the grounds stated in the Constitution of the country.

The United States of America and Argentina followed the presidential form of government. The US instead of imitating the parliamentary model, then emerging in England, followed the presidential model in 1787, when the new Constitution was written. Other models of the presidential system are found in most South American countries and a few African countries.

Parliamentary System

A Parliamentary system is a system of government in which the legislature holds supreme power to make and execute laws. There are members of the legislature and the Prime Minister is chosen by members of the legislature (Parliament) from among their own and in practice, the Prime Minister (chief executive) is the leader of the majority party in the legislature.

The Salient Features of Parliamentary System:

♦ There is dual executive: Council of Ministers and the President

♦ The Government is formed by the majority party. The government is collectively responsible, where the Council of Ministers works as a team and is responsible as a body for the general conduct of the affairs of government.

♦ The members of legislature are elected by the people and one of its members is appointed the chief executive.

♦ Separation of power is ideal but there are overlapping relations between the legislature and executive.

♦ The Prime Minister, being the head of the council of ministers, both the executive and legislative powers are vested in him.

♦ The roles of head of state and head of government are often held by different people. A country may have a Prime Minister who acts as its head of government and also a monarch or president, who acts as the head of state.

♦ The legislature can easily remove the Prime Minister in case of the disagreement in policy or a lack of effective leadership.

♦ The party in power or the party out of power can initiate a call for elections, though the opposition party can do so by first winning a 'no confidence' motion. If the Prime Minister loses the support of the majority in the legislature on a significant vote, he or she must resign, and elections are called immediately.

♦ Lower House of legislature can be dissolved.

The Parliamentary system also called sometimes a "Cabinet government, the term used by Sir Ivor Jennings (1903-1965) or the Prime Ministerial Government, used by Richard Crossman (1907-1974), is the more prevalent form of government. It can be republican and a constitutional monarch i.e., retaining their historical monarch with only ceremonial powers who has to abide by the constitution. The government is actually run by the Chief executive, usually called the Prime Minister. The countries like the United Kingdom, India, Canada, Australia and the Scandinavian countries Germany, Spain and Italy have Parliamentary systems. However in United Kingdom, now Monarchs are only Ceremonial and nominal head of government, devoid of any political power."

Do you know?

Sometimes a country that has both a Prime Minister and a President is called to consist of semi-presidential system of government, although it is more closely related to a parliamentary system because of the power held by the legislature and Prime Minister in such a system.

Organs of Government

The Government in India is formed through the Constitution of India, which is a living document and approved by Constituent Assembly, on November 26, 1949 and came into effect on January 21, 1950. The government of India is officially known as the Union Government and is also referred to as the Central Government. India, also known as Bharat, is a Union of States. It is a Sovereign Socialist Secular Democratic Republic with a parliamentary system of government.

There are three branches of the government in India that were established in order to check and balance the overall government. These three branches of government are the legislative, executive and the judiciary and are responsible for separate and independent area of administration.

Executive

In narrower sense, the term executive refers only to the Chief Executive Head of the state and his advisors and ministers. In the United States, the executive is known as the President. In other countries, the titles may include President, the King, Prime Minister and Chancellor. In India, the constitutional head of the Executive branch of the Union is the President; Art. 53 of the constitution provides that the executive power of the union shall be vested in the President. He is the head of State and either exercises his powers directly, or through officers that rank beneath him. The executive is responsible for the overall governance and daily administration of the country. The President acts in accordance with aid and advice given by the Prime Minister and his/her council of ministers (the cabinet) in accordance with Article 74 of the Constitution of India. The President is elected by an electoral college consisting of the elected members of both Houses of Parliament and the elected members of the Legislative Assemblies of the States for a term of 5 years.

Rashtrapati Bhavan

1. The President has power to appoint the following authorities of the country.
   - The Prime Minister of the country, who is the leader of majority party, on receiving the proposal from the majority party in the Lok Sabha.
   - The President also appoints the members of the Council of Ministers and distributes portfolios to these members based on the direction or opinion of the Prime Minister.
   - Governors of States;
   - The Attorney General;
   - The Comptroller and Auditor General;
   - The Chief Election Commissioner and other Election Commissioners;
   - Chief Justice and other judges of the Supreme Court and the High Courts in the states;
   - Chairman and members of the Union Public Service Commission.
   - Chief of Army, Navy and Air force.

2. President enjoys apart from power of appointment, the power of promotion, removal and suspension of civil servants.

3. The Executive/President is also responsible for:
   - Execution of laws made by the legislature and the decisions of the courts;
   - Maintenance of law and order;
   - Policy formation
   - Conduct of foreign affairs and appointment of Ambassadors and High Commissioners to other countries
   - Defense, as Supreme Commander of the Armed Forces.
   - Home Affairs;
   - Post and Telegraph
   - Railways, taxes, banking and currency, etc.

4. In times of emergency and grave national crisis, the President can declare martial law and suspend the rights of citizens. He can promulgate National Emergency (Article 352); State Emergency (President's Rule) (Article 356) and Financial Emergency (Article 360).

5. Article 72 of the constitution grants the power to President of India to grant a pardon, reprieve or remit the punishment or commute death sentences. At state level, similar and parallel power is vested in the Governors of each State under Article 161.

6. The President can summon and prorogue the two Houses of Parliament from time to time.

7. It has power to summon and prorogue the legislature. The Rajya Sabha is a continuing body but the President can dissolve the Lok Sabha on the recommendation of the council of ministers.

8. President can promulgate Ordinances having the same force and effect as laws passed by Parliaments. When the Parliament is not in session and the circumstances justify the need of immediate action.

9. The Bill passed by both Houses of Parliament needs assent by President to become an act.

10. Executive determines the economic policy of the country.

However, in India, the real executive power is vested in the Council of Ministers with the Prime Minister as its head and the power of president is also subject to Judicial Review. He does not sit or participate in the discussions in either of the two Houses. He can be impeached by the process initiated in either House of the Parliament only on the ground of violation of constitution.

In comparison, the President in USA is both, the head of state and head of government of the United States of America, and Commander-in-Chief of the armed forces. He is responsible for implementing and enforcing the laws written by Congress and appoints the heads of the federal agencies, including the Cabinet in United States but the President can also be impeached by the Senate.

Britain is a Parliamentary democracy, Queen is the head of the executive branch of the government, an integral part of the legislature, head of the judiciary, the commander-in-chief of all the armed forces of the Crown and the 'supreme governor' of the established Church of England. The executive power is exercised by Her Majesty's Government, on behalf of and by the consent of the Monarch, as well as by the devolved Governments of Scotland and Wales, and the Northern Ireland Executive, but like India, Prime Minister of the United Kingdom is the head of government.

The Legislative

The word Parliament is derived from the French word 'parter'. Parliament means meeting for discussion. The term 'Assemble' and 'Congress' are the terms that used as synonym for the term legislature in various countries. In India, Parliament is the legislative branch having two houses (bicameral) : the Lower House (Lok Sabha) and the Upper House, the Council of States (Rajya Sabha).

Parliament of India

1. The Parliament of India consists of the President and the Lok Sabha and the Rajya Sabha. The President of India is a titular head of Parliament. It is the main institution in the governance of the country and takes powers from various constitutional provisions for its election, business of House, cabinet functions, enactments, rules and procedures etc. The Lower House consists of directly elected members, it has 545 members including two nominated members (Anglo Indian community) by the President. The Upper Houses consist of indirectly elected members and at present out of 245 members, 233 represent the States and Union territories and 12 are members nominated by the President from amongst persons having special knowledge or practical experience in respect of such matters as literature, science, art or social service. The Council of Ministers, drawn from both Houses, is collectively responsible to Lok Sabha.

Legislative Assembly

2. The functions, organisation and nature of legislatures differ in every country depending upon the form of government. However, it plays significant role in parliamentary form of government. The most important powers and functions of the Indian legislature are following:

(i) **Law making on various subjects**–Parliament has absolute power to make, recommend and pass or negate bills as per the prescribed procedure of the constitution. All legislations when enacted are called act. These acts are enacted to achieve certain objectives. The law making procedure is dealt in detail in next chapter.

(ii) **Parliament has financial powers**– Article 265 of constitution provides that 'no tax shall be levied or collected except by authority of law and no expenditure can be incurred except with the authorisation of the Legislature (Article 266). The Lok Sabha has supremacy in financial matters.

3. It can amend the Constitution following the number of procedural restrictions.

4. Debates and discussions on policies and treaties and international matters come within deliberative functions performed by the Indian Parliament.

5. The legislature exercises regulatory functions and certain check over the executive. The executive is responsible and answerable to the parliament.

6. Parliament in exercise of judicial power can impeach the judges of Supreme Court, the members of U.P.S.C., the Comptroller and Auditor General.

7. Parliament takes part in the election of the President and Vice-President of India and also elects some of its members to various committees of the House. It elects its presiding and deputy presiding officers.

8. There are three Sessions of Parliament held in a year: (i) Budget Session (February-May); (ii) Monsoon Session (July-August); and (iii) Winter Session (November-December).

In United Kingdom, Parliament, is made up of the House of Commons, the House of Lords and the Queen, the Legislative power is vested in the two chambers of the Parliament as well as in the Scottish Parliament and Welsh and Northern Ireland Assemblies.

In United States, the Legislative Branch consists of the House of Representatives and the Senate, which together form the United States Congress. The Congress has the sole authority to enact legislation and declare war as per the Constitution.

Judicial Branch

The Judiciary is independent of the executive and the legislature, though the executive maintains a certain level of influence in the appointment of judges to the courts.

Supreme Court

The U.S. Judiciary has a court system comprising of a federal system and 50 state systems with each having its own structures and procedures. The U.S. Supreme Court has power of judicial review and its legal interpretations, has assumed supremacy. The legal system follows adversarial *process*. Under the U.K. Parliamentary system. Parliament is supreme and sovereign and the Judiciary has no power of judicial review of legislation.

The Indian justice system consists of a unitary system at both state and national level. There is Supreme Court of India at apex level, High Courts of India at the state level, and District Courts, Sessions Courts at the district level. India has chosen middle path between the British Sovereignty of Parliament and U.S. Judicial Supremacy. In India, all organs of government derive their powers and functions from the Constitution, there is no question of supremacy of any organ of government, both the Parliament and Supreme Court are supreme in their respective spheres. The Supreme Court has power to declare a law passed by the Parliament ultra vires if it violates the fundamental rights or basic features of the constitution. The Supreme Court plays an important role as protector of the fundamental rights of the citizens and dispensing justice to people. The powers and functions of courts in India is discussed in detail in chapter 3.

The division of power into separate branches of government is central to the republican idea of the separation of powers.

Doctrine of Separation of power : The conceptual framework

There are three organs of government as discussed above: 1. legislative, 2. executive and 3. judicial. The legislatures make/enact the laws; the executive enforces laws; and the judiciary interprets the laws. *William Blackstone* has pointed out in Commentaries on the Laws of England that "In all tyrannical government, the supreme magistrates, or the right both of making and of enforcing the laws is vested in one and the same man or one and the same body of men; and wherever these two powers are united together, there can be no public liberty".

The doctrine of the separation of powers emphasizes the structural classification of governmental powers in three organs *i.e.,* legislature, executive and judiciary. It implies that the powers and functions of each of these organs are separate and distinct and no single agency can exercise complete authority. These organs of the government act as checks and balances on each other to ensure that the rule of law prevails, the power is not vested in single authority and every act of government is in accordance with law thereby excluding any form of arbitrariness or abuse of power so that fundamental rights of individual can be protected.

Let us summarise below the system of governance followed in few selected countries:

Country	United States	Great Britain	India
Constitution	Federal constitution and each state has its own constitution.	Un-codified	Written
System of Government	Federal system, the States has unitary governments with bicameral legislatures (except Nebraska, which has a unicameral legislature.)	Unitary government	Quasi Federal
Form of Government	Democracy	Democracy	Democracy
	Constitutional republic	Constitutional monarch (head of state)	Republic.
	Presidential system (President as head of state and government)	Parliamentary system (Prime Minister as head of government)	Parliamentary form
Organs/branches of government	Legislative- Congress Executive- President Judiciary	Legislative-Parliament, Executive-Her Majesty's Government, on behalf of and by the consent of the Monarch, as well as by the devolved Governments of Scotland and Wales, and the Northern Ireland Executive. Judiciary	Legislative-Parliament Executive-President, Judiciary.

Origin of the Doctrine

The Doctrine was first evolved in ancient Greece and Rome. **Aristotle** in his treaties politics, for the first time classified the functions of the government into three categories *viz.,* deliberative (to discuss everything of common importance), official (executive) and judicial. The doctrine propounded by Aristotle divides the power according to class interest, comprising monarchy, aristocracy and democracy. Aristotle had argued that there could also be mixed forms of government with elements of all three, and that the best form of government was one where laws rather than people ruled. The work of **Marsilius of Padua** (1275-1342) in Defensor Pacis (The Defender of Peace) published in 1324 had envisaged ending of the medieval approach to the nature of law and a clear separation between the executive and the legislative functions in the fourteen century.

In the 17th century, the English philosopher **John Locke** (1632-1704), in his Second Treatise of Civil Government (1690), noted the distinction between three types of powers: legislative, executive and federative of the Commonwealth.

However, Locke did not mention separate judicial power in his classification and his analysis did not strictly expound the doctrine of separation of powers.

In **18th century**, the French philosopher, **Baron de Montesquieu** (1689-1755), expanded the study of John Locke and incorporated the ideas of a division of state and separation of powers. He is the modern exponent of the theory and articulated the fundamentals of the separation doctrine which become the basis of governance in democratic countries. In his book Espirit Des Lois (The Spirit of Laws), 1748, **Montesquieu** laid his view.

Some important features of doctrine of separation of power as enunciated by Montesquieu are given below :

♦ No one person or body should be vested with all three types of powers otherwise it will lead to tyranny.

♦ He combined the doctrine of the separation of powers, with the ideas of mixed government and mutual checks and balances among the three organs of government. He felt that spirit and manner in which the government functions would best safeguard the freedom and liberty of the individual.

♦ Emphasise is on judicial independence to secure liberty to individuals.

The strict interpretation of the separation of powers may provide that:

- The three branches of the government are equal in powers;
- none of them may exercise the power of the other;
- The same person should not be a member of any two of the branches.
- The independent and separate institutions should create a system of checks and balances between them.

Though the Montesquieu's theory was based on misinterpretation of English Constitution but it was widely welcomed.

The theory was criticised on various grounds :

- The communists and exponents of totalitarian theory out rightly rejected the doctrine. It is considered as negating the general spirit of the oneness of authority and is against the concept of unity of power on which the dictatorial regimes were based.
- The British political scientist Hermon Finer (1898-1969) in one of his writings on the theory and practices of modern government had observed that Montesquieu was searching for the means to limit the crown; to make a constitution to build canals which, but not over which, power should stream.
- It is regarded to be fallacious and dangerous by the democrats as they believe that under modern conditions articulation of powers is required to facilitate the smooth working of government and to meet the demands of a welfare society.
- John Stuart Mill has pointed out that "If the principle of separation of powers is applied in its complete form, integrating realities, government will come to a standstill."
- Laski has said that separation of powers would result in jealousy, suspicion and internal conflicts in the governmental machinery and lead to increasing inefficiency.
- Absolute separation of powers may be hazardous and prevents the unity and coordination needed to administer the legally expressed will of the State. It is often said that 'Power tends to corrupt, and absolute power corrupts absolutely'.
- Extreme checks and balances may lead to deadlocks preventing smooth and efficient working of government.
- The doctrine grants the equal power to three branches of government but in welfare of the state, the parliament has achieved overriding importance having the powers of executive.

Parliament Sovereignty, Judicial Independence and Separation of Power in Practice

United States

United States has the presidential system. The constitution did not specifically lay down that powers should be separate but simply, vested powers in three separate branches of government.

In the United States of America, concentration of power was avoided to ensure the preservation of liberty and an effective mechanism of 'check and balance' was formulated to makes three organs of government largely independent of one another.

The **Congress has the power to make law**, however the Supreme Court can determine whether the law is framed in conformity with the constitution. The President can send legislative proposals to the Congress though congress is not bound to follow suggestions by president but it becomes responsible for the refusal and has to justify itself before bar of public opinion. President has the power to veto a bill approved by the Congress, however congress can override it by a two-third vote in both houses.

The **President has executive power** and is not accountable to the Congress. But neither the President and nor his ministers can attend the Congress meetings to influence its deliberation and decisions. Congress may impeach and remove President, override presidential veto. The international agreements signed by the President need to be ratified by Senate.

Judiciary in U.S. enjoys considerable independence, the Supreme Court may declare executive/presidential action unlawful if not authorised by legislature; it has power to interpret the legal disputes arising by act of parliament and may declare act as unconstitutional. However the federal judges are appointed by President with consent of senate, president may pardon convicts of court. The congress decides the number of Supreme Court justices and may impeach and remove federal judges.

> **Do you know?**
>
> In federal constitution, judiciary is considered as guardian of constitution and has power to interpret law as an important part of its power of judicial review. In the US system, the Supreme Court with its power of judicial review and interpreting the Constitution has assumed supremacy.

United Kingdom

The U.K. has the parliamentary form of government and the crown is the titular head, the Parliament is considered supreme and sovereign. There are absolutely no limitations on its powers, at least in theory; in as much as there is no written Constitution, and the Judiciary has no power of judicial review of *i.e.*, no act passed by the British Parliament can be declared void or un constitutional by any court of law. The doctrine of separation of power plays a role in the United Kingdom's constitutional doctrine but it is said to have weak separation of powers with partial recognition.

U.K. has the cabinet system, where the powers of Parliament, executive and courts are closely entwined. The **Executive** comprises the Crown, the Prime Minister as head and the Cabinet ministers. The executive formulates and implements policy. The **legislature**, Parliament consists of the Crown, the House of Commons and the House of Lords. The executive and legislature are closely intertwined as the Prime Minister is the leader of majority party in legislature and a majority of his or her ministers are members of Parliament and sit in the House of Commons.

In judiciary, judges play the role in interpreting legislation in line with the intention of Parliament and in developing common law.

India

India has a written Constitution which is supreme and sovereign and the powers and functions of every organ are defined and delimited by the Constitution. The Indian Constitution has adopted the middle course between the American system of judicial supremacy and the English principle of parliamentary supremacy. In India Parliament enjoys wide powers but certain factors do restrict or limit its power. The parliament with certain restrictions can amend most parts of the Constitution. The Supreme Court is the guardian of Constitution and has power to judicial review. It can declare a law passed by the Parliament ultra vires which violates the basic structure of the Constitution, if it contravenes the fundamental rights of citizens or if it is beyond the competence of the legislature.

The Constitution of India does not have express provision recognising the doctrine of separation of powers in its absolute form but it embraces the idea of separation of powers in an implied manner.

Executive–Articles 53 and 154 respectively, provides that the executive power of the Union and the State shall be vested with the President and the Governor and they enjoy immunity from civil and criminal liability.

Article 50 lays down that State shall take steps to separate the judiciary from the executive to ensure the independence of judiciary.

Legislature–Article 105 gives judicial immunities to the conduct and behaviour of any member of parliament and article 122 of the Indian Constitution provides validity to the proceedings in Parliament and the same cannot be called into question in any Court of law clearly restricting the judiciary from intervention in the function of the legislature.

This is to ensure the separation and immunity of the legislatures from judicial intervention on the allegation of procedural irregularity.

Judiciary–According to Article 121 and 211 of the Constitution, the Judicial conduct of a judge of the Supreme Court and the High Courts' cannot be discussed in the Parliament and the State Legislature.

However the Constitution of India did not opt for the strict separation of powers and it can be seen in the diluted form. The three branches of government while acting within the ambit of their own power may perform overlapping functions and tend to interfere in the sphere of working of another organ; a strict demarcation of functions is not possible.

The executive may affect the functioning of the judiciary by making appointments to the office of Chief Justice and other judges. The heads of each governmental ministry is a member of the legislature, thus making the executive an integral part of the legislature.

The legislature besides exercising law making powers also exercises judicial powers in cases of breach of its privilege, impeachment of the President and the removal of the judges. It also exercises judicial powers while amending a law declared ultra vires by the Court and revalidating it; disqualifying its members and impeachment of the judges. Legislature by exercising the powers and privileges of the Parliament can impose punishment for exceeding freedom of speech in the Parliament but in conformity with due process.

The Article 118 and Article 208 of the constitution empower the Legislature at the Centre and in the States respectively, the authority to make rules for regulating their respective procedure and conduct of business subject to the provisions of the Constitution.

The higher judiciary is conferred with the power of supervising the functioning of subordinate courts. It also acts as a legislature while making laws regulating its conduct and rules regarding disposal of cases. The Supreme Court also has special advisory jurisdiction regarding matters referred to it by the President of India under Article 143 of the Constitution.

Besides the functional overlapping, the Indian system also lacks the separation of personnel amongst the three departments.

In the landmark case of *Indira Nehru Gandhi v. Raj Narain* AIR 1975 SC 2299- It was observed: "That in the Indian Constitution, there is separation of powers in a broad sense only. A rigid separation of powers as under the American Constitution or under the Australian Constitution is not applicable to India.

Constitution of India

Constitution in a democratic country like India is supreme law of land, a fundamental legal document made by its people; it lays down the basic structure, procedures, powers, and duties of government and the other public authorities–legislative, administrative and judicial; provides for fundamental rights and also the duties of the people. It contains the directive principles to be followed by the state in the governance of the country.

The Constitution of India was framed by the Constituent Assembly which deliberated over the precise constitutional future of India and enacted the Constitution on November 26, 1949 and it was brought into force on January 26, 1950 when India became a Republic. We will discuss in detail the drafting of Indian Constitution, sources of the Constitution in chapter 3 of this book.

The Constitution has 395Articles in 22 parts with 12 schedules and also 4 Appendices. All matters of public governance are regulated by the provisions of Constitution. The Constitution is the supreme and all the laws framed in nation falls under its supremacy. Article 13 of the Constitution states that all pre-constitutional laws, *i.e.,* Laws which were in force before the commencement of Constitution, are void to the extent to which they are inconsistent with the fundamental rights. However, a declaration by the court of their invalidity will be necessary [Article 13(1)]. Further, the laws made after adoption of the Constitution must be compatible with the Constitution, otherwise the law will be deemed to be void ab initio [Article 13(2)]. However article 13(4) states that nothing in this article shall apply to amendments made under Article 368.

The Preamble to the Indian Constitution reflects the basic structure of the Constitution and contains the ideals, objectives, rights and freedoms and basic philosophy of the Constitution which it intended to secure to its citizens. It represents the vision of the people of India and starts with 'We the people of India' and ends with 'Hereby adopt, enact and give to ourselves this constitution.' It means that constitution derives its authority from its people who are declared as sovereign.

In *Kesavananda Bharati v. Union of India* [(1973) Supp. SCR 1], the court had held that preamble of the Constitution is integral part of the Constitution. In *S. R. Bommai v. Union of India* [(1994) 3 SCC 1], the preamble has been held to be the basic structure of the Constitution.

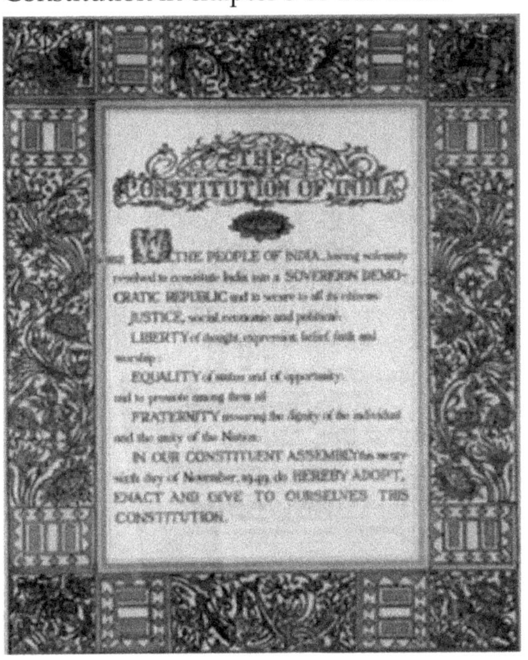

We, the People of India, having solemnly resolved to constitute India into a SOVEREIGN SOCIALIST SECULAR DEMOCRATIC REPUBLIC and to secure to all its citizens:

JUSTICE, social, economic and political;

LIBERTY of thought, expression, belief, faith and worship;

EQUALITY of status and of opportunity; and to promote among them all

FRATERNITY assuring the dignity of the individual and the unity and integrity of the Nation;

IN OUR CONSTITUENT ASSEMBLY, this twenty-sixth day of November, 1949, do hereby adopt, enact and give to ourselves, this Constitution.

The Preamble provides that India is :

Sovereign–State is independent authority free from any type of external control and is not dependent upon, or subject to any other external power or state. Legal sovereignty is vested in the people of India and political sovereignty is distributed between the Union and the States. Sovereignty has two aspects: external and internal.

Socialist and Secular–The word "socialist" and "secular" was added in 1976 by the 42nd Amendment to the Constitution. The main aim of the expression socialism was to secure to the people, justice and bring about a balance in the existing economic disparities and to ensure a decent standard of life to people. The word Socialist highlights the ideals of a welfare state. India is 'secular,' because it maintains neutrality in religious matters, protects all religions equally and doesn't oppose or support any religion, there is nothing like state-religion and the people are free to practice, propagate and worship any of their choice.

Democratic Republic–India has parliamentary form of government and is ruled by the elected representatives of the people. The head of the state is not a hereditary monarch but an elected representative. People govern themselves through their representatives elected on the basis of universal adult franchise. The government is for the people, by the people and of the people.

The Constitution aims to secure:

◆ Justice social, economic and political
◆ Liberty of thought, expression, belief, faith and worship
◆ Equality of status and opportunity
◆ Fraternity assuring dignity of the individual and unity and integrity of the nation.

Features of Indian Constitution

A. India has a parliamentary type of democracy and has cabinet type of government and the cabinet is composed of the Prime Minister, the chief of the executive and his senior colleagues who share the responsibility with him for the formulation and execution of the policies of the government. Indian Constitution has created three organs of governance: Executive, legislature and independent judiciary. The sovereign democratic republic, Parliamentary democracy and the three organs of the State form the basic structure of the Constitution. The Rule of law and judicial review also constitute to basic features of the Constitution.

B. Part I, article 1 of the Indian Constitution states that "India, that is Bharat, shall be union of states." The words "federation" or "federal" did not appear in the text of the Constitution of India but it consists of many features of a federal state however it is like Canadian federation and not like the America, it becomes unitary in times of war, emergency etc. There is single citizenship for all its citizens, in India; we are citizens of India only, not of the respective states to which we belong. All the citizens of 18 years of age and above have right to vote irrespective of their caste, creed, religion, status etc (see part II which deals with citizenship). Union/Centre has power : to make law on state subject which are of national importance; to give effect to international agreement; to declare emergency both political and financial and imposition of president rule in a state; to decide and demark territorial boundaries of a state. In *Kesvananda Bharati v. State of Kerala,* the majority of the Supreme Court judges were of the view that the federal features form the basic structure of the Indian Constitution. In *State of Rajasthan v. Union of India,* [1978] 1 SCR 1- Beg CJ, has described the Indian Constitution as "in a sense federal" however added, but the extent of federalism in it is largely watered down by the needs of progress and development of a country which has to be nationally integrated, politically and economically co-ordinated and socially, intellectually and spiritually uplifted. In *S.R. Bommai v. Union of India* on 11th March, 1994, it was observed that "the Constitution of India is differently described, more appropriately as 'quasi-federal' because it is a mixture of the federal and unitary elements, leaning-more towards the latter."

C. The Constitution of India is neither purely rigid nor purely flexible. There is a harmonious blend of rigidity and flexibility. Some parts of the Constitution can be amended by the ordinary law-making process by Parliament (power to amend lies with parliament alone and not in the state legislatures). Certain provisions can be amended, only when a Bill for that purpose is passed in each house of Parliament by a majority of the total membership of that house and by a majority of not less than two-third of the members of that house present and voting.

D. The Constitution recognises certain rights of the people as basic and fundamental imposing restrictions/limitations on the powers of the state.

Fundamental Rights

Part III of the Indian Constitution guarantees six categories of fundamental rights. These are :
  i. Right to Equality – Articles 14 to 18
  ii. Right to Freedom and Personal Liberty– Articles 19 to 22
  iii. Right against Exploitation – Articles 23 and 24
  iv. Right to Freedom of Religion – Articles 25 to 28
  v. Cultural and Educational Rights – Articles 29 and 30
  vi. Right to Constitutional Remedies – Article 32

Following are the Fundamental Rights in India :

Right to Equality	◆ Article 14 : Equality before law and equal protection of law. ◆ Article 15 : Prohibition of discrimination on grounds only of religion, race, caste, sex or place of birth. ◆ Article 16 : Euqality of opportunity in matters of public employment. ◆ Article 17 : End of untouchability. ◆ Article 18 Abolition of titles, Military and academic distinctions are, however, exempted.
Right to Freedom and Personal Liberty	◆ Article 19 : It guarantees the citizens of India the following six fundamentals freedoms : 1. Freedom of Speech and Expression. 2. Freedom of Assembly. 3. Freedom of form Associations. 4. Freedom of Movement. 5. Freedom of Residence and Settlement. 6. Freedom of Profession, Occupation, Trade and Business. ◆ Article 20 : Protection in respect of conviction for offences. ◆ Article 21 : Protection of life and personal liberty. ◆ Article 22 : Protection against arest and detention in certain cases.
Rights against Exploitation	◆ Article 23 : Traffic in human beigns prohibited. ◆ Article 24 : No child below the age of 14 can be employed.
Right to Freedom of Religion	◆ Article 25 Freedom of conscience and free profession, practice and propagation of religion. ◆ Article 26 : Freedom to manage religious affaris. ◆ Article 27 : Prohibits taxes on religious grounds. ◆ Article 28 :Freedom as to attendance at religious ceremonies in certain educational institutions.
Cultural and Education Rights	◆ Article 29 : Protection of interests of minorities. ◆ Article 30 Right of minorties to establish and administer educational institutions. ◆ Article 31 : Omitted by the 44th Amendment Act.
Right to Constitutional Remedies	◆ Article 32 : The right to move the Supreme Court in case of their violation (called soul and heart of the Constitution by B. R. Ambedkar) ◆ Forms of Writ check.

Do you know ?

The Right to Property was also guaranteed as a Fundamental Right under Article 31 of the Constitution but by 44th Constitutional Amendment Act, 1978, it was ceased to be fundamental and now it is only a legal right.

The State cannot take away the fundamental rights of the citizens. These rights are enforceable and justifiable against the State through courts. The aggrieved person has right to move directly to the Supreme Court for the enforcement of fundamental rights under article 32 (Right to Constitutional Remedies).

No fundamental right in India is absolute and reasonable restrictions can be imposed in the interest of the factors stated in the articles 19(2) and 19(3), respectively of the constitution. Article 19(2) empowers the State to impose reasonable restrictions on exercise of the right to freedom of speech etc., in the interest of the sovereignty and integrity of India, the security of the State, friendly relations with foreign States, public order, decency or morality, or in relation to contempt of court, defamation or incitement to an offence. Similarly, Article 19(3) enables the State to make any law imposing reasonable restrictions on the exercise of the right conferred in the interest of the factors stated therein. Fundamental Rights can be suspended during the time of emergency and rights of the citizen are curtailed temporarily except right to life and personal liberty (article-20-21).

Directive Principles

Part IV of the constitution provides for the list of directive principles. Directive Principles of State Policy are in the form of directives/instructions/guidelines to the governments at the center as well as in states. They aim at providing social and economic justice. The government has to incorporate these directive principles while making law formulating policies and taking decisions. **Directive principles were incorporated in our Constitution and cast duty on State to:**

i. Secure a social order for the promotion of welfare of the people. (Article 38)

ii. Follow certain principles of policy towards securing: adequate means of livelihood to its citizen; distribution of ownership and control of the material resources of the community to best sub serve the common good; there should not be concentration of wealth and means of production to the common detriment; equal pay for equal work for both men and women; the good health, freedom and dignity of its citizens ; protection of childhood and youth against exploitation and against moral and material abandonment. (Article 39).

iii. Provide equal justice and free legal aid. (Article 39A)

Source : Basu, Durga Das (1993). Introduction to the Constitution of India. New Delhi: Prentice Hall of India, 1993 Edition.

iv. Organise village panchayats. (*Article* 40).

v. Provide for right to work, to education and to public assistance in certain cases. (*Article* 41).

vi. Make provision for just and humane conditions of work and maternity relief. (*Article* 42).

vii. Determine Living wage, etc., for workers. (*Article* 43).

viii. Assure participation of workers in management of industries. (*Article* 43A).

ix. Provide uniform civil code for the citizens. (*Article* 44).

x. Make provision for free and compulsory education for children. (*Article* 45).

xi. Promote educational and economic interests of Scheduled Castes, Scheduled Tribes and other weaker sections. (*Article* 46).

xii. Raise the level of nutrition and the standard of living and to improve public health. (*Article* 47).

xiii. Organisation of agriculture and animal husbandry. (*Article* 48).

xiv. Protect and improve environment and safeguarding of forests and wild life. (*Article* 48A).

xv. Protect monuments and places and objects of national importance. (*Article* 49).

xvi. Separate judiciary from executive. (*Article* 50).

xvii. Promote international peace and security. (*Article* 51).

In India the State has made and is making many efforts to implement the Directive Principles of state policy.

Thus the directive principles can be said to be the "goals" to be achieved by Part III of the Constitution. They are intended to ensure "distributive justice" for removal of inequalities and disabilities and to achieve a fair division of wealth amongst the members of the society. In *Unnikrishnan v. State of AP & Ors* 1993 SCR

(1) 594 - it was held that Parts III and IV of the Constitution are supplementary and complementary to each other and that Fundamental Rights are but a means to achieve the goal indicated in Part IV. The fundamental rights must be construed in the light of the directive principles.

Fundamental Duties

Fundamental duties in article 51 A were incorporated in constitution by 42nd Amendment Act (part IV A). The rights and duties are correlative. The purpose of incorporating these duties in the Constitution is just to remind the people that while enjoying their right as citizens, it shall be the duty of every citizen of India to do the various things specified in Clauses (a) to (j) of the article. The duties as such cannot be judicially enforced.

<table>
<tr><td colspan="2">It shall be the duty of every citizen of India :</td></tr>
<tr><td>i.</td><td>to abide by the Constitution and respect its ideals and institutions, the National Flag and the National Anthem;</td></tr>
<tr><td>ii.</td><td>to cherish and follow the noble ideals which inspired our national struggle for freedom;</td></tr>
<tr><td>iii.</td><td>to uphold and protect the sovereignty, unity and integrity of India;</td></tr>
<tr><td>iv.</td><td>to defend the country and render national service when called upon to do so;</td></tr>
<tr><td>v.</td><td>to promote harmony and the spirit of common brotherhood amongst all the people of India transcending religious, linguistic and regional or sectional diversities; to renounce practices derogatory to the dignity of women;</td></tr>
<tr><td>vi.</td><td>to value and preserve the rich heritage of our composite culture;</td></tr>
<tr><td>vii.</td><td>to protect and improve the natural environment including forests, lakes, rivers and wild life, and to have compassion for living creatures;</td></tr>
<tr><td>viii.</td><td>to develop the scientific temper, humanism and the spirit of inquiry and reform;</td></tr>
<tr><td>ix.</td><td>to safeguard public property and to abjure violence;</td></tr>
<tr><td>x.</td><td>to strive towards excellence in all spheres of individual and collective activity so that the nation constantly rises to higher levels of endeavour and achievement.</td></tr>
</table>

Article 326 of the Constitution provides that the elections to the House of the People and to the Legislative Assembly of every State shall be on the basis of adult suffrage *i.e.*, the person who is citizen of India.

◆ is not be less than 18 years of age (by constitutional 61st Amendment Act, 1988, age of 21 years is reduced to 18 years) and

◆ is not otherwise disqualified under this constitution or any law made by the appropriate Legislature on the ground of non-residence, unsoundness of mind, crime or corrupt or illegal practice, shall be entitled to be registered as a voter at any such election.

There shall be one general electoral roll for every territorial constituency for election to either House of Parliament or to the House or either House of the Legislature of a State and no person shall be ineligible for inclusion in any such roll or claim to be included in any special electoral roll for any such constituency on grounds only of religion, race, caste, sex or any of them (article 325).

Parliament has power to make provision with respect to elections to either House of Parliament or to the House or either House of the Legislature of a State including the preparation of electoral rolls, the delimitation of constituencies and all other matters necessary for securing the due constitution of such House or Houses to Legislatures (article 327) and State has power to make provision with respect to elections to House or either House of the Legislature of the State including the preparation of electoral rolls and all other matters necessary for securing the due Constitution of such House or Houses (article 328).

Articles 330 and 332 of the Constitution which mandate the reservation of seats for: Scheduled Castes and Tribes in the House of the People and Legislative Assemblies of the States respectively and Article 331 provides that notwithstanding anything in article 81, the President may, if he is of opinion that the Anglo-Indian community is not adequately represented in the House of the People, nominate not more than two members of that community to the House of the People.

Schedules to the constitution are the lists categorising and tabulating the bureaucratic activity and policy of the government. These schedules are amendable by parliament.

i. First Schedule (under Articles 1 and 4) gives a list of the States and Union Territories of India.

ii. Second schedule under Arts. 59(3), 65(3), 75(6), 97, 125, 148(3), 158(3) consists of Parts A to E.

◆ Part A contains provisions for fixing the remuneration and emoluments payable to the President and Governors.

- ◆ Part B has been deleted by the Constitution (Seventh Amendment) Act of 1956.
- ◆ Part C contains provisions as to the Speaker and the Deputy Speaker of the House of the People and the Chairman and the Deputy Chairman of the Council of States and the Speaker of the Legislative Assembly and the Chairman and the Deputy Chairman of the Legislative Council.
- ◆ Part D contains provisions as to emoluments of the judges of the Supreme Court and of the High Courts.
- ◆ Part E contains provisions as to the Comptroller and Auditor General of India.

iii. Third Schedule contains forms of Oaths and Affirmations- Articles 75(4), 99, 124(6), 148(2), 164(3), 188 and 219.

iv. Fourth Schedule allocates seats for each State and Union Territory, in the Council of States (Articles 4(1) and 20).

v. Fifth Schedule under Articles 244(1) deals with administration and control of Scheduled Areas. This schedule provides for amendment by a simple majority of Parliament and takes it out of the ambit of Article 368 (Amendment of the Constitution).

vi. Sixth Schedule provides for the administration of Tribal Areas in Assam, Meghalaya and Mizoram (Articles 214(2) and 275(1)). This schedule can also be amended by a simple majority of Parliament.

vii. Seventh Schedule (under Article 246) gives three Lists : 1. Union List contains 97 subjects in which the Union government has exclusive authority; 2. State List contains 66 subjects which are under the exclusive authority of State Governments; 3. Concurrent List contains 47 subjects, where the Union and States have concurrent powers.

viii. Eighth Schedule (under Articles 344(1) and 351 (1) gives list of languages recognised by the Constitution : 1. Assamese, 2. Bengali, 3. Gujarati, 4. Hindi, 5. Kannada, 6. Kashmiri, 7. Malayalam, 8. Marathi, 9. Oriya, 10. Punjabi, 11. Sanskrit, 12. Sindhi, 13. Tamil, 14. Telugu, 15, Urdu, 16. Konkani, 17. Manipuri, 18. Nepali.

ix. Ninth Schedule (under Article 31(B) was added by the Constitution (First Amendment) Act, 1951 covers validation of Acts and Orders relating to land tenures, land tax, railways, industries, etc., passed by the State Governments, and Union Government which are beyond the jurisdiction of Civil Courts.

x. Tenth Schedule (under Articles 101, 102, 191 and 192) contains provisions as to disqualification on the ground of defection.

xi. Eleventh Schedule (under Article 243 G) enlists functional areas or subjects that are necessary for implementation of schemes for economic development and social justice in each Panchayat.

xii. Twelfth Schedule contains provisions as to power, authority and responsibilities of municipal committees: Nagar panchayats for transitional area, municipal council for smaller urban areas and Municipal Corporation for large urban areas.

LET US SUM UP

⇨ The concept of state has emerged out of society which is governed by certain legal norms and sets of rules and regulations, in words of Aristotle, state is "a body of citizens sufficing for the purposes of life" and every state is a community and every community is established with a view to some good.

⇨ Though there is no accepted definition of the state, and various philosophers and Jurists have attempted to define the term state and have propounded different notions of state as given below:

⇨ Ethical notion- propounded by Plato and Aristotle and supported by Rousseau, Kant, Hegel and T. H. Green.

⇨ Legal notion - Bodin, Hobbes, Bentham and Austin.

⇨ Necessity of state to maintain law and order- Adam Smith, Bentham and Herbert Spencer.

⇨ State as both evil and unnecessary- anarchist view.

⇨ State as a mechanism representing the interests of every member of the state -MacIver and Laski , the Pluralist view.

⇨ State has absolute powers and unlimited control over the individuals who have no rights - Hegel and Nietzsche, Bernhardi, Treitschke, Mussolini and Hitler, the totalitarian view.

⇨ Minimal role of state - *Classical* liberals, Locke, Robert Nozick , Ayn Rand, Murray Rothbard and David Friedman.

⇨ State as welfare state- Modern liberalism, J. S. Mill, T. H. Green, MacIver and Laski.

⇨ There are different theories on origin of state as represented in tabular form below:

Theory	Philosophers	Basic concept
The organic theory	Cicero, Bluntschli, Rousseau, *Herbert Spencer, Albert Schaffle*	State is natural institution- the body politic is compared with the human body
The divine theory	Thomas Hobbes, James, Roberfilmers and Bossuet.	State established and governed by God. King is appointed by the God and is his agent and responsible to god for his actions.
Social contract theory	Richard Hooker, Grotius, Thomas Hobbes, John Locke, J. J. Rousseau.	State is formed by social contract of people for serving them.
Patriarchal theory	Sir Henry Maine, Donisthorpe, Duguit.	Society originated through families held together by the authority and protection of the eldest male descendant.
Matriarchal theory	McLennan, Jenks , Morgan, R. N. Gilchrist	In primitive family the kinship was traced through females and not through males
Theory of Force	Individualist school	Force and compulsion played an important part in the consolidation and erection of new state.
Historical or evolution theory		State had emerged out of historical and evolutionary process - Kinship, Religion and Political Consciousness.

⇨ The historical or evolution theory is the most scientific, popular and modern theory of origin of state.The modern nation-states had evolved over a period of span and in the world polity various types of states had existed at different times as a result of several factors such as kinship, religion, property, war, technical development and political consciousness *viz;* Tribal State, Oriental Empire, Greek City-State, Roman Empire, Feudal State. The Feudalism was succeeded by nation-states and the international law consisting of treaties, regulations, customary norms, and codes of conduct to govern relationships among state was developed.

⇨ According to *Bornhak*: three factors are necessary to the concept of the state: a definite territory, a population attached there to, and the subjection of both to a supreme magistracy. It can be said that A *state* is a legal and political entity comprised of the following essential elements:

(a) a number of people or a permanent population; (b) a definite territory; (c) a government; and (d) sovereignty (independence of external control).

⇨ The Constitution of India has defined the word 'State' for the purpose of Part III (fundamental rights of citizens) and Part – IV (Directive principles of state policy). Article 12 of the Constitution provides that state is: the Government and Parliament of India; the Government and Legislature of each State; all Local Authorities within the territory of India or under the control of the Government of India; other Authorities within the territory of India or under the control of the Government of India. *In Pradeep Kumar Biswas v. Indian Institute of Chemical Biology (2002) 5 SCC 111,* Supreme Court has laid down guidelines for determining what authorities can come under State under Article 12 of Indian Constitution.

⇨ The term Nation is very near in meaning to the term state and they are often used interchangeably but the 'Nation' is broader in significance, it is the state plus something else.

⇨ Seton Watson had noted that a 'scientific' definition of nation had never been achieved and probably never will be. Each nation is unique in the way its elements are combined, let alone how successfully they have jelled into a durable identity. The most significant elements in nation-building are language, religion, and historical experience, but there are also more unquantifiable ones such as custom and usage or the sense of togetherness.

⇨ There are various forms of government: Monarchy, rule by one, Aristocracy, rule by few people, Democracy. In perverted form the monarchy and aristocracy takes the form of Tyranny and oligarchy.

⇨ The French writer, Montesquieu, classifies governments into (1) Republics (with democratic and aristocratic), (2) Monarchies, and (3) Despotisms.

- Monarchy is the oldest type of government; sovereign power resides on one person. It could be royal and pure monarchy, absolute monarchies, the ocratic monarchies, limited, elective, mixed, and constitutional monarchies. It may also be despotic or tyranny.

- In aristocrat state, a minority Landowners, Nobles, Priests collectively enjoys sovereign power and imposes law on the rest.

- In democracy all the people, or a majority among them, exercise sovereign power collectively, people are free to express their views and rule themselves by consensus. Democracy may be pure or direct democracy or representative or indirect democracy.

- In the dictatorship form of government, an individual (a dictator) or small groups of an authoritarian party govern people by the use of intimidation and terror.

- The countries in world polity may follow unitary or federal system; they may have presidential or parliamentary form of government. In unitary form of government, the governing power resides and concentrated in a centralized government and all the local governments are subordinates for better administration and are subject to a central authority. In federal system there is division or distribution of the powers, decisions and functions of government between the centre at national level and its constituents at regional, state and local level.

- In presidential system of government, an executive branch exists and presides separately from the legislature and executive is chosen directly/indirectly by the citizens for a fixed period and is not responsible to the legislature. The legislature cannot dismiss it in normal circumstances. The President formulates the national policy, has power to mobilises military troops and declare state emergency.

- In parliamentary system, the legislature holds supreme power to make and execute laws. There are members of the legislature and the prime minister is chosen by members of the legislature (Parliament) from among their own and in practice the Prime minister (chief executive) is the leader of the majority party in the legislature.

- The United States of America, Argentina and few African countries have presidential form of government. The countries like the United Kingdom, India, Canada, Australia and the Scandinavian countries Germany, Spain and Italy have parliamentary systems.

- The legislature, executive and the judiciary are three organs of government. The Parliament of India consists of the President and the Lok Sabha and the Rajya Sabha. Parliament has Law making, financial powers and discusses the various policy agenda on various issues and concern of nation. The real executive power, in India is vested in the Council of Ministers with the Prime Minister as its head and the power of president is also subject to Judicial Review. The Supreme Court has power to declare a law passed by the Parliament ultra vires if it violates the fundamental rights or basic features of the constitution. All organs of government derive their powers and functions from the Constitution and therefore there is no question of supremacy of any organ of government in India. India is considered as quasi federal state.

- The Doctrine of the separation of powers emphasizes the structural classification of governmental powers in three organs i.e., legislature, executive and judiciary. It implies that the powers and functions of each of these organs are separate and distinct and no single agency can exercise complete authority.

- According to Wade and Philips, the theory of separation of the powers signifies that the same person should not form part of more than one of the three organs of the government; one organ of the government should not interfere with any other organ of the government; one organ of the government should not exercise the functions assigned to any other organ.

- The Doctrine was first evolved in ancient Greece and Rome. In the 17th century, John Locke in his Second Treatise of civil Government (1690), noted the distinction between three types of powers: legislative, executive and federative of the Commonwealth. Baron de Montesquieu in the book, The Spirit of Laws expanded the study of John Locke in 18th century and incorporated the ideas of a division of state and separation of powers. According to him:

"When the legislative and executive powers are united in the same person, or in the same body of magistrates, there can be no libert… Again, there is no liberty, if the judiciary power be not separated from the legislative and executive. Were it joined with the legislative, the life and liberty of the subject would be exposed to arbitrary control; for the judge would then be the legislator. Were it joined to the executive power, the judge might behave with violence and oppression. There would be an end to everything, were the same man, or the same body, whether of the nobles or of the

people, to exercise those three powers, that of enacting laws, that of executing the public resolutions, and of trying the causes of individuals."

⇨ The Montesquieu's theory was based on misinterpretation of English constitution but was widely welcomed and was re-in forced by English jurist Blackstone and Alexander Hamilton. The doctrine of separation of powers was incorporated in "French Declaration of Rights of Man" and was adopted byAmerica after the end of the war of independence by 1787.

⇨ The theory of separation of power was out rightly rejected by communists and totalitarians. However the doctrine is inevitable and is useful for maintaining individual liberty though it cannot be exercised in the strict sense of term and the functions of three organs of government cannot be divided into water tight compartments. In England, USA, and India, no separation of powers in the strict sense of term exists though in U.S.A., a rigid separation of powers is provided for in the constitution.

⇨ Constitution is a fundamental legal document made by its people providing for basic structure, procedures, powers, and duties of different organs of government and the other public authorities. The Indian constitution is supreme and provides for fundamental rights of the people, Directive principles of state policy to be followed by the state in the governance of the country and also lay down the duties of the people towards each other and nation.

Fundamental rights	Directive principles
Part –III of constitution. (Article 14 to 32)	Part –IV of constitution. (Article 39 to 51)
Enforceable and justifiable against the State through courts.	Non-justiciable but are fundamental in the governance of the country and act as directives or guidelines.
Fundamental right in India is not absolute and reason-able restrictions can be imposed in the interest of the sovereignty and integrity of India, the security of the State, friendly relations with foreign States, public order, decency or morality, or in relation to contempt of court, defamation or incitement to an offence.	The Directive Principles of state policies are intended to ensure distributive justice for removal of inequalities and disabilities and state has made many efforts to implement them and many laws hav ebeen enacted to implement them.

We, the People of India, having solemnly resolved to constitute India into a SOVEREIGN SOCIALIST SECULAR DEMOCRATIC REPUBLIC and to secure to all its citizens:

JUSTICE, social, economic and political;

LIBERTY of thought, expression, belief, faith and worship;

EQUALITY of status and of opportunity; and to promote among them all;

FRATERNITY assuring the dignity of the individual and the unity and integrity of the Nation;

IN OUR CONSTITUENT ASSEMBLY, this twenty-sixth day of November, 1949, do hereby adopt, enact and give to ourselves this Constitution.

⇨ The Constitution of India was framed by the Constituent Assembly and was enacted in November 26, 1949 and was brought into force on January 26, 1950. The Constitution is the supreme and all the laws framed in nation fall under its supremacy. It has 395 Articles in 22 Parts with 12 Schedules and also 4 Appendices.

⇨ India has a parliamentary type of democracy and has cabinet type of government and the cabinet is composed of the Prime Minister, the chief of the executive and his senior colleagues. There is single citizenship for all its citizens, in India. The Constitution of India is neither purely rigid nor purely flexible and is described as more appropriately a 'quasi-federal' because it consists of both, the federal and unitary elements. The Parliament may in exercise of its constituent power and amend by way of addition, variation or repeal any provision of this Constitution in accordance with the procedure laid down in article 368 of the constitution.

⇨ The Preamble to the Indian constitution representing the vision of people provides for the basic structure of the constitution and contains the ideals, objectives, rights and freedoms and basic philosophy of the Constitution which it intended to secure to its citizens.

⇨ Fundamental duties in article 51A were incorporated in constitution by 42nd Amendment Act (part IVA). The Part III and Part IV are considered complementary and supplementary to each other by Indian judiciary.

⇨ Article 326 of the Constitution provides that the elections to the House of the People and to the Legislative Assembly of every State shall be on the basis of adult suffrage.

Terminal Questions

1. Define state. Discuss in brief the main elements that constitute state.

2. Examine briefly various theories regarding the nature of state.

3. What constitute to be state as per article 12 of the Constitution?

4. Write short notes on the following:
   (a) Monarchy   (b) Democracy

5. Distinguish between federal and unitary form of government.

6. The Indian constitution is Quasi-federal in nature. Examine

7. Discuss and evaluate the impact of the theory of separation of powers.

8. Discuss the relationship between the fundamental rights and directive principle of state policy with the help of case laws.

9. What are the basic structures of Indian constitution? Describe in brief.

10. Discuss the procedure through which parliament can amend the constitution in India.

●●

2   Nature and Sources of Law

Nature of Law

Law is socially significant, indispensable and spread or flows throughout in all realms of behavior: social, cultural; moral, religious, etiquette and so on. The Justinian digest defines law as 'the standard of what is just and unjust'.

The Ancient Hindu law, viewed law as the command of God and not of any political sovereign, law is the part of 'Dharma'. (Sewell and Debrett, 1796)

The Aristotle, the ancient Greek philosopher defined law *'as an embodiment of reasons whether in individual or the community'*. Salmond in Jurisprudence defined Law as 'the body of principles recognised and applied by the state in the administration of justice'. The American jurist Benjamin Cardazo and Oliver Holmes while defining law also emphasised the role of courts.

Cardozo(1924)	Defines Law as a "principle or rule of conduct so established as to justify a prediction with reasonable certainty that it will be enforced by the courts if its authority is challenged."
Holmes (1897)	Stated that "The prophecies of what the courts will do in fact and nothing more pretentious, are what I mean by the law."

The anthropologist, Malinowski was of the view that law operates in common day activities of people and the essence of law is embodied in principle of reciprocity, on the other hand, Radcliffe- Brown and Hoebel see it as administration of state power but they were criticised as they failed to distinguish between law and government.

Malinowski (1926)	"Law is the specific result of the configuration of obligations, which makes it impossible for the native to shirk his responsibility without suffering for its future." "The rules of law– are sanctioned not by a mere psychological motive, but by a definite social machinery of binding force, based--upon mutual dependence and realised in the equivalent arrangement of reciprocal services".
Radcliffe-Brown as cited by Hoebel (1954:26)	Viewed Law as "The maintenance or establishment of social order within territorial framework by the exercise of coercive authority through the use or the possibility of use of the physical force. "
E. Admanson Hoebel (1954:28)	Has argued that "A social norm is legal if it neglects or infraction is regularly met, in threat or in fact, by the application of physical force by an individual or group possessing the socially recognised privilege of so acting".

The law as defined by British philosophers : Jeremy Benthamn, John Austin and H.L.A. Hart is given below:

Jeremy Benthamn (1970)	An assemblage of signs declarative of volition conceived or adopted by the sovereign in a state, concerning the conduct to be observed in a certain case, by a certain person or class of persons, who in question are supposed to be subject to his power.
John Austin	A rule laid down for the guidance of an intelligent being by an intelligent being having power over him.
H. L. A. Hart (1961)	As a union of primary and secondary rules. The Primary rules impose duties on people to behave in certain ways and are turned into laws via secondary rules which are power-conferring rules.

Theories of Law and different Schools of Jurisprudence

There are general philosophical theories of jurisprudence that attempts to define law and the nature of law. This theory of law advanced by legal theorists are of particular value and helps to understand the different facets of law and give a complete and rounded picture of the concept of law. Some theories try to define law by reference to its formal characteristics and to state what distinguishes law from other related phenomena. Others concentrate rather on the content of law and inquire what law ought to be rather than what it is. Yet others stress the operation of law in society and attempt to describe the function of law as it works in actual practice. Conflicts between such theories then are not altogether real, in so far as each theory is dealing with a slightly different aspect of law and are discussed below :

The Natural Law Theories

It provides that Law is 'lexnaturalis', it is universal law and is set by nature. It refers to objective moral truths or behavior which can be known or discovered by use of reason to analyse human nature. Socrates (470 -399 B.C.) and Plato believed that like natural physical law, there is natural moral law, the man's insight is the basis to judge the law and make know the absolute and eternal moral rules.

The natural theory as known today was codified by *Thomas Aquinas* (1225-74). He distinguished four different kinds of law, the eternal, the natural, the divine and the human law.

Hobbes accepted the fundamental law of nature by proclaiming that self-preservation is the great lesson of natural law and peace is the necessary condition for self-preservation. However he conceives "social contract" to justify authoritarian government or absolutist sovereign (see Leviathan, Pt. I. Chap 13).

Locke believed in "common good" and the sovereign or legislature constituted for the purpose of safeguarding life, property and liberty cannot take away these essentials as it would amount to violating the conditions of the social trust under which the legislature or sovereign holds its power (see Locke, *Two Treatises of Government*). The Locke's concept of separation of powers was further developed by Montesquieu who interposed judiciary as the final arbiter of maintaining balance between legislature and executive.

Grotius has also emphasised natural law principles and developed the concept of natural rights which was carried forward by Pufendorf with emphasis on the doctrine of legal equality amongst men.

Thus the theory of natural law defines law according to its content and believed that the law must include all moral principles to provide validity to the legal norms that are promulgated by human beings and law is just and legitimate if it promotes the common good.

Analytical Legal Positivism School

The theory of natural law has been fiercely challenged by the legal positivism tradition promulgated by scholars such as *Jeremy Bentham* (1748-1832) and *John Austin* ((1790-1859). *Jeremy Bentham* expounded the Theory of Utility for the purpose of legislation, whereby the law should aim at *"the greatest happiness of the greates number"*. In his work, *Introduction to the Principles of Morals and Legislation, Bentham has* expressed that the principle of utility should be the basis of morality and law. According to him *'utility'* promotes pleasure and prevents pain and all the questions of right and wrong should be decided on the touchstone of utility. Hobbesin Levathan has propounded that the individual subordinates himself to the sovereign, who can create and enforce laws according to a social contract with the people.

The idea that law is the command of the sovereign though, was advanced by *Bodin, Hobbes* and *Bentham*, but found its chief expression in Austin, whose theory of law is contained in *The Province of Jurisprudence Determined, first published in 1832*. Law, as per Austin is a body of rules determined and enforced by a sovereign political authority and it is not dependent on the morality of its content to be legitimate and draws its validity from the power of the sovereign, the only ruler, who must always be obeyed by subjects. According to Austin, the opinions or sentiments of an undetermined body of men , the law by analogy (fashion or honour) and law by metaphor (gravity) are improperly called law. The laws properly so called is divided into (1) laws of God set by God for men and (2) Human laws, set by men for men. Human laws are further divided in to positive law and other laws (positive morality) that are not set by men as political superior. According to *Austin*, positive Law (Laws strictly so called; the subject matter of jurisprudence) in a society have three characteristic features:

- A type of commands
- Laid by legally unlimited political sovereign;

♦ Coercive orders that impose duties or obligations on individuals and are enforceable by threat of force or sanction.

> *Who is* sovereign? To Austin, a sovereign is any person, or body of persons, whom the bulk of a political society habitually obeys, and who does not himself habitually obey some other person or persons *i.e.*, sovereign is a determinate person or group who have supreme and absolute *de facto* power and they are obeyed by all or most others but do not themselves similarly obey anyone else.
>
> *What command is law?* all commands are not law. For, to qualify as law, a general command obliging a class to act or forbearance must have been given by a political superior, or sovereign.
>
> *What is meant by Sanctions?* They are a logical part of the concept of law; they consist of the penalties inflicted on the orders of the sovereign for the violation of the law in other words of institutionalized punishments.

Thus Positivism regards law as the expression of the will of the state through the medium of the legislature. It is objected that this theory conflicts with ordinary usage by denying the name "law" to rules which are generally classified as legal, *e.g.*, rules of customary law, International law and much of constitutional law as none of these rules originate from a sovereign command. In the modern legal systems the procedures for legislation may be complex making it impossible to attribute sovereignty to any commander in this personal sense, especially where the power is divided into different organs of government. Further, it would be impossible for the supreme legislature/parliament to enact every legal rule and much law making will in fact be done by subordinates to whom legislative powers have been delegated.

> **Do you know?**
> Indian legal system has 'diffused' sovereignty that may be said to vest in the organs of government and is attributed to the persons in capacity of the post it holds in any of these organs and did not correspond with Austin's concept of sovereignty and did not vest in individual as an individual per se.

Modern Legal Positivist Approach

The Modern legal positivist approach was represented by Austrian jurist Hans Kelsen (1881-1973), H.L.A. Hart (1907-92), British philosopher and Joseph Raz.

Hans Kelsen propounded the Pure Theory of Law, a science of norms. The theory addresses the dynamic conception of law which addresses the process by which legal norms are created and provides a process oriented account of how these norms attain validity. According to Kelsen :

1. The entire legal system is a hierarchy of norms or pyramid of norms. (however this is static concept of law).

2. As a general rule, in the hierarchical structure of the legal system, the norms must derive their validity from other, "higher" norms and ultimate are controlled and dependent on the basic norms.

3. The basic norm, he calls it Grundnorm is the norm that one's respective legal system ought to be complied with.

4. For setting out the conditions for valid law, the theory of law must be "pure" and legal norms should be distinguished from other fields such as ethics, sociology, and psychology.

5. "A legal norm is no longer considered to be valid, if it remains permanently ineffective. Effectiveness is a condition of validity in the sense that effectiveness has to join the positioning of a legal norm if the norm is not to lose its validity. Kelsen further explains that "effectiveness" denotes two factors: whether a norm "is applied by the legal organs (particularly the courts)," and whether a norm "is obeyed by the individuals subjected to the legal order."

H.L.A. Hart describes his own viewpoint as a "soft positivism", he defines legal positivism as the theory that there is no logically necessary connection between law and morality but admits that rules of recognition may consider the compatibility or incompatibility of a rule with moral values as a criterion of the rule's legal validity.

Criticism of Analytical Positivism Theory

One of jurist *Joseph Raz* has criticised earlier analytical positivist jurist for overemphasising on nature of law instead of taking into account law as a system. He describes *law as system of norms providing a method of settling disputes authoritatively.* According to him, law consists of authoritative positivist considerations enforceable by the courts.

However, the theory of analytical school of law was rejected by jurists such as *Ronald Dworkin, Fuller and Finnis a*s it lays more emphasis on 'law as a command' and did not consider morality and custom as a source of law. Ronald Dworkin, has argued that moral considerations are important tools for judges to arrive at just decisions while deciding disputes involving statutory or case law. A legal system is more than just rules; there are principles, policies and binding legal standards which operate alongside rules. *Raz,* in 'The concept of a legal system'(1970) has stated that: The three most general and important features of the law are that it is normative, institutionalised and coercive. It is normative; it serves and is meant to serve as a guide for human behaviour. It is institutionalised, its application and modification are to a large extent performed or regulated by institutions. And it is coercive in that obedience to it and its application are internally guaranteed ultimately by the use of force. Naturally every theory of legal system must be compatible with an explanation of these features and every theory of legal system should take into account these features.

Historical and Anthropological Approaches

The representatives of historical and anthropological approaches are Von Savigny, Sir Henry Maine and others : EaHoebel, M. Gluckman, S. Diamond.

According to *Von Savigny* (system):

◆ Law has its existence (Daseyn) in the general will (Gesammtwille);

◆ Customary observance is not the cause of Law, but the evidence of its existence. Thus, according to him the common consciousness of the *Volk* (the people) can be the only true source and substance of this positive law;

◆ It is primarily via *custom*, habits, practices and beliefs of the people;

◆ The law is a matter of unconscious and organic growth and is therefore found and not made.

◆ The law like language develops with the life of people.

◆ Law is not universal and varies with people, time and needs of the community.

The Savigny's thesis was criticised as not taking into account other factors that influence law, the Volkgeist cannot be considered as exclusive source of law and customs are not solely based on popular consciousness of community.

Maine in his works, especially in *Ancient Law* (1861) has contrasted early societies in which social relations are dominated by *status* with "progressive" (complex) societies in which social relations are predominantly determined by contract.

According to Maine, the source of law in early societies took various forms such as: Law made by ruler under divine inspiration, customs, knowledge and administration of customs by priests followed by codification.

In the progressive societies, the law is developed by fiction, followed by equity and finally legislation. Maine's contribution to English jurisprudence is immense and triggered the anthropological research of law. However the **historical theories have been criticised** on the ground of its vague, parochial and unscientific explanation of the law.

Sociological Jurisprudence

Sociology as science dates back to writing of *Augustecomte* and *Spencer* who delineated stages of social phenomena and development but did not lay down any theory for sociology of law. The *Ihering* (1818-1892), a social utilitarian has laid down first foundation of Sociological Jurisprudence, and propounded theory *'law as means to an end'*. Ihering states that legal relations are in their essence relations of dominion or power; which are the sole starting points of the whole of private law.

Emile Durkheim (1858-1917) conceived division of labour in society and propounded that: Law reflects all the essential varieties of social solidarity which is mechanical and organic.

Leon Duguit (1859-1928), follows the views of the French sociologist. Emile Durkheim and considers that norms of objective law are based on a law of social solidarity. Social solidarity occurs when people have common needs which can be satisfied jointly, and when people have different needs and different abilities which can be satisfied through the exchange of mutual services. Duguit has argued that the law follows directly from the public solidarity and therefore stands above the state; the legal norm arises spontaneously in social interactions and Legislator merely states, but does not create it.

According to Austrian legal scholar *Ehrilch (1862-1922)*, sociology of law begins with the ascertainment (legal investigation) of the *living law*, the concrete which can be observed and not the abstract. He claims that 'the centre of gravity of legal development lies not in legislation, nor in juristic science, nor in judicial decision, but in society itself.

Max Weber (1864-1920) was first to develop a systematic sociology of law and graded the rational quality of law and its stages and concluded that there is casual connection between law and capitalism.

Roscoe Pound (1870-1964) has given distinct dimension to the sociology of law.

1. He concentrated on the functional aspects of law.

2. According to him law is designed for social needs, 'the end of law should satisfy a maximum of wants with minimum of fiction'.

3. He stated: 'Law is social engineering', *i.e.,* tasks of law is social engineering.

> 'Social engineering means a balance between the competing interests in society', in which
>
> Applied sciences are used for resolving individual and social problems.

4. He classifies interest in to three categories:
   i. Individual interest ;
   ii. Public interest and
   iii. Social interest

> *What is interest?* -Interest may be roughly defined as anything that is of general advantage to a person. Bodily security, property, reputation and freedom of speech are all interests in this sense, since all of these are to a man's advantage or in his interest but all such interests may not necessarily receive recognition and protection by law. What interests are the subject of legal recognition in a society are questions partly for sociology, partly for law and partly for ethics; and the reconciliation of conflicts between competing interests is in a broad sense part of the problem of justice.

The **Duguit's theory** has been criticised for excluding all metaphysical considerations from law, overlooking the state activities. Ihering pointed out that task of law is to reconcile conflicting interest but did not state in what direction it should be done. Ehrlich was criticised to be sketchy and for not making distinction between social and legal norms. The term social solidarity and social engineering are considered as a vague expressions creating confusion.

Realist School

The Positivism regards law as the expression of the will of the state through the medium of the legislature. Theories of legal realism too, like positivism look on law as the expression of the will of the state, but see this as made through the medium of the courts. The realist school concentrates more on what the courts actually do in reaching the final decision and evaluates any part of law in terms of its effect. The realist school has been divided into two parts:

- ◆ Scandinavian Realism
- ◆ American Realism

American Realism is a combination of the analytical positivism and sociological approaches and focuses on empirical factors underlying a legal system. Realist thinking was introduced to American jurisprudence by *Oliver Wendell Holmes,* according to him;

   i. The life of law is logic as well as experience.
   ii. The real nature of the law cannot be explained by formal deductive logic.
   iii. Judges make their decisions based on their own sense of what is right.
   iv. In order to see what the law is in reality, he adopted the standpoint of a hypothetical 'Bad man' facing trial. Therefore his theory is known as Bad Man Theory.

For Gray, the law was simply what the court decided and everything else including statutes, were simply the sources of law. (Gray, 1924).

Karl Llewellyn described the basic functions of law is to do 'law-jobs' in a society (Llewellyn, 1940).

Jerome Frank has stated, "Law is what the court has decided in respect of any particular set of facts prior to such a decision, the opinion of lawyers is only a guess as to what the court will decide and this cannot be treated as law unless the Court so decides by its judicial pronouncement." (Jerome Frank, 1930).

Scandinavian realism-law is nothing but social facts. The rules of law are independent imperatives issued from time to time by various constitutional agencies. The theorists like Hagerstrom, [Inquiries into the Nature of law and Marais (trans. Broad; ed. Olivecrona)]; Olivecrona, [Law and Fact]; Lundstedt, [*Legal Thinking Revised] had* contended that there are no such things as rules, but that conformity with a rule consists really in habitual behavior accompanied by a feeling of being bound to act in this habitual way. *Hägerström's* philosophy advances a naturalistic approach that conceives the positive law as a system of rules in terms of behavioural regularities among human beings and legal knowledge as an empirical inquiry into the causal relations between legal rules and human behaviour. This approach is followed by his pupils, the Swedish lawyers A. V. Lundstedt and Karl Olivecrona and Ross.

Olivecrona has stressed in *Law as Fact* that:

   i. Law as fact is something which has to be observed and the legal conceptions such as "command-duty", "legal rights and duties" are fantasies of mind;
   ii. The psychological pressures are the real reasons for law;
   iii. Law chiefly consists of rules about force.
   iv. He rejected the theory that morals influence the law. It is regular using of force and propaganda associated with it that establish moral standards.

v. "Rules of law" are imperatives distinct from commands, etc.

Olivercrona, in Legal Language and Reality had stated that the purpose of all legal enactments, judicial pronouncements, contracts, and other legal acts is to influence men's behavior and direct them in certain ways.

Lundstedt had said that law is found on social needs and not justice. The Danish theorist *Alf Ross* (B. 1899), though sharing some of these views regards laws as directions to the judges rather than as mere statements of fact and the test of validity of law lies in predictability of decisions *i.e.*, in accepting the system of norms as a scheme of interpretation, the actions of judges or decisions of the courts are meaningful responses to given conditions and within certain limits predict them. (See Ross, On Law and Justice).

The realist theories, defines law in terms of its actual functioning and operation and like positivism, look on law as the expression of the will of the state, but see this as made through the medium of the courts.

The Functions and Object of Law

The purpose of law is to provide Legal rights, Justice, stability and peaceful change. As per *Hobbes*: 'Law was brought into the world for nothing else, but to limit the natural liberty of particular men, in such manner, as they might not hurt, but assist one another, and join together against a common enemy (Leviathan, p. I38).

The immediate objects of Law are the creation and protection of legal rights. The theorist, Aquinas and Salmond have claimed justice as the goal of law: indeed for them it is a logical part of the very notion of law. For Aquinas, following Augustine, an unjust law is no law, while to Salmond, law is those principles that are applied by the state in the adminis-tration of justice. Others, such as the positivists, who would deny any essential or logical connection between the two concepts, would nevertheless regard justice as highly relevant to a critical evaluation of law (P.J. Fitzgerald, 1966).

Nature of Law as per Different School of Thought

We can summarise the nature of law as follow-ing:

♦ Law as the dictate of reason- natural law.

♦ Law as the command of the sovereign– Impera-tive law.

♦ Law as the practice of the court legal- realism.

♦ Positive law is the rules of ordinary human law.

♦ Law as means to creation and protection of legal rights, Justice, stability and peaceful changes.

♦ Law to maximise the fulfillment of the interests of the community and its members and to promote the smooth functioning of the machinery of the society.

♦ Law is territorial in nature with some exceptions to the rule.

♦ Law is response to social needs-Hoebel, 1954.

♦ Law reflects the intellectual, social, economic and political climate of its time and also the ideas, ideals and ideologies which are part of a distinct legal culture–Friedman,1984.

♦ Law is the most specialised and highly furnished engine of control employed by society–E. A. Ross, 1922.

Classification of Law

The classification of law is not a new concept and is categorised by various jurists in many ways. For the proper and legal understanding of the concept of law, it is essential that students must know the types of law which will help in better understanding of the systematic arrangement, interrelation and application of legal rules backed with state's enforcement mechanism.

Branches of Law

♦ The ancient Hindu law classifies law and matter of disputes under eighteen heads (Manusamriti). The Arthashastra had distinguished between the civil and criminal law. The ancient Indian law is discussed in detail in next chapter.

♦ The content of law can also be categorised as procedural or substantive and the distinction may also be made between public and private law and the same is discussed below in brief.

The Substantive and Procedural/Adjective Laws

These are the two important branches of Law and the terms "substantive" and "adjective" been invented by Bentham in 1843 but was criticised by Austin that the distinction cannot be made the basis of a just division. It is not easy to state with precision, the exact nature of the distinction between the two branches and there may be some overlapping but without laws of a substantive nature, procedural law would not have much to regulate, and in absence of procedural law, fair and consistent application of substantive law is not possible.

♦ The *Substantive laws* are statutory laws derived from common law, statutes, constitution, precedents, from writings of various professional texts and it defines and determines the rights and obligations of the citizen which is to be protected by civil and criminal law and includes the sphere of both public and private law.

Examples : Indian Contract Act, 1872; Transfer of Property Act 1882; Indian Penal Code 1860, Hindu Marriage Act, 1955,

♦ The *Procedural Laws* (or Adjective Law) are derived from constitutional law, statutes enacted by legislature and deals with the enforcement and administration of substantive law that is guided and regulated by the practice, procedure and machinery. It is the law of action that includes all legal proceedings, civil or criminal. Procedural law or adjective law comprises the rules by which a court hears and determines what happens in civil law suit, criminal or administrative proceedings. The rules are designed to ensure a fair and consistent application of due process (in the U.S.) or fundamental justice (in other common law countries) to all cases that come before a court.

Examples : Code of Civil Procedure, 1908; Code of Criminal Procedure, 1973; Indian Evidence Act, 1872; Limitation Act, 1963;

♦ There may be a law which may be procedural as well as substantive. For Example : Evidence law.

♦ *In Hitendra Vishnu Thakur and Ors. etc. v. State of Maharashtra and Ors.* (1994) 4 SCC 602-held that: Law relating to forum and limitation is procedural in nature, whereas law relating to right of action and right of appeal even though remedial, is substantive in nature. Further, every litigant has a vested right in substantive law but no such right exists in procedural law.

Public and Private law

Public law is that part of law, which governs relationships between the state (government/government agencies) with its subject and also the relationships between individuals directly concerning the society. In public law the State is not only arbiter, but is also one of the parties interested and therefore persons concerned in a Public- law right are necessarily dissimilar as one of them being always the State.

It includes the following heads:

♦ *Constitutionat Law:* Constitutional law postulates the supremacy of law in the functioning of state. It provides for the organs of the government. It establishes the structure, procedures, powers and duties, of the organs of government and spells out basic human rights which are fundamental in the governance of Nation in the form of Fundamental Rights and Directive Principles of State Policy. In words of Salmond, constitutional law is the body of those legal principles which determine the constitution of a state- which determine, that is to say, the essential and fundamental portions of the state's organisation.

♦ *Administrative Law:* Administrative law includes the making and promulgation of laws. The Administrative laws are enforced by the executive branch of a government in the form of regulations, orders, and decisions. It deals with the extent of powers held by the administrative bodies and the mechanism whereby their actions can be controlled. It also provides for legal remedies in case of any violation of the fundamental rights of its people.

Source : Different branches of the leagal system. Join http://www.excellup.com

♦ *Criminal Law:* Criminal law denotes wrongs against the state, community, and public. It generally is substantive law, deals with defining

Procedural Law versus Substantive Law

	Procedural Law	Substantive Law
Concept	Comprises of set of rules that govern the court; process or the procedure which the case moves through.	Deals with statutory law that is applied by courts in a particular case.
Enforcement	Provides mechanism for enforcement and administration of substantive law.	Defines the rights and duties of citizens to be protected by law.
Function	Can not function independently.	Can function independently.
Role in legal prcess	Can be applied both in legal and non-legal context.	Cannot be applied in non-legal context.

crime and acts prohibited by law as an offence (Indian Penal Code). The Adjective criminal law, Penal Procedure, provides for the machinery of the prosecution and punishment of offenders.

Criminal law is important for maintaining law and order in the society. A crime is a "public" offense as opposed to an "individual" or "private" wrong and it is considered as crime against the whole society.

> "Public Offense" is an act committed or omitted in violation of a law forbidding or commanding it which can be punished upon conviction with either death, fine, imprisonment, removal from office or disqualification to hold any office of honour (defines in Section 15 of California Penal Code).

Criminal law deals with conduct or acts that the law defines as offences. For example, theft, harassment a woman her dowry, murder.

Public Law also deals with regulation of public utilities, law relating to the proprietary powers of the state and its political sub-divisions.

- *Private Law* concerns with defining, regulating, governing and enforcing relationships between individuals with one another or private relationships between citizens and companies/ associations/corporations that are not of public importance. It is concerned with both substantive and procedural rules.

In the case of private law, the role of the state is merely to recognise and enforce the relevant law and to adjudicate the matters in dispute between litigating parties through its judicial organs (*e.g.* courts). Both of the persons concerned in private law have rights and duties and the State is present but only as arbiter of the rights and duties which exist between one of its subjects and another. If there is harm or injury to right of individual. The petition has to be filed before relevant court by affected party for the specific relief.

Private Law may include Civil Laws such as :
  i. Law of Obligations/Law of Contract
  ii. Law of Tort
  iii. Law of Property
and Personal Laws such as :
  i. Marriage
  ii. Divorce
  iii. Succession and
  iv. Family Laws–family rights against abduction and adultery

General Classification of Law

Law in modern state can be generally classified in terms of its usage into two classes (1) International Law and (2) Municipal Law.

International Law

International law consist of those rules, regulations and principles of general application that deals with conduct of nation's and international organisations in their international relations which are recognised and are binding upon each other through reciprocity.

Today, this branch of law has grown manifold and has acquired increasing importance on account of globalisation and other related factors.

> ### International Court of Justice (ICJ)
> **Some Important Points:**
> - The International Court of Justice was established by the Charter of the United Nations June 1945, which provides that all Member States of the United Nations are *ipso facto* parties to the Court's Statute.
> - The composition and functioning of the Court are organised by this Statute, and by the rules of the Court which are drawn up by the Court itself.
> - The Statute can be amended only in the same way as the Charter, *i.e.,* by a two-thirds majority vote in the General Assembly and ratification by two-thirds of the States (Art 69).
> - It is the principal judicial organ of the United Nations (UN);
> - It began to work in April 1946.
> - The seat of the Court is at the Peace Palace in The Hague (Netherlands).
> - The Court's role is to settle, in accordance with international law, legal disputes submitted to it by States and to give advisory opinions on legal questions referred to it by authorised United Nations organs and specialised agencies.
> - The Court is composed of 15 judges, who are elected for terms of office of nine years by the United Nations General Assembly and the Security Council.
> - It is assisted by a Registry, its administrative organ.
> - Its official languages are English and French.
> Source: http://www.icj-cij.org/

Legal Personality and International Public and Private Law

The States, International Organisations established by States through international agreements are legal persons that can have rights and obligations under international law. This branch of law that relates to the body of rules and regulations, governing the relationship between nations falls under the sphere of *Public International law*. The Countries mutually recognise the sets of rules which are binding on them in their transactions on a reciprocal basis.

Besides, the states may also have international obligations to regulate the conduct of their nationals, especially if they are carrying out activities outside their territory. *The Private International Law* is that part of law which deals with cases having a foreign element and relates to the rights of private citizens of different countries. Example: Marriages and adoption of individuals belonging to different nations.

Municipal Law

Municipal laws are basically domestic or national laws, *as an entity independent of other states or nations.* They regulate the relationship between the State and its citizens and determine the relationship among citizens. Municipal law can be further classified into two segments: public and private law as discussed above. The law is also substantive and adjective. Municipal law includes not only law at the national level, but law at the state, provincial, territorial, regional or local levels.

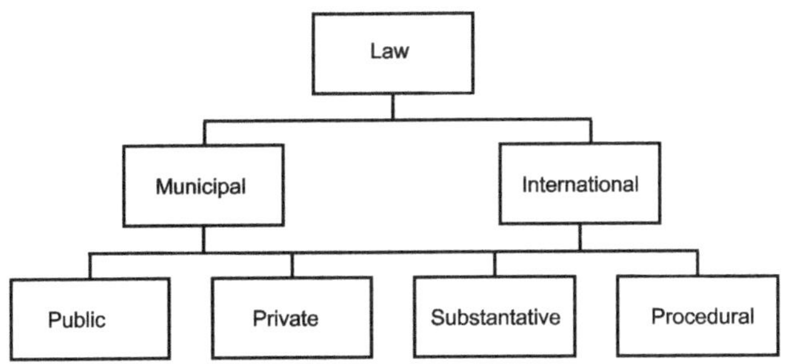

Source of Law

According to Gray, 'Source means the raw materials both statutory and traditional, from which judges derive the grounds for deciding the cases brought before them. **Austin** has divided sources into 'formal' and 'material' sources. The formal sources meant giving legal stamp of the state authorities. The material sources mean content of law and legal precept. (kaul,Ak:383)

Salmond (edn 2009): Sources of law can be classified as either legal or historical. The former are those sources which are recognised as such by the law itself. The latter are those sources lacking formal recognition by the law.

Salmond's classification can be explained in the following graphic manner:

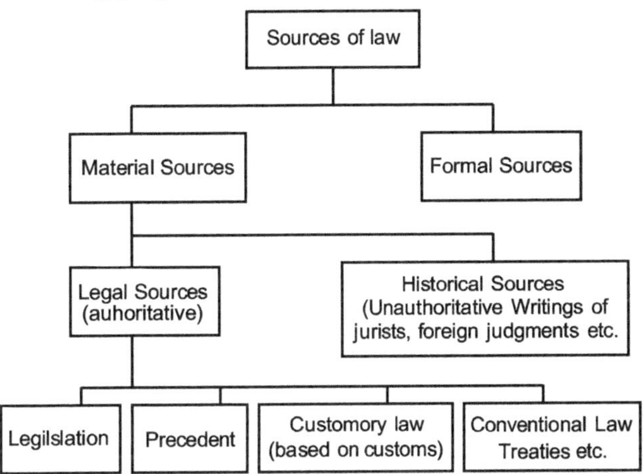

Allen: law and its sources connote those agencies by which rules of conduct acquire the character of law by becoming objectively definite, uniform, and above-all, compulsory.

Holland (2007: 55) -The term source has been used to denote/indicate the following:

1. The quarter whence we obtain our knowledge of law *e.g.*, Statute Book, Reports, Esteemed Treatises.

2. The ultimate authority which gives them the force of law *i.e.*, the State.

3. Causes that brought in to existence rules which have subsequently acquired that force-custom, religion, scientific discussion.

4. Organs through which state either grants legal recognition to rules previously unauthorised or itself create new law by adjudication, equity, legislation.

Von-Savigny: The sources of law are faith, custom, and the common consciousness of the people.

Henry Maine: the source of law in early societies took various forms such as custom, followed by codes and in the progressive societies by fiction, equity and finally, legislation.

For **Realist school** of thought, the source of law is the judicial decision and 'law jobs'.

For **Sociological jurists**: interests are the chief subject-matter of law and the task of law in society is the satisfaction of human wants and desires by converting the lawyer as a social engineer to satisfy the wants and desires of the society.

According to **Roscoe Pound**: sources of law implies the factors which legal precepts owe their content, the agencies that develop them and formulate them as something behind which the law making and law administering authorities may put the power of state behind them (Roscoe pound, Jurisprudence) According to Pound, there are seven sources of law: Usage; Religion; Moral and Philosophical Ideas; Adjudication; Scientific Discussions; Legislation; Custom.

Thus, every school of philosophy provides for a different meaning of the term sources of law as also seen in definitions of law. It is however necessary to know the sources i.e. from where the law has originated as the binding rule of conduct in a society. There may be variation in sequencing of various sources of law, but generally they are applicable to most legal systems.

Sources of International Law- Article 38(1) of the Statute of the International Court of Justice, provides for the list of sources of law that the court shall apply:

a) International conventions (treaties), whether general or particular, establishing rules expressly recognised by the contesting states;

b) International custom, as evidence of a general practice accepted as law;

c) The general principles of law recognised by civilised nations;

d) The judicial decisions and the teachings of the most highly qualified publicists of the various nations, as subsidiary means for the determination of rules of law. (This is Subject to the provisions of Article 59- The decision of the Court has no binding force except between the parties and in respect of that particular case).

Major Sources of Law

Let us now discuss the major sources of law with special reference to India:

Legislation (process, delegated and subordinate legislation)

The term "legislation" describes the deliberate creation of legal precepts by a body of government which gives articulate expression to such legal precept in a formalised legal document. (Vago Steven, 1988). The term *'legislation'* is derived from the Latin word *legis* which means *'law'* and *latum* which means *"to make"* or *"set"*. Therefore, the word *'legislation'* means the *'making of law'*. Legislation is that source of law which consists in the declaration of legal rules by a competent authority. In a wide sense, it includes all methods of law-making and in modern state emerged as major, nearly exclusive source of law. Every Act of parliament is an instance of legislature, irrespective altogether of its purpose and effect.

> **Do You Know?**
>
> Legislation is not merely a source of new law, but is equally effective in amending or abolishing existing laws in a country.

Types of Legislation

Legislation is either supreme or subordinate.

The **supreme legislation** is that which proceeds from the supreme or sovereign power in the state, and is therefore incapable of being repealed, annulled or controlled by any other legislative authority.

The **delegated legislation** (also referred to as secondary legislation or subordinate legislation) is law made by an executive authority under powers given to them by primary legislation in order to implement and administer the requirements of that primary legislation. Since delegated legislation proceeds from any authority other than the sovereign power and is dependent for its continued existence and validity on some superior or supreme authority, it is called subordinate legislation. As the legislature is required to make laws in a large number of subjects and due to paucity of time, pressure of work, technicality of subjects, to meet unforeseen/emergency situations, the legislature makes laws in the skeleton form and expressly delegate by an enabling act also known as the parent act or empowering act a power to make delegated legislation on a government minister or another person or body, the executive-to exercise power of the rule making, delegated to it by legislature. There are subordinate legislation in the form of rules, regulations, orders, ordinances, as well as by-laws made by Central and State Governments and local authorities like Municipal Corporations, Municipalities, Gram Panchayats and other local bodies. This subordinate legislation makes the implementation of law easier and flexible and is made under the authority conferred or delegated either by Parliament or State or Union Territory Legislatures.

Legislation in India–Legislation has been an important source of law in India. The acts like Indian Penal Code, 1860; Indian Evidence Act, 1872; Indian Contract Act, 1872; Government of India Act, 1919; Government of India Act, 1935, exist even from in British era. The constitution of India is the guiding light in all matters executive, legislative and judicial in the country. According to the doctrine of separation of powers, the legislature cannot exercise executive or judicial power; the executive cannot exercise legislative or judicial power; and the judiciary cannot exercise the other two powers. In India, the doctrine of parliamentary supremacy exists and all forms of legislative activities recognised by law, other than the power of parliament, are considered subordinate and subject to parliamentary control. The Indian Parliament is competent to make laws that may extend throughout or in any part of the territory of India on the matters enumerated in the Union List and also on matters that are not included in the State List or the Concurrent List; State Legislatures are competent to make laws applicable within its territory on matters enumerated in the State List. However, on the matters enumerated in the Concurrent List, both the Union and the States have power to legislate and in the event of repugnancy, laws made by Parliament prevail over law made by State Legislatures to the extent of the repugnancy.

Case Law–Stare decisis(s), precedents within the hierarchy of courts

In earlier human civilisation, the dispute between two parties is referred to a third party who acts as the arbiter (tribal chief or a priest) and his decision is generally obeyed by both the parties. With the passage of time, the judicial organ of the state is given power to decide cases between the parties. While deciding a case and pronouncing a judgment, when there is no legislature on particular point, the judges generally apply their own common sense of right and wrong and of justice. This is known as Judge-made laws or case laws. Such decisions become authority or guide for subsequent cases of a similar nature and they are called *precedents*.

◆ Precedent is one of the important source of law though is considered less authoritative source of law than a statute. The judicial precedent is a judgement or a decision of a court of law and is cited as an authority for deciding a similar state of fact in the same manner or on the same principle or by analogy.

◆ The principle by which a judicial decision becomes a precedent is known as "Stare Decisis", an abbreviation of the Latin phrase, *stare decisiset non quietamovere* (to stand by precedents and not to disturb settled points). Generally speaking, *stare decisis* means that a point of law once settled by a judicial decision must be followed in a subsequent case on similar point of law.

◆ *In Krishna Kumar v. UOI 1990 (4) SCC 207 at 226-27*–Supreme Court held that there cannot be a judicial precedent on a question of fact. It is only the legal principle laid down on the basis of fact and the law that becomes judicial precedent.

◆ The rule is only ratio *decidendi* of previous case is binding not the obiter *dicta*. Ratio *decidendi* of a case is "any rule of law considered *necessary* by the Judge for the decision of the case: it is that part of the *decision* which has binding effect and the *facts* of the case plays a large part in its identification". (R. Cross, 1977).

Ratio *decidendi*	Obiter *dicta*	Ratio *legis*
It is the reason for (or of) deciding. (Paul Wilson case, 1983)	Statement of law which goes beyond the occasion, and lay down a rule that is irrelevant to the purpose in hand.	The reason behind the law.
The decision of any issue in the course of judicial proceedings. (G.W. Paton)	Expression of a brief viewpoint.	Occasion of making a law.
The necessary core of the decision. (H.J. Abraham)	Is more or less extraneous, presumably unnecessary-to-the decision- point made by the author of an opinion. (H.J. Abraham)	
Legal Binding rule.	has no binding effect and may have persuasive influence.	Applies to statutory law.

The Hierarchy of Authority

The general rule is that a court is bound by the decisions of all courts higher than itself. Article 141 of the Constitution provides Law declared by Supreme Court to be binding on all courts within the territory of India. Supreme Court is at apex level followed by High Court and at the lowest level are Subordinate Courts (at District and subordinate level). Elaborate discussion has been done in the chapter 3 of this book.

Rules applicable on courts with regard to hierarchy of authority:

♦ The decision of a superior Court is binding on all inferior court but the Supreme Court is not bound by its own decisions and may reverse a previous decision. However, the Court will surely be slow to do so unless such previous decision appears to be obviously erroneous. (*Dwarkadas v. Sholapur Co.*, AIR 1954 SC 119 (137))

♦ The rule is that courts are bound only by decisions of higher courts and not by those of lower or equal rank. High Court judge cannot question a decision of the Supreme Court.

♦ Section 3 of the Code of Civil Procedure, 1908 provides that a District Court is subordinate to the High Court and every Civil Court inferior to a District Court and every Court of Small Causes is subordinate to the High Court and the District Court.

♦ The Courts of subordinate jurisdiction do not create binding decision even for courts lower in rank.

♦ Let us see the rules applicable on courts with regard to hierarchy of authority as deduced from various judgments of the court: *Seshamma v. V.N. Rao* (1940) 1 MLJ 400 (412) (FB); *Subbarayudu v. State*1955 ALT 53 (FB); *Atma Ram v. State of Punjab*, AIR 1959 SC 519 (527); *Jai Kuer v. Sher Singh*, AIR 1960 SC 1118 (1122); *Tribhovandas v. Ratilal*, AIR 1968 SC 372 :

  ♦ A Single Judge shall not differ from the judgment of another Judge of the Court. If he does not agree, he shall refer the matter to a Bench of two Judges. He must follow the decision of a Divisional Bench exercising appellate jurisdiction.

  ♦ If there is a conflict of Bench decisions, single judge should refer the case to a Bench of two Judges who may refer it to a Full Bench.

♦ A Division Bench cannot dissent from another Division Bench decision. Ordinarily, one Divisional Bench must respect another Divisional Bench but if it differs, the case should be referred to a Full Bench. Division Bench must follow a Full Bench decision of the same Court.

Judicial review and law making power of courts

Jacob, 1984:38 has noted that the courts are often called upon to interpret the Constitution. Every controversial statute and a variety of controversial executive actions are challenged in the courts on grounds of unconstitutional. The power of judicial review of legislation is given to the judiciary by the Indian Constitution vide articles: 13, 32, 131-136, 143, 226, 145, 246, 251, 254 and 372.

The Courts also get opportunity to engage in lawmaking when Judges determine the effect of legislative decisions while interpreting ambiguous statutes. However there is prevalent theory of case law that a judge does not make law but merely declares it and the overruling of a previous decision is a declaration that the supposed rule was never a law. The supporters of this view are Jurists like *Edward Coke and Mathew Hale*. According to them judicial decisions are not sources of law but, they are simply the proof of what the law is. On the other hand, jurists like *Dicey, Gray, Salmond*are are of the opinion that judges do make law, the judges while interpreting the law enacted by the legislative bodies, contribute to the existing body of law. A large part of the English law is judge-made law.

The legislation is the most authoritative source of law. The judicial decisions may be Authoritative, Conditionally authoritative or persuasive precedent as distinguished below :

Authoritative Precedent	Conditionally authoritative Precedents	Persuasive Precedent
Are that which judges must follow whether they approve of it or not.	They are ordinarily binding on the Court before which they are cited, but are liable to be disregarded in certain circumstances.	Are those precedents which the judges may take in to consideration if they are sound and reasonable but are under no obligation to follow.
These are Legal sources of law and are allowed by the law courts as of right. Example: decision of the Supreme Court.	The decision of a Single Judge of a High Court is absolutely authoritative on the subordinate Courts, but is conditionally authoritative if cited before a Division Bench of the same High Court by way of overruling or dissenting.	These are Historical sources of law have no such claim, although they influence the course of legal developments. Example: Foreign judgments; the decisions of one High Court are only persuasive precedents in other High Courts; obiter dicta.

<table>
<tr><td>

Do you know?

The distinction between authoritative and persuasive precedents is somewhat rendered difficult because of the fact that the same precedent may be authoritative in one court and persuasive only for the other.

</td></tr>
</table>

Customs

Customs are the oldest source of law. A custom is a norm or rule which is not written but has been established by a long usage or practice common to many or to a particular place or class or habitual with, and has obtained the force of law. It exists as law in every country but tends to lose its importance relatively to other kinds of law. Customary law is brought in by long usage and observed as law. Paul Bohannan (1973) has argued that laws are a special kind of "reinstitutionalised custom." Customs are norms or rules about the ways in which people must behave if social institutions are to perform their function and society is to endure.

There is a very long history of recognition of local customary law in civil matters in India, in particular, in matters of *family law and succession*. Article 13(3) (a) of Indian Constitution provides that "law" includes custom or usage having in the territory of India, the force of law.

Proof of existence of custom

In view of the above, the proof of local custom has become a matter of considerable importance and is litigated in many cases. Proof of custom has been aided by the provisions of the Indian Evidence Act 1872. Section 48 of the act provides that when the Court has to form an opinion as to the existence of any general custom or right, the opinions, as to the existence of such custom or right, or persons who would be likely to know of its existence if it existed, are relevant *i.e.*, considered admissible

Explanation – The expression "general custom or right" includes customs or rights common to any considerable class of persons.

<table>
<tr><td>

Illustration:

The right of the villagers of a particular village to use the water of a particular well is a general right within the meaning of this section.

</td></tr>
</table>

Section 49 of the act deals with opinion as to usage, tenets, etc., when are considered relevant by courts- Section 49 has been held to apply to proof of customary adoption, to family customs of primogeniture, and so on. [AIR Manual, 179-80].

Section 57 deals with facts of which Court must take judicial notice.

Essentials for the custom as source of law:

♦ Where custom is set up to prove that it is at variance with the ordinary law, it has to be proved that it is *not opposed to public policy* and that it is *ancient, invariable, continuous, notorious,* not expressly forbidden by the legislature and not opposed to morality or public policy [*Mookka Kone v. Ammakutti Ammal (AIR 1928 Mad 299 (FB))*]

♦ The custom could properly be proved by general evidence given by members of the family or tribe without proof of special instances. Further when there is clear evidence of such general statements, which is all one-sided, it is open to the Court to rely on that and give a decision upholding the custom. Thus, proof of actual instances of such a custom taking effect is not necessary. (*Privy Council, Ahmad Khan v. Channi Bibi 1925, 52 IA 379, 3834; Ajai Verma v. Vijai Kumari (1939) 41 BOMLR 700).*

♦ Custom, being in derogation of a general rule, is required to be construed strictly (*Dr. Surajmani Stella Kujur v. Durga Charan Hansdah AIR 2001 SC 938*).

♦ A custom is a particular rule which has existed either actually or presumptively from time immemorial, and has obtained the force of law in a particular locality, although contrary to or not consistent with the general common law of the realm. It must be certain in respect of its nature generally as well as in respect of the locality where it is alleged to obtain and the persons whom it is alleged to affect.

♦ *Custom is authoritative,* it stands in the place of law, and regulates the conduct of men in the most important concerns of life; fashion is arbitrary and capricious, it decides in matters of trifling importance, manners are rational, they are the expressions of moral feelings.(*Bhimashya & Ors. v. Smt. Janabi @ Janawwa,* (2006) 13 SCC 627).

♦ Custom is one of the three sources of Hindu Law. Custom may override a statute subject; of course, to a clear proof of usage--- Hindu law recognises three types of customs: local custom, class custom and family custom.(*Smt. Ass Kaur (Deceased) By L. Rs v. Kartar Singh (Dead) By L.Rs. & Ors 2007 AIR 2369-para 9,10,11*)

♦ The various case laws *Effuah Amissah v. Effuah Krabah, AIR 1936 P.C. 147; T. Saraswati Ammal v. Jagadambal & Anr., AIR 1953 SC 201; Ujagar Singh v. Mst. Jeo, AIR 1959 SC 1041; R.B.S.S. Munnalal and Others v. S.S. Rajkumar and Others [AIR 1962 SC 1493], and Siromani v. Hemkumar & Ors., AIR 1968 SC 1299); Laxmibai (Dead) Thru Lr'S. & Anr. v. Bhagwanthbuva (Dead) Thru Lr'S. 2013* - provides that:

i. A custom must be proved to be ancient, certain and reasonable.

ii. The evidence adduced on behalf of the party concerned must prove the alleged custom and the proof must not be unsatisfactory and conflicting.

iii. A custom cannot be extended by analogy or logical process and it also cannot be established by a priori method. Custom cannot be a matter of theory but must always be a matter of fact and one custom cannot be deduced from another. It is a well-established law that custom cannot be enlarged by parity of reasoning.

iv. When a custom has been judicially recognised by the Court, it passes into the law of the land without necessity of proof in each individual case. Customs are also recognised under Indian Easements Act, 1882 according to section 18 of the Indian Easements Act, 1882, an easement may be acquired in virtue of a local custom. Such easements are called customary easements.

Illustrations :

(a) By the custom of a certain village every cultivator of village land is entitled, as such, to graze his cattle on the common pasture. Having become the tenant of a plot of uncultivated land in the village breaks up and cultivates that plot he thereby acquires an easement to graze his cattle in accordance with the custom.

(b) By the custom of a certain town, no owner or occupier of a house can open a new window therein so as substantially to invade his neighbour's privacy. A builds a house in the town near B's house. A thereupon acquires an easement that B shall not open new windows in his house so as to command a view of the portions of A's house which are ordinarily excluded from observation, and B requires a like easement with respect to A's house.

Source: Section 18, Indian Easement Act, 1882.

http://lawzonline.com/bareacts/indian-easements-act/Section18-indian-easements-act.html-

v. The court can also take judicial notice of such customs in terms of Section 57 of the Evidence Act, 1872. As and when custom has repeatedly been recognized by the courts, the same need not be proved.

vi. Material customs must be proved properly and satisfactorily, until the time that such custom has, by way of frequent proof in the Court become so notorious, that the Courts take judicial notice of it.

Do you know?

Both, practice and custom are general or particular but the practice is absolute and may be adopted by a number of persons without reference to each other but on the other hand, the custom is relative and is always followed either by limitation or prescription. The practice of gaming has always been followed by the vicious part of society, but it is to be hoped for the honour of man that it will never become a custom.

LET US SUM UP

⇨ The philosophical theories of law advanced by legal theorists are of particular value and help to understand the nature, concept and function of law. **The Natural Law theory** provides that Law is *'lexnaturalis'*, it is universal law and is set by nature. Thomas Aquinas, proponent of natural law theory distinguished four different kinds of law, the eternal, the natural, the divine and the human law. Hobbes conceives "social contract" to justify authoritarian government or absolutist sovereign.

⇨ The Locke's laid down the concept of separation of powers which was further developed by Montesquieu who interposed judiciary as the final arbiter of maintaining balance between legislature and executive.

⇨ Grotius emphasised natural law principles and developed the concept of natural rights which was carried forward by Pufendorf with emphasis on the doctrine of legal equality amongst men.

⇨ The idea that law is the command of the sovereign was advanced by legal positivist such as Bodin, Hobbes and Bentham, but found its chief expression in Austin's theory of law contained in *The Province of Jurisprudence Determined*.

⇨ Positivism regards law as the expression of the will of the state through the medium of the legislature. The Modern legal positivist was jurist Hans Kelsen, H.L.A. Hart, and Joseph Raz. Hans Kelsen propounded the Pure Theory of Law, a science of norms, where the Grundnorm is a basic norm; the norms derive their validity from other, "higher" norms in a legal system. According to Hart, a legal system arises from the combination of primary and secondary rules. Joseph Raz describes law as system of norms providing a method of settling disputes authoritatively.

➪ The main representatives of historical and anthropological approaches are Von Savigny and Sir Henry Maine. As per Savigny, Law has its existence in the general will and customary observance is not the cause of Law, but the evidence of its existence. Maine contrasted earlier societies with progressive societies; the source of law in early societies took various forms such as customs, followed by codes and in the progressive societies by fiction, equity and finally legislation.

➪ *Jhering* laid down first foundation of Sociological Jurisprudence, and propounded theory 'law as means to an end'. Duguit had argued that the law follows directly from the public solidarity and therefore stands above the state. *Ehrilch*, sociology of law begins with the legal investigation of the *living law*. Roscoe Pound propounded that 'Law is social engineering which means a balance between the competing interests in society'.

➪ In the twentieth century, the Philosophical School has taken various shapes such as revival of Natural law, American realism, Scandinavian realist, Marxist theory of law and state, critical legal studies, feminist jurisprudence and theories of justice.

➪ Theories of legal realism like positivism also looked on law as the expression of the will of the state, but see this as made through the medium of the courts.

➪ The Marx and Engels believed that capitalist societies and capitalism will give way to communist society and communism and the society will be a classless society. The critical legal studies have raised the debate about law, legal institutions and legal reasoning in the overall structural design of a society.

➪ There are four schools of feminist thought: *liberal, radical, cultural and postmodern. Rawls* in his theory of justiceas fairness envisions a society of free citizens holding equal basic rights cooperating within an egalitarian economic system.

➪ Law is a means for creation and protection of legal rights, justice, stability and peaceful changes. It is territorial in nature with some exceptions to the rule.

➪ The Case of the Speluncean Explorers is a hypothetical legal case reflecting the five separate judicial opinions on the issue based on divergent philosophical theories of jurisprudence.

➪ Thus out of the five judges, two upheld the conviction and two set aside the conviction, whereas one judge declared his withdrawal from the decision of this case. The Supreme Court being evenly divided, the conviction and sentence of the trial court stood affirmed.

Judge	School of thought followed	Decision	
Chief Justice Truepenny	Positive school	Upheld conviction	Felt guilty of inflicting undeserved punishment; relinquishing his positive approach of law he recommended chief justice to extend executive clemency to the defendants
Foster, J.	Natural and Realistic school	No conviction	Felt defendant were in State of nature and form their law by agreement; applies purposive interpretation of law; follows realist school and referring to broad purpose of criminal legislation declared that statute did not apply to case of self defence.
Tatting, J.	—	Withdraw	Criticised Foster, J. but was unable to resolve his dilemma to convict or acquit the defendants.
Keen, J.	Positive school	Affirmed conviction	He also criticised Foster, J., he did not like the idea of judicial activism and preferred to interpret and decide case as per the letter and spirit of law.
Handy, J.	Sociological school	Acquittal	Take into account the opinion poll of the people and justified it as to maintain credibility of judiciary among the public.

➭ The important branches of law are public and private law, and the procedural and substantive law. In general, law is divided in to Municipal and International Law.

➭ International law consists of those rules, regulations and principles of general application that deals with conduct of Nation's and International organisations in their international relations which are recognised and are binding upon each other through reciprocity.

➭ Municipal laws are domestic or national laws regulating the relationship between the State and its citizen.

➭ Public law deals more with issues that affect the general public (may be individual, citizen or corporation) or the state itself *and* is concerned with the structure of government, the duties and powers of officials, and the relationship between the individual and the state.

➭ The private law focuses more on issues affecting private individuals, or corporations. *Private* law is concerned with both substantive and procedural rules governing relationships between individuals.

➭ Substantive law defines the crime or the wrong and also their remedies; it determines the subject-matter of litigation. It consists of Substantive Civil and Substantive Criminal Law and includes all categories of public and private law.

➭ Procedural Law is law of action that includes all legal proceedings, civil or criminal. It determines what facts constitute proof of a wrong and lays down the rules with the help of which law is enforced.

➭ Public law includes the following heads: Constitutional Law, Administrative Law, Criminal Law and Criminal Procedure. It may also include law of the state considered in its quasi private personality, procedure relating to the state as so considered and Judge made law.

➭ The Private law may include: Law of obligations/ Law of contract (organises and regulates legal relations between individuals under contract); Law of tort (addresses and remedies issues for civil wrongs, not arising from any contractual obligation); Law of property; Law of succession; family laws- family rights against abduction and adultery.

➭ Sources of law are formal and material; either legal or historical. After referring to writings of different jurists, it can be said that, the sources of law may include: faith, custom, and the common consciousness of the people, equity, legislation, judicial decisions.

➭ Legislation is the source of law which consists in the declaration of legal rules by a competent authority-parliament. Legislation is either supreme or subordinate. The supreme legislation is that which proceeds from the supreme or sovereign power in the state and the delegated legislation (also referred to as secondary legislation or subordinate legislation) is the law made by an executive authority under powers given to them by primary legislation in order to implement and administer the requirements of that primary legislation. The subordinate legislations are in the form of rules, regulations, orders, ordinances, as well as by-laws made by Central and State Governments and local authorities like Municipal Corporations, Municipalities, Gram Panchayats and other local bodies.

➭ In India, the doctrine of parliamentary supremacy exists and all forms of legislative activities recognized by law, other than the power of parliament, are considered subordinate and subject to parliamentary control. The Executive, Judiciary, Municipal Authorities, Private individuals may have power to exercise delegated legislation.

➭ The Legislature is not competent to delegate to the executive or any other body, its essential legislative function, namely, the determination of the legislative policy and its formulation, as a rule of conduct.

➭ While deciding a case and pronouncing a judgement, when there is no legislature on particular point, the judges generally apply their own common sense of right and wrong and of justice. This is known as *Judge-made laws or case laws*. Such decisions become authority or guide for subsequent cases of a similar nature and they are called *precedents*. The principle by which a judicial decision becomes a precedent is known as "Stare Decisis", to stand by precedents and not to disturb settled points.

➭ The legislation is the most authoritative source of law. The judicial decisions however may be *Authoritative, Conditionally authoritative or persuasive precedent.*

➭ The general rule is that a court is bound by the decisions of all courts higher than itself only and not by those of lower or equal rank. The ratio *decidendi* of previous case is binding, not the obiter *dicta.* High Court judge cannot question a decision of the Supreme Court. However Courts of subordinate jurisdiction do not create binding decision even for courts lower in rank.

➪ A custom is the oldest source of law and is a norm or rule which is not written but has been established by a long usage or practice in a particular place, class or community. In India, a custom must be proved to be ancient, certain and reasonable, further the proof of custom has been aided by the provisions of the Indian Evidence Act 1872. The custom could properly be proved by general evidence given by members of the family or tribe without proof of special instances but when a custom has been judicially recognised by the Court; it passes into the law of the land without necessity of proof in each individual case.

➪ In *Bhimashya & Ors. v. Smt. Janabi @ Janawwa,* (2006) court has held that *Custom is authoritative,* it stands in the place of law, and regulates the conduct of men in the most important concerns of life; fashion is arbitrary and capricious, it decides in matters of trifling import; manners are rational, they are the expressions of moral feelings.

➪ The term 'equity' means 'just', 'fairness' and 'good conscience'. When the existing law is inadequate or silent with regard to a particular case, the judges generally apply their common sense, justice and fairness in dealing with such cases.

➪ Law reform is the process of examining existing laws with the aim of maximising justice and responding to the changing values and concerns within society. The Efficacy of Law as an Instrument of change and varies according to the conditions present in a particular society. The Law Ministry and the Law Commission initiate policy reform while State legislatures and Parliament develop the legislative framework. There are four methods for law reform: Repealing law, Creation of new Law, Revising existing laws and Codification.

➪ Through judicial decisions, the Courts can also shape the law and reform it.

Terminal Questions

1. Discuss the nature of law as conceptualised by legal positivist.

2. What do you mean by the term sources of law? List the sources of law identified by jurists of different schools of law.

3. Explain in brief:
   (a) Ratio decidendi
   (b) Custom
   (c) Equity

4. Discuss the law making process in India.

5. Distinguish between supreme and subordinate legislation.

6. Write short note on the following:
   (a) Conditional legislation
   (b) Ancillary legislation

7. Discuss the doctrine of precedent and Stare decisis, in I*ndia.*

8. Discuss the essential elements of recognising the custom as valid source of law in India.

9. Elaborate on law reforms in India.

●●

3 | Historical Evolution of Indian Legal System

Ancient Indian Law

In India, civil law system was in existence during the Bronze Age and the Indus Valley civilisation (3300 BC) followed by the Iron Age Vedic Period. The ancient Vedic society had a structured social order, Brahmins were considered responsible for maintaining spiritual Hindu system, and they had control on rituals and penance. The king (raja) was the supreme head and the danda (punishment) was the only way to maintain order.

The ancient Indian law was of two types namely secular and religious. The secular law however varied from ruler to ruler and also as per regions. The Mauryas Empire (321-185 BCE) was well known for its judicial system (described in Arthashastra) and the secular court system also prevailed during Mughals period (16th–19th centuries) with the latter giving way to the current common law system.

The term Hindu law, was prevalent in India from the ancient Vedic times was used in general by the scholars to refer the diverse Indian Law and is accepted by them that the word "Hindu" is derived from the river Sindhu otherwise known as Indus which flows from the Punjab (*Sastri Yagnapurushadji and Others v. Muldas Bhudardas Vaishya and another* 1966(3) SCR 242). The expression "Hindu" was first used by the Persians and then by the Greeks to refer to the ethnic group of people or Indians. B. G. Tilak in "Gitarahasaya", has given broad description of the Hindu religion.

"Acceptance of the Vedas with reverence; recognition of the fact that the means or ways of salvation are diverse; and realisation of the truth that the number of Gods to be worshipped is large, that indeed is the distinguishing feature of Hindu religion".

In between 13th and 16th centuries, the word "Hindu" was widely used to distinguish them from the Mohammedan or Islamic law within India. In the nineteenth century, the expression "Hinduism" was used during the British Rule in reference to the Hindu religious, philosophical and culture group as distinct from Christianity and Islam. However, the meaning of the term `Hinduism' embraces within self, so many diverse forms of beliefs, faiths, practices and worship that it is difficult to define the term `Hindu' with precision. (*Commissioner of Wealth Tax, Madras & Ors. v. Late R. Sridharan* (1976) Supp. SCR 478,). Hinduism is also known by the names *Sanatana-Dharma* and *Vaidika-Dharma*.

Hindu Law

Hindu law can be divided into three categories: The Classical Hindu Law; The Anglo Hindu Law and Modern Hindu Law.

Classical Hindu Law–the classical Hindu law was based on religion, where Smritis and Shrutis had played an important role. It may include: ancient Indian law (dharma) and diverse legal practices as existed between 500 B.C. till 1772. The diverse practices were followed by various communities based on locations, work and caste: like merchants, military groups, and priests.

Anglo-Hindu Law –The law as evolved from the classical Hindu law during the British rule in India from 1772 to 1947 is regarded as the Anglo Hindu Law. In the first phase, the periods between 1972 and 1864 the personal laws were applied by the British for administration of justice in India. The court pandits were used in the British courts to aid the British judges with the interpretation of the Dharmashastra texts and implementation of the Classical Hindu Law. *Gradually, the* case law (precedents) were developed having authoritative value and the Anglo-Hindu law was codified by legislative measures, therefore in second phase the period between 1864 and 1947, the departure from the Dharmashastra tradition was seen and the system of court pandits was ended. The law reforms were introduced to have uniform laws except for laws related to family or personal matters like marriage, inheritance and succession of property. The Laws were codified in the form of the English Legal System or the modern form of law.

Modern Hindu Law–After independence in 1947, in the family or personal matters, customary laws of the relevant religious groups or traditional communities continued to be applied and the four major legislations governing the family and personal matters of the Hindus were codified: Hindu Marriage Act (1955), Hindu Succession Act (1956), Hindu Minority and Guardianship Act (1956), and Hindu Adoptions and Maintenance Act (1956). We will discuss Ancient Indian Law in Modern Legal Framework and Hindu laws in Modern India in detail, later in this chapter.

Ancient Indian Law (Dharma)

It has following features:

◆ It was customary law (sadchara). Mayne in his treatise on 'Hindu Law & Usage' has stated that "Hindu law is the law of the Smritis as expounded in the Sanskrit Commentaries and Digests which, as modified and supplemented by custom, is administered by the courts."

◆ The ancient Indian law is Dharma Shastra (religious ethics). The term '*Dharma*' is a Sanskrit word having wider connotation to means righteousness, duty and law.

◆ The ancient Indian law also consists of the Arthashastra.

◆ Ancient Indian Law (Hindu law) was codified in Manusmriti and the Arthashastra by Kautilya, which describes the rules of governance and law.

◆ The Vedas and other scriptures defined the role of king, his courtiers and public. King was considered as incarnation of God. To punish the wrong-doers was considered as the sacred duty of the king. The king is the fountain of justice (dharmapravartaka).

The Sources of ancient Indian law- The sources of ancient law are: (1) Shrutis are called Vedas or *Amnaya*. (2) Smritis (3) Achara (4) other sources of law are Itihasas, Puranas, Agamas etc.

◆ *Shruti* is concerned with 'what is heard' or 'the revealed' and includes: Vedas, Aranyakas and Upanishads in this class. Veda literally means knowledge. Vedas is collections of hymns, praises, and ritual instructions, the *mantras*. They were never written, never created and are embodiment of divine knowledge; eternal and impersonal. The primary Vedas are Rig Veda, Atharva Veda, Yajur Veda and Sama Veda. They throw light on the *Srishti* (the creation), the Brahman, the *atman*, the life and all the related issues of spiritualism. The *Shrutis* are Prabhu-Samhitas or the Commanding Treatises with

great authority and therefore considered as the supreme and ultimate authority.

◆ *Smriti* literarily means 'which is remembered'. It consists of 1,010 slokas (verses), created probably during Gupta period. Smritis are secondary scriptures, the books written by certain Sanskrit Scholars in ancient times. The main Smritis or Dharma Sastras are Manu, Narada, Yajnavalkya; Visnu Brahaspati; Katyayana; Parasara, Atri, Harita, Usana, Angira, Yama, Apastamba, Samvarta, Vyasa, Daksa, Gautama, Satatapa, Vasistha, Devala, Sankha-Likhita, and Saunaka. The most important and famous text are those of Manu and his Manava Dharma-shastra (Laws of Manu). It is also called the Manusmriti. The Puranas, Ithihas as also belong to this category.

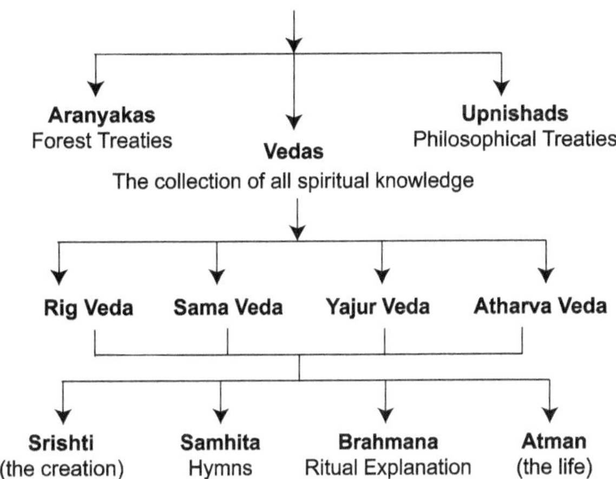

◆ The *Shruti* literature is veritable and inviolable but the *Smriti* literature may get modified under the influence of time and place. The *Smriti* literature is based on the *Shruti* and therefore the *Smriti* is to be interpreted in consonance with the *Shruti*. The Smriti stands next in authority to the Shruti.

◆ *Dharmasutra* (righteousness string) are the first four texts of the *Dharmashastra, it is* guidebooks on dharma providing rules of conduct, rites and duties for all the *ashrama's:* the student-hood; householdership; retirement or forest dwelling and renunciation. It also lays down the rites and duties of kings, rules of crimes and punishments, court proceedings. There are sections that deal with rules about one's diet, daily sacrifices, caste identifying dress, symbols, marks and funeral practices. The most important *Dharmasutra* texts are the sutra of *Apastamba, Gautama, Baudhayana and Vaisistha.*

> According to Ashramas, there are four stages: the first stage is Brahmacharya or student-hood that takse about males life till 24 years. The male is send to Gurukuls at the age of 5 years to learn science, literature, law, dharma and other disciplines. The second stage is Grihastha, house holder. It is between 25 years to 49 years, the male householder is supposed to fulfil household duties as father, son and husband. The third stage is Vanapratha, Hermit (between 50 years to 74 years). The person gradually withdraws from the world, life and luxuries. The last stage of life involves Sanyasa (from 74 to demise). It is the absolute withdrawal from world. The person practices meditation at this age to seek spiritual freedom, Moksha. (see for more details Chakkarath, p. 39; Rama, p. 467; Kriyanasnda, p. 154)

♦ *Achara* are customary laws, norms followed by particular community or a group. The 'Achara' also derives its authority by virtue of its connection with the *Vedas*. Where both the *Vedas* and the *Smritis* are silent on an issue, the norms of the community can be considered as *dharma*.

♦ Purans contain mythological account of ancient times to popularise the religion of the Vedas. It deals with the creation and destruction; renovation of worlds, the genealogy and deeds of Gods and Goddesses. Puranas can be divided into Mahapuranas (Brahma, Vishnu and Shiva) and Upa Puranas. Both the categories have 18 Puranas each. Examples of popular Puranas: Srimad Bhagvad Gita and the Vishnu Purana.

♦ The Itihasas are considered as friendly treatise (Suhrit-Samhitas) and four books can be placed under this head: The Valmiki's Ramayana, the Yogavasishtha, Mahabharata and the Harivamsa. Both Purans and Itihasas belong to same class of Suhrit-Samhitas.

♦ The Agamas include the Tantras, Mantras and Yantras and are theological treatises and practical manuals of divine worship. The Agamas deals with (i) *Jnana* or Knowledge, (ii) *Yoga* or Concentration, (iii) *Kriya* or Esoteric Ritual and (iv) *Charya* or Exoteric Worship. The Agamas are divided into three sections: the Vaishnava Agamas or Pancharatra Agamas glorifying God as Vishnu, the Saiva Agamas glorifying God as, the Sakta Agamas or Tantras glorify God as the Mother of the Universe (*Devi).* The Agamas are vedic in character and spirit though do not derive their authority from the Vedas and were regarded as authoritative.

Law and Legal System in Medieval India

In medieval period, the laws that were prescribed or promulgated were not codified in the modern sense but were classified under several heads *viz.*

1. The Canon Law-personal law of the Muslims;

2. The Common Law- consists of Islamic Law of Crimes, Tort, Nuisance, etc., and applied to all the subjects of the state irrespective of religion;

3. The regulations known as Tashriyah (religious) and Ghair Tashriyah (Secular) - proclamations, known as Farmans and Dasturul;

4. Local customs, Qanun e Urf.

5. Precedents.

> **Sources of Islamic Law**
>
> **Main/primary source**: Quran (the divine law); Sunna (traditions of Prophet Muhammad recorded in the Hadith literature.
>
> **Other sources**: Sahabah (Concurrent opinion of the Prophet's companions), Ijma (gathering/ consensus of opinion), and Qiyas.

M. Basheer Ahmad, in the book "The Administration of Justice in Medieval India" referring to Barni; Briggs; Kennedy; Elliot III; Mirat; Alumgir Namah, 595; Ain I; Ain II; Farameen; Baqiat; Ibn Batuta; Storia I has noted the following:

♦ Before the Mughal advent, several dynasties reigned in India in different parts till 1526 and some till 1680 A.D. They dominated the Northern, Central, Eastern and the Southern wings of the country. The Mahmud (1246-1266), Balban (1266-1286), Muhammad Tughlaq Shah (1320-1325), Firoz Tughlaq (1351-1388), Bahlol Lodi (1451-1489) and Sikander Lodi (1489-1517), maintained a high level of judicial administration and as a result of their close observance of the rules of Shara', they considered the dispensation of justice a religious duty (Lazim e-din-e Haq dad dehi wa insaf sitani ast). The Kings of Bengal in the East and the Sultans in the Deccan occupied important positions. With the exception of the two states of Bijapur and Golconda in the south where the Kings were Shiahs, the rulers in the rest of the country were Muslims of the Sunni persuasion, and the followers of the Hanafi School.

- Sultan as the head of state is under religious duty and the supreme authority to administer justice. He was elected by the leading men at the Capital, as was the case when the early Caliphs of Islam were selected. This was usually done in the presence of the Chief Justice who was known as Qaziul Quzat and other officers.

- The Sultanat (Empire) was divided into Subahs (Iqtas), Sarkars and Parganahs.

- The Sultan was assisted by a Council of Ministers responsible to him for such departments as Finance, Army, Accounts, General Administration, Ecclesiastical, Law and Justice.

- Qazi is in charge of administration of Justice and Faujdar maintains Law and Order. The Chief Ministers (Wazirs) of the Sultans were in some cases invested with judicial powers in addition to their executive duties (see State versus Sh. Haidari, Ibn Batuta (Lee) page 146; State versus Khwajah Ahmad, Shams Siraj Afif, page 508) .

- The Chief Justice or the Qaziul Quzat was the titular head of the Empire judiciary from 1206-1248. In about 1248 A.D. Sultan Nasir Uddin created the superior post of *SadreJahan*which becames the de jure head of the Empire judiciary.

- The Mohammad Tughlaq (1320-1325), created three separate court having different jurisdictions: Diwaniqaze; Diwani Mazalim and Diwani Siyasat, the Court of Correction for "hardened criminals". This institution, however, was abolished by his successor Firoz Tughlaq. (See Barni, pages 572- 573).

- The Mughal *dynasty* was founded by Babur *ruled (1526-1530)*, who defeated the last Lodi Sultan of Delhi and brought the Sultanate, to an end. He was succeeded by Muhammad Humayun (1530-39 and 1556). The Mughal rulers did not adopt the title of Sultan and preferred to be known as 'Badshahs' or sometimes 'Shahenshahs.

- Sher Shah (1540-1545) introduced the system of having separate Courts of first instance for civil and criminal cases in the Parganahs. For the purposes of efficient administration, the whole Empire was partitioned into 47 Divisions called sarkars, each having a Shiqdar-i-Shiqdaran, or Shiqdar-in-Chief, and a Munsif-i-Munsifan, or Munsif-in-Chief.

- The Subahdar, provincial governor, was in charge of a Division and was responsible only to the Crown for his actions, civil as well as military.

The emperor is the highest authority in all judicial matters.

- A Sarkar was comprised of number of Parganahs, each having a Shiqdar/Shiqahdars (police chief and were given magisterial powers), an Amin, a Munsif, a Khazanchl, a Hindi writer and a Persian clerk to write accounts. The Civil cases of Parganah were heard by Amin and criminal cases by a Qazior Mir-i-Adal. Several Parganahs also had a civil Judge called a Munsif-i- Munsifan. At the capital, there was chief quazi (sadr).

- Parganahs were subdivided by Sher Shah into Mahals or groups of villages for Revenue purposes. The heads of the village councils were recognised- Moqaddams, there were also a Chaudhri and a Patwari.

- The Emperor, like the Sultans of Delhi, was the head of the judicial and the executive departments and the Commander-in-Chief of the whole army and Navy and had all civil and military authorities. The Emperor had a council of ministers who were independently responsible to him for their respective departments, but the most influential among them was the Wazir or Vakil-e-Mutlaq (Sujan Rae) or Dastur-e-Muazzam (Ruqaat-e-Alamgir). He was like the modern Prime Minister, usually in constant touch with the head of the State. Except the judicial department, he had a controlling hand in all other spheres of administration, and the other ministers approached the Emperor through him in the normal course of business. The Revenue, Finance and cultural departments were under the Diwan-e-ala final court of Justice for Revenue cases.

- The Moghuls had many diwans which were also military commanders. Diwan-e-ala was the highest diwan under which there was the 'diwan-e- tan' (incharge of salaries) and 'diwan-e-khalsa' (incharge of State/Crown lands). There were waqia-navis for keeping record of farmers and mustafa's for auditing of income and expenditure. The duties of the Prime Minister under the Mughal emperors were confined to executive matters as were those of the Chief Justice to judicial.

- The Mughals ruled India effectively until 1750 A. D. and nominally up to 1857, when the last Mughal Emperor was succeeded by Queen Victoria as Empress of India.

Let us see in table below to understand the administration system under Mughals:

S. No.	Provinces (Subahs):	Districts (Sarkars):	Parganahs:	Villages:
1	Provincial heads Subahdar or the Governor.	Chief officers Qazi- in charge of administration of Justice.	staff of officers Qazi-e-parganah- Incharge of Justice.	Panchayats- an assembly usually of five men, in charge of Justice.
2	Qazi-e-Subah or the Chief Qazi.	Faujdar- maintained Law and Order.	Amil-e-Parganah-collectionof Land Revenue under his supervision.	Headman- President of the Panchayat, (Moqaddam or Chaudhri) and Incharge of Law and Order (Farameen).
3	Diwan-e-Subah or the Chief Revenue Officer.	Amalguzar or Amils in the Deccan (Collections) settled revenue.	Qanungoe - was the refuge of the husband men they assisted the Amil.	Patwari- representative of the Revenue Department and Recorder of rights.
4	Sadr-e-Subah- represented the Sadr us Sudur in the Province and supervised the work of the District Sadars and Mohtasibs in the Province.	Bitikchi- Assistant to Amalguzar.	Amin, Munsif and Karor -Land Revenue and rent cases.	Village guard or Chaukidar or Rahdar-Inchargeof traffic and of Saraes where travelers lodged for the night.
5	Bakhshi-e-Subah-incharge of Pay and Accounts.	Fotedar or Khazana-dar (Treasurer).	Karkun- Land Revenue Department.	
6		Sadr-Ecclesiastical Department.	Wasan Kash.	
7		Sadr Amin- Land Revenue Cases.	Faujdar or Shiqahdar- Incharge of law and order in the Parganah.	
8		Karkun or Karori- Collection of Revenue.	Kotwal-represented Faujdar in the Parganah in case no Shiqahdar was appointed.	
9		Kotwal-Police.		

English Law in India (British era)

The Charter of 1600 established the English East India Company in India. The charter of 1661 provided that the English and the Indians residing under the company came under its jurisdiction. The administration of Justice in British India during the period (1661 till 1726), there was no codified law and the laws of equity, good conscience and justice in conformity with the laws in England were followed. The three major presidencies in British India were Bombay Presidency, Madras Presidency, Calcutta Presidency.

- In presidency of Calcutta, the judicial system was simple, the collectors enjoyed all powers based on the authority given by Company and zamindar's till the charter of 1726 was passed.

- Madras had two courts:

The Choultry Court

- The courts are akin to today's Magistrat Courts, presided over by an Adigar, it has jurisdiction in petty cases, both civil and criminal.

Agent in Council of Fort St. George

- Deals with offences by British subjects in which Indians were not concerned.

The Charter of Charles II in 1661

Under this charter, *the Court of Governor and Council* was created which were designated as the High Court of Judicature in 1678. The old Choultry court was also reorganised and the number of judges increased to three from two and it was made compulsory that not less than two of the judges should sit for trial of cases and registration of bills of land and other property. The court was empowered to try civil cases up to 50 pagodas and petty criminal cases. Appeals against orders of the Choultry court lay with the High Court of Judicature. *An admiralty court* (civil and criminal jurisdiction) was established in 1686 and *Mayor's Court* (civil and criminal jurisdiction) in 1688 under Charter 1687 (applied to Madras only) was granted to the East India Company to establish a Corporation with a Mayor and twelve Aldermen. The Admiralty Court hears the appeals from the Mayor's Court, but later this jurisdiction of the Admiralty Court was transferred to the Governor and Council and the court gradually disappeared.

The Charter of 1668

The Company was conferred powers to make laws for the Bombay by the charter of 1668. A *Court of Judicature* was established to deal with civil and criminal cases and there was a provision to prefer appeal to the Deputy Governor and Council against the decision of Court of Judicature. In 1718, the representation to the Indians was given by appointment of four Indian Judges, known as Black Justices, in the Court. Under the Judicial Plan 1672, a Court of Conscience was established to deal with petty civil cases.

Mayor's Court and Charter of 1726 and 1753

The Company was granted charter by King George I in 1726 to establish Mayor's Courts in Madras, Bombay and Calcutta bringing uniformity in judicial system and superseding all the other courts of Bombay, Madras and Calcutta. The Mayor court was a court of crown not of company with *civil jurisdiction* in addition to testamentary and probate. The Governor and Council were given criminal jurisdiction (court of record) and civil appeal was allowed to the Presidency Government against the decisions of the Mayor's Court and further, in the court of King-in-Counsel in England (Court of Privy Council.) The Laws under this Charter was also applied in conformity with the laws in England on the principles of equity and justice.

There are many discord and difficulties under the charter, the system remained suspended while the French had occupied Madras in 1746 which they later surrendered in 1749. Then the Charter of 1753 was passed in order to remove the difficulties of the preceding Charter.

The Charter of 1753 provides for the following:

♦ The Mayor Court will work under the subjection of the Governor and Council in order to avoid disputes between the two; it reaffirmed the provisions of appeal to Privy Council from Mayor's Courts.

♦ It expressly states that Suits and actions between the natives were excluded from the jurisdiction of the Mayor's Court unless both parties submitted before court, dispute for its determination.

♦ Court of Requests was created to hear small civil cases *i.e.,* petty civil cases having low pecuniary jurisdiction.

This Charter also suffers from many defects and judiciary is dominated by executive, courts have limited jurisdiction to Presidency Towns and fails to deliver impartial judgment due to lack of legal knowledge and no representation of Indian Judges as opposed to earlier provisions in some courts in Bombay.

Regulating Act of 1773 (East India Company Act, 1772)

The financial break-down of the company was the immediate cause for the enforcement of the Regulating Act of 1773.

♦ The Regulating Act set up a Governor General and Council nominated partly by the East India Company and partly by the government.

♦ Warren Hastings was appointed Governor General and his councilors were Clavering Monson, Barwell and Philip Francis.

♦ A system was set up whereby government of Britain regulated the work of the East India Company but did not take power for itself.

♦ The Act also provided for the establishment of a Supreme Court at Calcutta. The court was a court of record, with the power to punish for its contempt and consisted of a Chief Justice and three assistant judges.

♦ Supreme Court had civil, equity, criminal, ecclesiastical and admiralty jurisdiction. It could determine any suits or actions against any of his Majesty's subjects in Bengal, Bihar and Orissa, the matters pertaining to Hindus and Muslims were decided as per their personal laws.

♦ Appeals against decisions of this Court and through the Court could be filed in all civil and criminal cases respectively before the King-in-Counsel. The court however could not deal with matters relating to Governor General and council in their official capacity.

However a parallel system of judiciary was running in the **Mofussil areas.** In 1765 company obtained Diwani of Bengal, Bihar and Orissa from Mughal emperor, at that time *Diwani* decided civil and revenue disputes and *Subhadhar or Nazim* administered criminal justice.

First Judicial Plan 1772

It was prepared by committee of circuit under Warren Hastings. It provided for the Courts of Original Jurisdiction as discussed below:

i. *Mofussil Faujdari Adalat-* the court of criminal jurisdiction was presided over by quazi and Mufti assisted by two maulvies.

ii. *Mofussil Diwani Adalat-* the court of civil jurisdiction and Small Cause Adalat. The collector was judge of this court. Personal law was applied with the help of pandits/quazis as per the religion (Hindu/Muslim).

iii. *Small cause Adalat–*head farmer of purganah decided civil dispute up to amount of Rs. 10.

iv. *Appellate Adalats-* i) Sadar Nizamat Adalat, the criminal court of appeals and is presided by Daroga-i-adalat assited by chief Kazi, chief Mufti and three Maulvies. The governor and council exercise general supervision. ii) Sadar Diwani Adalat, Civil Court of appeals and is composed of Governor and council.

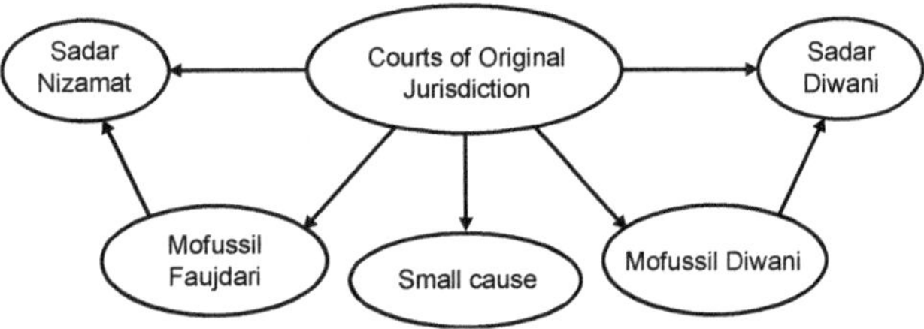

The Judicial Plan 1774

The Collectors started monopolising the trade in the districts. Therefore, need for new plan arose and the judicial plan 1774 was formulated. Under this system, *Diwan or Amil,* acted as the judge of the Mofussil Diwani Adalat. The Mofussil areas of Bengal, Bihar and Orissa were divided into six districts with a Provincial Council in each district acting as the Appellate Court. *Sir Impey* as judge of Sadar Diwani Adalat introduced number of reforms in administration of justice: Diwani Adalats were directed to hear case in open, the number of adalats were increased and the code of civil procedure was compiled in 1781. Sir Impey was particular about administering of oath to the witnesses, as a lot of importance is given in the law of evidence, to the credibility of the witnesses. He increased the number of Diwani Courts from 6 to 18 to prevent inconvenience of litigants. During Impey's regime, Code of Civil Procedure was drafted with 95 clauses which was a welcome step.

(See B. M. Gandhi, 2012).

The Act of Settlement 1781

The act aimed at removing the ambiguities created by the former Act, but was not successful in its entirety. With the increase in activities of the Company, an urgent need of a lawyer-judge was felt to deal with new cases. For the administration of criminal justice in a more efficient manner, Warren Hastings drew a scheme in 1781 under which, for apprehending criminals, Judges of the Mofussil Diwani Adalats were authorised to work as Magistrates and a department headed by the Remembrance of criminal Courts was opened to look after the working of the said courts.

Pitts India Act (1784)

According to this Act, a Board of Control (constituting six members, two members of the British Cabinet and four of the Privy Council), was established in England for better control of acts and operations of the Company related to the civil, military and revenues.

It provided for a joint government of the Company (represented by the Directors), and the Crown (represented by the Board of Control). Later on, the Board of Control became the real ruling authority over the Indian terrorists, the Council was reduced to three members and the Governor General was empowered to overrule the majority. The independent powers of Governors of Bombay and Madras were taken off.

Judicial Plans 1787, 1790, and 1793

Lord Warren Hastings remained the Governor General between 1772 and 1785. In 1786, Lord Cornwallis was appointed as the Governor General, who became the effective ruler of British India under the authority of the Board of Control and the Court of Directors. The Governor General Lord Cornwallis introduced changes in the judicial system in 1787, 1790, and 1793 and reorganised the civil and criminal judiciary in India. In 1787, all revenue and judicial functions were vested with collectors as represented below:

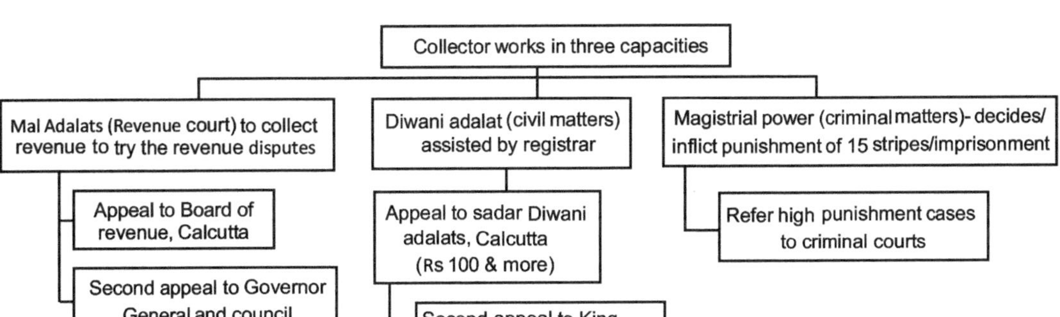

In the year 1790 the policy of 1787 was annulled. To improve the administration of justice in the Mofussil, reforms in the criminal law was introduced by Cornwallis. The scheme was formulated where the magistrates in the district are at the lowest level, then the courts of circuits and ultimately there was the Sadar Nizamat Adalat under the control of Governor General and his Council at Calcutta (initially at Murshidabad), it was assisted by the Muslim law officers who were to expound the law.

But in the year 1793 new plan was introduced bringing extensive reforms in legal system. There was separation of judicial and executive powers, the function of collector was limited to collection of land revenue and power to decide such cases and administration of civil justice was taken away; the personal liability to pay damages to injured parties was fixed on Collectors in case of violation of laws and regulations; the Supreme Court was divested of all its powers except for the power of appeal; to enhance efficiency of courts, the professional lawyers or vakeels were allowed to appear in the courts on behalf of the parties to contest their cases. Reforms were made in procedural law and the hierarchy of courts was formulated for civil matters as represented below in descending order but not many reforms were introduced in substantive criminal law. The power of administration of civil justice was given to the Diwani adalats. The Diwani adalat's was created in each district of Patna, Murshidabad and Dhaka. First courts of appeals were created with seats at Patna, Dhaka, Calcutta and Murshidabad.

Hierarchy of Courts

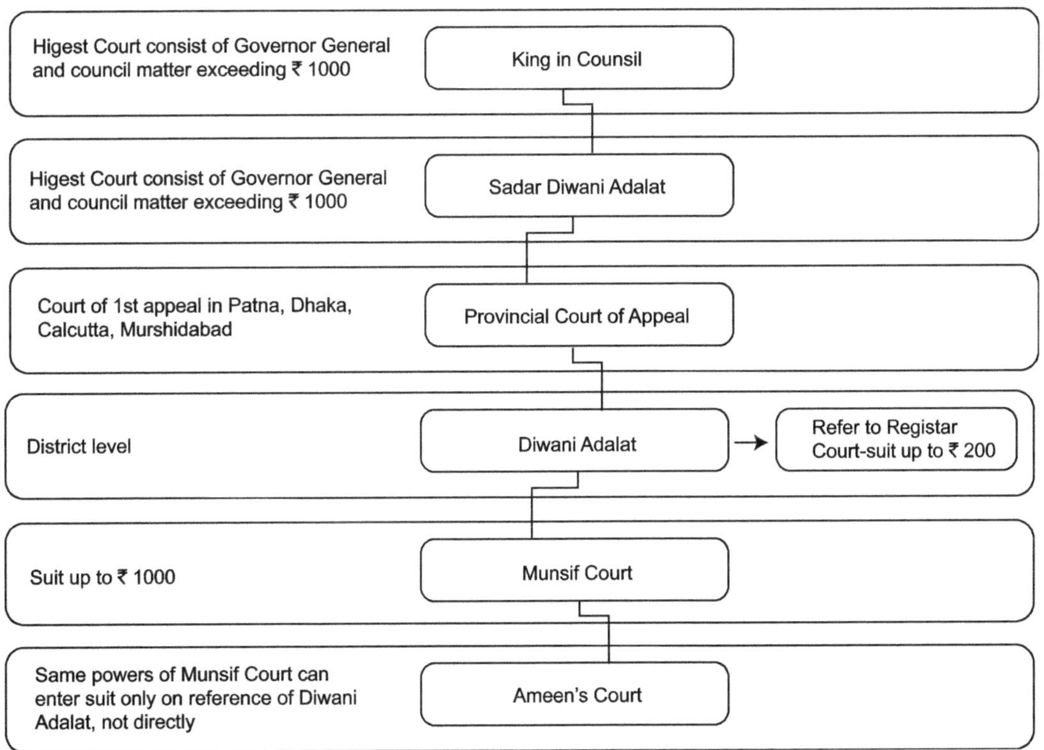

The Charter Act of 1813 and 1833

The charter of 1813 abolished the monopoly of trade of the East India Company except in Tea and its trade with China; proclaimed sovereignty of crown over possessions (territorial and revenue); granted one lakh for improvement of education. Charter Act of 1833 has an objective of securing a uniform and simple system of law in India through the process of integration of the general system of codes. It marked the beginning of Central Legislative Council in India and the Governor General was known as Government of India and his council as the Indian Council; the act vested the legislative power exclusively in Governor General in Council and deprived of the Government of the Residencies of their legislative functions; the Indian Civil Services was founded; it also provided for the constitution of a Law Commission in India under Macaulay.

The Charter Act of 1853

The existing legislative machinery under the Charter Act of 1833 was not adequate and there was demand for the decentralisation of powers and representation of people of India in the management of their affairs, the Charter of the Company was renewed in 1853. The Act also empowered the Crown to appoint a Law Commission in England to examine the reports and the drafts of the Indian Law Commission which had by then ceased to exist.

Charter of 1861 and subsequent Charters

After the mutiny of 1857, the Company's Government came to an end through the Queen's Proclamation of 1858 and the administration of the country was placed in the hands of the Crown through the Secretary of State for India. For this purpose the Indian Councils Act, 1861 and 1892 were passed. **Under the Indian Councils Act, 1861,** the function of the Council was strictly limited to legislation; provided for issuance of Ordinances by the Governor which could remain in force for a maximum of 6 months; no distinction was made between the Central and Provincial subjects. **The Indian Councils Act, 1892** was enacted on the demand of the Indian National Congress to expand legislative council, the number of non-official members was increased both in central and provincial legislative councils; allowed the councils to discuss annual financial statement, allow members to put questions on internal matters, but supplementary questions were not allowed. The Indian Councils Act, or the Morley Minto **Reforms, of 1909** further increased the size of the legislative councils at the Center (from 16 to 60) and the Provincial Legislatives (50 in the provinces of Bengal, Madras and Bombay, and 30 for the rest of the provinces); Right of separate electorate was given to the Muslims; at the Center, official members were to form the majority but in provinces non-official members would be in majority; Two Indians were nominated to the Council of the Secretary of State for Indian Affairs; The Governor General was empowered to nominate one Indian member to his Executive Council.

But there is no true representation and the Government of India Act in 1919 was passed to make the provincial governments more responsible to the popular representatives and the control of British Parliament and the secretary of state be relaxed *i.e.,* emphasis is on the maximum autonomy to provinces with the target of achieving self-government. The system of double government (dyarcy) introduced by the Government of India Act (1919) for the provinces of British India. The dissatisfaction from this act led to the Government of India Act, 1935 which aimed to establish federalism; provides for diarchy at centre and creation of post of Crown Representative. Though it also proclaimed the supreme authority of Crown over India, but relaxed its control, in certain spheres, for a more popular government. The Secretary of state remained in overall control, with a new body of advisers in lieu of the old council.

Establishment of High Courts and the Federal Court

The India High Courts Act, 1861 was enacted which provides for creation of High Courts in various provinces abolishing Supreme Courts at Calcutta, Madras and Bombay and also the Sadar Adalats in Presidency towns. It was the amalgamation of King's Courts and Company's Courts. The Calcutta, Madras and Bombay high courts were established by the Royal Charter in the year 1862. By the subsequent charters High Courts were formed in Allahabad (1875), Patna (1912), Lahore (1865), a High Court of Judicature for the North Western Provinces (1866) etc.

Jurisdiction of High Court–High Court had ordinary original, appellate and extraordinary original jurisdiction in civil cases while exercising ordinary original jurisdiction the courts was to apply the law of equity. The High Courts were empowered to make rules and orders for regulating all its proceedings in civil matters.

Extraordinary and appellant jurisdiction in criminal cases the courts while exercising extraordinary original jurisdiction applied the law of the corresponding local court. In case of appellate jurisdiction, the Courts applied the law of equity as administered by court of original case filing and good conscience. Acting as the court of appeal, reference or revision in criminal cases, the courts applied the Indian Penal Code.

The Charter of 1866 conferred Civil, Criminal, Testamentary and Interstate as well as Matrimonial jurisdictions upon High Court. Testamaentary jurisdiction of High Court includes examination of wills, granting or rejecting probates, letters of administration ect. The significant feature of the Charter was the amalgamation of the dual system of administration of justice and transference to the New High Court qua some matters, of the jurisdiction exercised by the Calcutta High Courts and that of the Sadar Courts with regard to the rest. The conferment of guardianship, lunacy, and testamentary and interstate jurisdictions, on this High Court was made by incorporating the powers exercised by the High Court at Fort William.

The India High Courts Act 1861 provided for the right to appeal from High Courts to Privy Council from all of its judgments except in Criminal matters. In addition to this, there was a provision of special leave to appeal in certain cases to be so certified by the High Courts.

The Legal Practitioners Act of 1846 opened up the profession regardless of nationality or religion and the respective High Courts were responsible for enrolment of law practitioner's. The High Court was vested with power of superintendence of lower courts under Government of India Act, 1935.

Federal Courts

The High Courts were the highest Courts for all cases till the creation of Federal Court of India under the Government of India Act 1935. A Federal Court was to consist of Chief Justice and not more than six judges. This court had original, appellate, and advisory jurisdiction. Federal Court had exclusive original jurisdiction to decide disputes between the Center and Constituent Units or units *inter see*, the disputes between provinces and federal states; it can hear appeal against judgments from High Courts. The provision was made for filing of appeals from Federal Court to the Privy Council. The Federal Court also had jurisdiction to grant Special Leave to Appeal and for such appeals a certificate of the High Court was essential.

Law reforms introduced by British Government

The British Government had adopted the policy of non-interference in personal laws of Hindu and Muslims and therefore did not introduce legislative measures in the earlier phase of their rule but gradually after 1854 some law reforms were introduced during British regime and codification was done in the field of personal laws for example:

♦ In 1856, the widow remarriage was regularised by the Hindu Widow Remarriage Act 1856 and subsequently under Civil Marriage Act, 1872. Section 1 of the Hindu Widow Remarriage Act, 1856 read as follows:

No marriage contracted between Hindus shall be invalid, and the issue of no such marriage shall be illegitimate, by reason of the woman having been previously married or betrothed to another person who was dead at the time of such marriage, any custom and any interpretation of Hindu Law to the contrary notwithstanding.

♦ The Hindu Inheritance (Removal of disabilities) Act, 1928 was enacted to amend the Hindu Law relating to exclusion from inheritance of certain classes of heirs, and to remove certain doubts.

♦ In 1929, the Child Marriage Restraint Act to restrain the solemnisation of child marriage was passed.

♦ The Hindu Law of Inheritance (Amendment) Act, 1929 to alter the order in which certain heirs of a Hindu male dying intestate are entitled to succeed to his estate.

♦ Women's Right to Property Act, 1937 to provide widows, the right to enjoy deceased husband's property even if any male heir exists.

♦ The Muslim Personal Law (Shariat) Application Act, 1937 was passed to make provision for the application of the Muslim Personal Law (Shariat) to Muslims.

♦ The dissolution of Muslim Marriage Act 1939 was formulated to provide muslim women right to dissolution of marriage on certain grounds stated there in.

♦ There were no legal practitioners before the establishment of Major's Court in 1726.

♦ The Legal Practitioners Act, 1846 allowed anyone to be an advocate. Before that Indians were not allowed to be an advocate in the Courts.

♦ As per Advocates Act, 1961, advocates enrolled in any State or Central Bar Councils are permitted to practise the profession of law.

♦ Bar Council of India lays down the standard of professional conduct and the rules for affiliating colleges and universities whose degrees qualify for enrollment.

◆ Solicitor and Attorney system is abolished in 1970. Only Bomany Incorporated Law Society conducts exam for solicitors.

◆ In our legal system there are two set of lawyers–(i)senior advocates, (ii) advocates.

Drafting of the Indian Constitution

The Constitution of India lays down the basic principles to be followed in all matters-executive, legislative and judicial, in the country. The process of evolution of Constitution had began in the year 1895 when freedom fighters: Annie Besant and Lokmanya Tilak had put forward a document called Constitution of India Bill [also known as Home Rule Bill] envisaging freedom of expression and equality before law. In February 1924 Motilal Nehru introduced and passed a resolution outlining the procedure for drafting and adopting a Constitution for India in the Central Legislative Assembly and the committee under the Chairmanship of Motilal Nehru, to determine the principles of Constitution for India was appointed in 1928 which submitted its report on 10th August and recommended equal rights to men and women regardless of caste, class, religion or region, free elementary education, freedom of expression to all.

The Constituent Assembly

The Constituent Assembly, as per the scheme recommended by cabinet Mission, consisted of indirectly elected representatives of the provincial legislative assemblies. Initially, total membership of the Assembly was 389: 292 members were elected through the Provincial Legislative Assemblies; 93 members represented the Indian Princely States; and 4 members represented the Chief Commissioners' Provinces but due to constitution of separate constitutional assembly for Pakistan as a result of the partition under the Mountbatten Plan of 3 June, 1947, the representatives of some Provinces ceased to be members of the Assembly and the membership of the Assembly was reduced to 299.

The first session of the Constituent Assembly took place at Constitution Hall, New Delhi, on December 9, 1946 and was attended by 207 members (Dr. Sachchidananda Sinha was the first President of the Constituent Assembly when it met on December 9th, 1946). Later Dr. Rajendra Prasad was elected President of Constituent Assembly.

The Constituent Assembly formed different sub committees dealing with different aspects of the Constitution. The Drafting Committee was set up in August 1947 under Chairmanship of Dr. B. R. Ambedkar. The Constituent Assembly met 11 times,

Over 165 days between 1946 and 1949 and after several deliberations and modifications; the Constituent Assembly approved the draft Constitution on 26th November, 1949 which became law on January 26, 1950.

Sources of Indian Constitution

The Constituent Assembly, while drafting the Indian Constitution relied upon the following sources:

1. **Government of India Act of 1935-** The Act was passed by the British Parliament and remained in force until 1950 when the Indian Constitution was adopted.

   ◆ The Act introduced provincial autonomy and proposed to form an All India Federation. All the provinces were to be the members of a federation. (Refer : *Key John India :* Grove Press Books. New York 2000)

   ◆ The federal polity proposed for a bicameral legislature at the centre consisting of Federal Assembly (Lower House) and Council of States (Upper House). The total number of members of the Federal Assembly were 375 (250 were elected by the people of British Provinces and 125 from Indian States). The federation consists of 11 provinces, 6 chief commissioners' provinces and other states and the bicameral legislature (*viz,* Legislative Assembly and Legislative Council) was introduced in six provinces (Bengal, Bihar, Bombay, Uttar Pradesh, Madras and Assam) and the other five Provinces, Punjab, Central Provinces, Orissa, and North-West Frontier Provinces (N.W.F.P.) and Sind were to have Legislative Assembly only.

   ◆ But the parts of the Act that establish federation of India did not come in to operation due to opposition of rulers of princely states.

   ◆ It divided subjects in to three lists: Federal, Provincial and Concurrent List. The provinces were given autonomy with respect to subjects delegated to them. The provision was also made for Residuary Subjects to be looked after by the Governor General.

   ◆ The Act introduced Dyarchy (diarchy) system at the centre but in the Provinces, the system of Dyarchy was replaced by the provincial autonomy.

   ◆ The India Council of the Secretary of State for India was replaced by an Advisory Council.

   ◆ A Federal Court consisting of one Chief Justice and more than 6 judges and Federal Public Service Commission was established.

2. **Constitutions of other countries**–The different parts of Indian Constitution are borrowed from the Constitution of other countries and are given below :

S.No.	Constitution of the country	Features adopted
1.	British Constitution	Parliamentary form of government; Bicameral Parliament; Cabinet System of Ministers; Speaker in Lok Sabha; single citizenship; the Rule of law; law making procedure; procedure established by Law; prerogative writs.
2.	Irish Constitution	Directive principles of state policy; Method of election of President; nomination of members in the Rajya Sabha by the President.
3.	United States Constitution	Federal structure of government; due process of law; power of Judicial Review; independence of the judiciary; Fundamental Rights; President as supreme commander of armed forces; removal of president, judges of supreme court and High court.
4.	Canadian Constitution	A quasi-federal form of government- distribution of powers between centre and the states and placing residuary powers with the centre.
5.	Australian Constitution	Provision of trade and commerce between different states of the country; Power of the National legislature to make laws for implementing treaties; Concurrent list.
6.	French Constitution	Ideals of Liberty, Equality and Fraternity.
7.	Japan Constitution	Fundamental Duties.
8.	USSR (Russia)	Five year pan
9.	Weimar Constitution	Emergency Provisions

3. The Objectives Resolution drafted by Pandit Jawaharlal Nehru laid down the philosophy behind the Constitution and expressed through its various provisions.

On 13 December, 1946, Pandit Jawaharlal Nehru moved the Objectives Resolution.

1. This Constituent Assembly declares its firm and solemn resolve to proclaim India as an Indepen-dent Sovrign Republic and to draw up for her future governance, a Constitution;
2. WHEREIN the territories that now comprise British India, the territories that now form the Indian States, and such other parts of India as are outside British India and the States as well as such other territories as are willing to be constituted into the Independent Sovereign India, shall be a Union of them all; and
3. WHEREIN, the said territories, whether with their present boundaries or with such others as may be determined by the Constituent Assembly and thereafter according to the law of the Constitution, shall possess and retain the status of autonomous units, together with residuary powers and exercise all powers and functions of government and administration, save and except such powers and functions as are vested in or assigned to the Union, or as are inherent or implied in the Union or resulting there from; and
4. WHEREIN, all power and authority of the Soverign Independent India, its constituent parts and organs of government, are derived from the people; and
5. WHEREIN, shall be guaranteed and secured to all the people of India, justice, social economic and political : equality of status, of opportunity, and before the law; freedom of thought, expression, belief, faith, worship, vocation, association and action, subject to law and public morality; and
6. WHEREIN, adequate safeguards shall be provided for minorities, backward and tribal areas, and depressed and other backward classes; and
7. WHEREBY, shall be maintained the integrity of the territory of the Republic and its sovereign rights on land, sea, and air according to justice and the law of civilised nations; and this ancient land attains its rightful and honoured place in the world and make its full and willing contribution to the promotion of world peace and the welfare of mankind.

This Resolution was unanimously adopted by the Constituent Assembly on 22 January, 1947. Late in the evening of 14 August, 1947 the Assembly met in the Constitution Hall and at the stroke of midnight, took over as the Legislative Assembly of an Independent India.

Source: http://parliamentofindia.nic.in/ls/debates/facts.htm

The Preamble to the Constitution :

"WE, THE PEOPLE OF INDIA, having solemnly resolved to constitute India into a SOVEREIGN SOCIALIST SECULAR DEMOCRATIC REPUBLIC and to secure to all its citizens: JUSTICE, social, economic and political; LIBERTY of thought, expression, belief, faith and worship; EQUALITY of status and of opportunity; and to promote among them all FRATERNITY assuring the dignity of the individual and the unity and integrity of the NATION; IN OUR CONSTITUENT ASSEMBLY this twenty-sixth day of November, 1949, do HEREBY ADOPT, ENACT AND GIVE TO OURSELVES, THIS CONSTITUTION."

Salient features of the Constitution of India

- It is the longest, written constitution consisting of 395 Articles and twelve schedules. It reflects ideology of a nation and is supreme law of land.
- It provides for Fundamental Rights and protection of civil liberties; Directive Principles of state policy; ensures supremacy of people of the country.
- It provides: freedom of religion, freedom of speech and expression, freedom of association and peaceful assembly; eradication of inequality; non-discrimination on the ground of caste, sex, language, religion and culture; right to constitutional remedies for the protection of civil right.
- The Constitution provides for a secular state (which is neutral in matters of religion and is neither religious nor irreligious, or anti-religious) and for a democratic republic (*i.e.,* the sovereignty rests with the people of India and they govern themselves through their representatives elected on the basis of universal adult franchise).

Do you know?

The Fundamental Rights are in part III of the Indian Constitution (Art. 14-35). They are enforceable in court of law, aggrieved person can directly move to the Supreme Court under Article 32 and High Court under Art. 226.

On the other hand, Directive Principles of state policy (Art. 36-51), part IV of the constitution are not enforceable by any court but are fundamental in governance of the country and it is the duty of the State to apply these principles in making laws. Further, 10 Fundamental duties that are expected to be performed by every citizen are added by 42nd Amendment in 1976. (Article 51(A)). The 11th Fundamental Duty is added by 86th Amendment Act, 2002.

- The President of India, the highest official of the state (is elected for a fixed term) with the provision for parliamentary democracy; separation of power between executive and legislative.
- The Indian Constitution seeks to establish the fundamental organs of government and lays down their structure, composition, powers and principles governing their operations.
- Article 1 of the Constitution of India lays down that: "India, that is Bharat, shall be a Union of States." The term 'Federation' has not been used but the government is federal because it consist of the features of federal state like: two sets of governments and distribution of powers between the two; written constitution, which is the supreme law of the land and an independent judiciary to interpret the constitution and settle disputes between the centre and the states. But in spite of all these essential features of a federation, Indian Constitution, unlike U.S.A., the federation provides for single citizenship and integrated judiciary for the whole country.
- The Indian Constitution is partly rigid and partly flexible as the parliament has power to amend the Constitution and procedure by way of addition, variation or repeal of any provision of the Constitution in accordance with the procedure laid down in article 368 of the constitution. An amendment of the Constitution can be initiated only by the introduction of a Bill for the purpose in either House of Parliament, and when the Bill is passed in each house by a majority of the total membership of that house present and voting, it is presented to the President for his assent and thereupon the Constitution stands amended in accordance with the terms of the Bill, provided that if such amendment seeks to make any change in (a) Article 54, Article 55, Article 73, Article 162 or Article 241, or (b) Chapter IV of Part V, Chapter V of Part VI, or Chapter I of Part XI, or (c) any of the lists in the Seventh Schedule, or (d) the representation of States in Parliament, or (e) the provisions of this article, the amendment shall also require to be ratified by the Legislature of not less than one half of the States by resolution to that effect passed by those Legislatures before the Bill making provision for such amendment is presented to the President for assent.

LET US SUM UP

⇨ A legal system is a system for the interpretation and enforcement of laws in a particular country.

➪ Hindu Law in India has emanated from the Vedas (shrutis), the Upanishads and other religious texts, Manusmriti, Arthashastra, Smiritis of Vishnu, Narad, Parashar, Apastamba, Vashisht, Gautam, etc.

➪ In ancient India, administration of justice is doneby king on the basis of eternal law and according to principles drawn from local usages and from the institutes of the sacred law. At the time of Maurya's Empire, as described in Arthashastra, there were administrative units called Khrvatika, Sangrahana, Dronamukha, Sthaniya and Janapadasandhishu. The King, Prince, ministers, and other state officials have to observe strict discipline and code of conduct.

➪ As per Brihaspati, there were three kinds of tribunals: stationary; movable courts held under royal signet in absence of King and commissions under the Kings presidency. The court presided over by the king himself is called Sasita. In villages, Kulani (local village council like modern panchayat were in existence, consisting of five or more members).

➪ In Sultanate, Sultan as the head of state is under religious duty and the supreme authority to administer justice. The empire was divided into Subahs (Iqtas), Sarkars and Parganahs. The Sultan was assisted by a Council of Ministers responsible to him for such departments as Finance, Army, Accounts, General Administration, Ecclesiastical, Law and Justice. Qazi is in charge of administration of Justice and Faujdar maintains Law and Order.

➪ The Sher Shah introduced the system of having separate courts of first instance for civil and criminal cases in the Parganahs having a civil Judge called a Munsif. The Mughals ruled India effectively until 1750 A. D. and nominally up to 1857, when the last Mughal Emperor was succeeded by Queen Victoria as Empress of India.

➪ The Charter of 1600 established the English East India Company in India. The charter of 1661 provided that the English and the Indians residing under the Company came under its jurisdiction, under the charter, the Court of Governor and Council was created which were designated as the High Court of Judicature in 1678. During the period, (1661 till 1726) there was no codified law and the laws of equity, good conscience and justice in conformity with the laws in England were followed.

➪ Under the Charter of 1668, the company was conferred powers to make laws and a Court of Judicature was established to deal with civil and criminal cases and there was a provision to prefer appeal to the Deputy Governor and Council against the decision of Court of Judicature.

➪ Under Charter of 1726, the Mayor's Courts were established in Madras, Bombay and Calcutta bringing uniformity in judicial system and superseding all the other courts of Bombay, Madras and Calcutta. This was a court of Crown not of company. The Mayor Courts have civil jurisdiction; the Governor and Council were given criminal jurisdiction and civil appeal was allowed to the Presidency Government against the decisions of the Mayor's Court and further in the court of King-in-Counsel in England (Court of Privy Council.)

➪ The Regulating Act, 1753 provided for the establishment of a Supreme Court at Calcutta. The court was a court of record, with the power to punish for its contempt. It had civil, equity, criminal, ecclesiastical and admiralty jurisdiction. Appeals against decisions of this Court and through the Court could be filed in all civil and criminal cases respectively before the King-in-Counsel. Appeal lies to Privy Council from all its judgments except in criminal matters.

➪ The charter of 1798 established the Recorder's Court at Madras and Bombay under the authority of act of 1797 replacing Mayor's court. This Court had similar jurisdiction and was subject to the same restrictions as the Supreme Court of Calcutta. Appeal from the judgment of this court lies to Privy Council.

➪ Charter Act of 1833 with the objective of securing a uniform and simple system of law in India through the process of integration of the general system of codes, marked the beginning of Central Legislative Council in India and the Governor General was known as Government of India and his council as the Indian Council; the act vested the legislative power exclusively in Governor General in Council and deprived of the Government of the Residencies of their legislative functions; the Indian Civil Services was founded; it also provided for the constitution of a Law Commission in India under Macaulay.

➪ The India High Courts Act 1861 was enacted which provides for creation of High Courts in various provinces abolishing Supreme Courts at Calcutta, Madras and Bombay and also the Sadar

Adalats in Presidency towns. It was the amalgamation of King's Courts and Company's Courts. High Court had ordinary original, appellate and extraordinary original jurisdiction in civil cases and extraordinary and appellant jurisdiction in criminal cases.

⇨ Federal Court of India were created under the Government of India Act 1935, had original, appellate, and advisory jurisdiction. It had exclusive original jurisdiction to decide disputes between the Centers and Constituent Units or units *inter sec*; appeals from Federal Court lies to the Privy Council.

⇨ The Supreme Court as an apex court was established with the commencement of the Constitution of India in 1950; High courts (state level) have become the courts of record with appellate and original jurisdiction; then there are Subordinate Courts (at District and subordinate level).

⇨ The sources of Indian Constitution are: Government of India Act of 1935, Constitutions of other countries and objectives resolution.

⇨ Indian Constitution reflects the ideology of a nation and is the supreme law of land, providing Fundamental Rights and protection of civil liberties; consists of Directive Principles of state policy; ensures supremacy of people of the country; provides: freedom of religion, freedom of speech and expression, freedom of association and peaceful assembly; eradication of inequality; non discrimination on the ground of caste, sex, language, religion and culture; right to constitutional remedies for the protection of civil right.

⇨ Constitution provides for a secular and democratic state with the provision for parliamentary democracy; there is separation of power between executive and legislative. The Indian Constitution seeks to establish the fundamental organs of government and lays down their structure, composition, powers and principles governing their operations. The constitution can also be amended as per procedure laid down in article 368 of the constitution.

⇨ In modern Indian legal system, the Mimansa Rules of Interpretation can be used in case of ambiguity and conflict in legal text. Further, the rules of governance laid down by Kautliya, Arthshastra can also be useful in formulating policies and initiatives for social and economic parity of the nation. The sources of Hindu law remains Vedas, Manu Samriti, Shrutis, customary law but radical changes have been made by the codification of Hindu law.

Terminal Questions

1. Explain the following in brief :
   (a) Legal System
   (b) Sources of Hindu Law
   (c) Sources of Islamic Law.

2. Describe the important features of Ancient Indian law.

3. Discuss the rules of governance and law as laid in Arthashastra by Kautilya.

4. Elaborate on the Law and Legal System as prevalent in Medieval India.

5. Discuss the Administration of Justice in British India.

6. Write the important provisions of Charter of 1753.

7. Write a short note on contributions of Law Commissions in codification of laws in India.

8. What are the basic features of Indian Constitution? Discuss.

9. Write a note on the following:
   (a) Supreme Court of India
   (b) High Court of India
   (c) Lok Adalats.

●●

Judiciary : Constitutional, Civil and Criminal Courts and Process

Introduction

The Indian legal system has evolved through a complex procedure and derives its authority from the Constitution of India. In the previous chapter we have studied the historical processes relating to development of legal institutions and administration of justice in ancient India, medieval period and British era. The Legislature, Executive, and the Judiciary are the three organs of state and are substantiated by the doctrine of the separation of powers that implies separate and distinct powers and functions of each of these organs with no single agency having complete authority. In India parliament is supreme law making agency but judiciary in exercise of power of judicial review can declare a law passed by the Parliament ultra vires as being violative of the basic structure of the Constitution (as evolved in *Kesavananda Bharati v. State of Kerala And Anr* AIR 1973 SC 1461) if it contravenes the fundamental rights of citizens, Supreme court being the protectors of civil liberties of citizens or if it is beyond the competence of the legislature. The Supreme Court in deciding the validity of legislation follows the principles of interpretation of law as envisaged in the doctrine of pith and substance (the true object of the legislation or a statute, relates to a matter within the competence of the legislature which enacted it); doctrine of severability (the violating part of any provision of a statute is declared unconstitutional and void *to the extent of such inconsistency,* but the remainder remains enforceable and valid) and the doctrine of colourable legislation etc. It prevents legislatures to make laws indirectly that they would otherwise not be able to create directly due the constitutional constraints.

Classifications and Hierarchy of Courts under Indian Legal System

The present judicial system for the administration of justice is pyramidal in nature with the Supreme Court is established as an apex court followed by the 24 High Courts, subordinate courts at the district level : civil and criminal courts, family courts and specialised tribunals. The court structure in India is practically same in all the states with some variations in designations of courts which are derived principally from the Code of Civil Procedure, 1908 (CPC) ; the Code of Criminal Procedure, 1973 (Cr.P.C) as amended from time to time and also guided by local statutes listing the functions and jurisdiction of such courts.

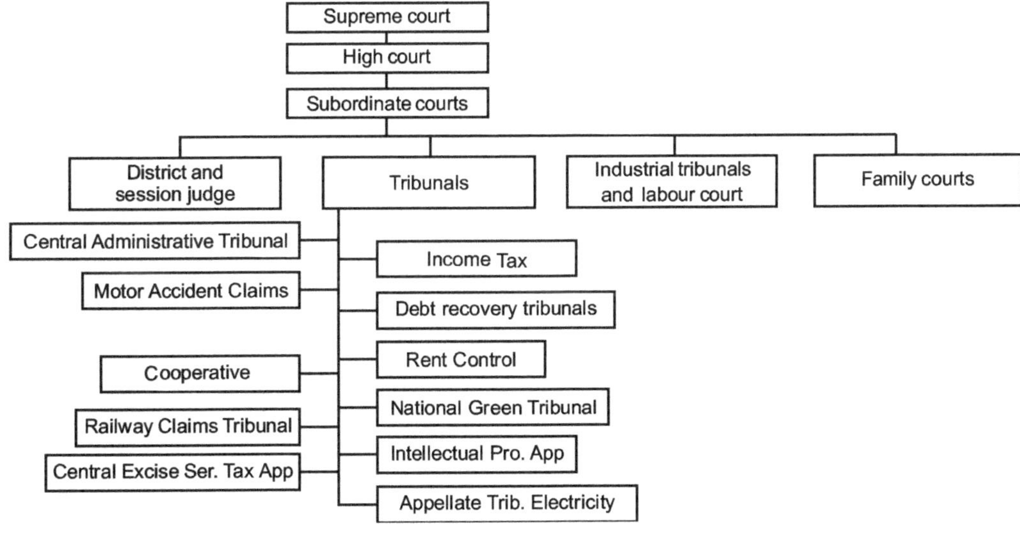

Judicial independence and impartiality

We have studied in the previous chapters that judiciary, as separated from legislative and an executive organ of government is independent with power to have judicial review of the legislation enacted by the Parliament. It has to act impartially in relation to the issues and the parties in a particular case. The Constitution provides for independence of the Judges of the higher courts, *i.e.*, the Supreme Court and the High Courts, Article 124(2) in The Constitution of India 1949 provides that "Every Judge of the Supreme Court shall be appointed by the President by warrant under his hand and seal after consultation with such of the Judges of the Supreme Court and of the High Courts in the States as the President may deem necessary for the purpose and shall hold office until he attains the age of sixty five years provided that in the case of appointment of a Judge other than the chief Justice, the chief Justice of India shall always be consulted". The procedure for voluntary resignation by a Judge, as well as for compulsory removal of judges respectively from their offices is prescribed under proviso [a] to clause (2) of Article 124, Article 217 (1) proviso (a), which provides that a Judge may, by writing under his hand addressed to the President, resign his office and further Cl.(4) of Art. 124 provides that a Judge can be removed from office before he attains the age of sixty five years on grounds of proved misbehavior or incapacity.

In S.P. Gupta v. Union of India [(1981) Supp. SCC 87] in paragraph 27, the Court held that "if there is one principle which runs through the entire fabric of the Constitution it is the principle of the rule of law, and under the Constitution it is the judiciary which is entrusted with the task of keeping every organ of the State within the limits of the law and thereby making the rule of law meaningful and effective. Judicial review is one of the most potent weapons in the armoury of law. The judiciary seeks to protect the citizen against violation of his constitutional or legal rights or misuse or abuse of power by the State or its officers. The judiciary stands between the citizen and the State as a bulwark against executive excesses and misuse or abuse of power by the executive. It is, therefore, absolutely essential that the judiciary must be free from executive pressure or influence which has been secured by making elaborate provisions in the Constitution with details. The independence of judiciary is not limited only to the independence from the executive pressure or influence; it is a wider concept which takes within its sweep, independence from any other pressure and prejudices. It has many dimensions, *viz.*, fearlessness of other power centers, economic or political, and freedom from prejudices acquired and nourished by the class to which the judges belong. Judicial individualism - whether needs protection? Independent judiciary is, therefore, most essential when liberty of citizen is in danger. It then becomes the duty of the judiciary to poise the scales of justice unmoved by the powers (actual or perceived) undisturbed by the clamour of the multitude. The heart of judicial independence is judicial individualism. The judiciary is not a disembodied abstraction. It is composed of individual men and women who work primarily on their own."

Supreme Court : Its constitution, powers and jurisdiction

In the previous chapters, we have already studied the establishment and Constitution of Supreme Court under Art 124 of the constitution including qualification required to be a Judge of the Supreme Court, retirement and removal of judges and also the Jurisdiction and powers of the Supreme Court. Let us note some important points with respect to function and powers of Supreme Court including judicial review that make it independent from the other organs of government.

Supreme Court is the Court of record and the judgments of the court have authoritative value and are binding on Lower Courts.

Article 129 of the constitution states that the Supreme Court shall be a court of record and shall have all the powers of such a court including the power to punish for contempt of itself.

> **Do you know?**
>
> A Court of Record is a Court whose records are of evidentiary value and cannot be questioned when produced before any Court.- *Wharton's Law Lexicon, 14th Edition, p.275*

Further, Article 141 of the Constitution of India provides that the law declared by Supreme Court is binding on all courts. The 'law declared' in a judgement (*ratio decidendi*) is binding upon courts. It is the essence of a decision and the principle upon which, the case is decided and which has to be ascertained in relation to the subject matter of the decision.

Supreme Court has the jurisdiction which can be categorised as original, appellate and advisory.

Establishment and Constitution of Supreme Court- (Artical 124 of the Constitution)

Composition of the Court and appointment of judges - It consists of the Chief Justice and twenty five other Judges appointed by the President of the country. The Chief Justice is appointed by the President with the consultation of such of the Judges of the Supreme Court and the High Court's as he deems necessary for the purpose. But in appointing other Judges, the President shall always consult the Chief Justice of India. Under Article 124 (2) of the Constitution, the President, in appointing other judges of the Supreme Court is bound to consult the Chief Justice of India. But in appointing the Chief Justice of India he is not bound to consult anyone.

Qualification of Judges–As per Artical 124(3) of the Constitution, the person to be qualified for appointment as a Judge of the Supreme Court must be:

- a citizen of India;
- has been a Judge of a High Court at least for five years, or a Judge of two or more such Courts in succession;
- has been for at least ten years an advocate of a High Court or of two or more such Courts in succession;
- is in the opinion of the President, a distinguished jurist.
- a person who has been a Judge of the Supreme Court is debarred from practicing in any court of law or before any other authority in India. (Artical 124(7) of the Constitution)

Retirement and removal of Judges

- Supreme Court Judges retire upon attaining the age of 65 years.
- A Judge of the Supreme Court cannot be removed from office except by an order of the President passed after an address in each House of Parliament supported by a majority of the total membership of that house and by a majority of not less than two-thirds of members present and voting, and presented to the President in the same Session for such removal on the ground of proved misbehavior or incapacity. (Article 124(4) of the Constitution)

Do you know?

The 'law declared' is the principle culled out on the reading of a judgment as a whole in light of the questions raised, upon which the case is decided. See: *Ambica Quarry Works v. State of Gujarat & Ors (1987) 1 SCC 213 and Commissioner of Income Tax v. Sun Engineering Works (P) Ltd. (1992) 4 SCC 363.*

The 'law declared' has to be construed as a principle of law that emanates from a judgment, or an interpretation of a law or judgment by the Supreme Court, upon which, the case is decided. See *Fida Hussain & Ors. v. Moradabad Development Authority & Anr. (2011) 12 SCC 615.*

Original Jurisdiction

Under Original Jurisdiction, the Supreme Court of India can decide any disputes, if and so far as the dispute involves any question (whether of law or of fact) on which the existence or extent of a legal right depends, between the centre and the one or more States or between the Centre and any State or States on the one side and one or more other States on the other or between the two or more states (see article 131 of the constitution).

Article 32 of the Constitution gives an extensive original jurisdiction to the Supreme Court to issue directions, orders and writs in regard to enforcement of Fundamental Right.

The court can issue following writs:

Habeas Corpus- is order by a Supreme Court or High Court to the detaining authority to produce the arrested person before it so that it may examine whether the person has been detained lawfully or otherwise.

In *Ummu Sabeena v. State of Kerala and others*, (2011) 10 SCC 781, Court has observed that–

"...the writ of habeas corpus is the oldest writ evolved by the common law of England to protect the individual liberty against its invasion in the hands of the executive or may be also at the instance of private persons. This principle of habeas corpus has been incorporated in our constitutional law and we are of the opinion that in a democratic republic like India where Judges function under a written Constitution and which has a chapter on fundamental rights, to protect individual liberty the Judges owe a duty to safeguard the liberty not only of the citizens but also of all persons within the territory of India. The most effective way of doing the same is by way of exercise of power by the Court by issuing a writ of habeas corpus."

Kanu Sanyal v. District Magistrate AIR 1973 SC 2684. The Supreme Court, in this case pointed out that while dealing with a petition for writ of Habeas Corpus, the court may examine the legality of the detention without requiring the person detained to be produced before it.

It is the general rule that the petition is filed by a person whose right has been infringed but the writ of Habeas Corpus is an exception to that the rule and can be filed by the person imprisoned or by any interested person on behalf of the prisoner or detainee.

Mandamus–Mandamus means "we order". It is an order from a superior court to a lower court or tribunal, coropration, or public authority or state authority to perform an act, which falls within its duty.The writ can not be issued against president, governors of state or state legislature to prevent them to execute law alleged to be violative of the constitution.

Prohibition–an order from a superior court to inferior court, tribunal or quasi judicial body (commissions established by law; administrative officers) forbidding or stoping an act outside its jurisdiction., *i.e.*, prohibiting an act,which exceeds to their jurisdiction.

Certiorari– is an order by Supreme Court or any High Court for quashing the order already passed by an inferior court, tribunal or quasi judicial body in excess of jurisdiction or outside its jurisdiction. The writ is corrective in nature

Quo Warranto–Quo Warranto means "by what warrant?". It is an order issued by Supreme Court or any High Court to restrain a person from holding a public office to which he/she is not entitled to. The writ is applicable to the public offices only.

Appellate Jurisdiction

Under Appellate jurisdiction, the Supreme Court can hear appeals that lie from any judgement, decree or final order of a High Court in the territory of India, whether in a civil, criminal or other proceeding, if the High Court certifies under article 134A that the case involves a substantial question of law as to the interpretation of this Constitution. (Article 132).

The appellate jurisdiction of Supreme Court in appeals from High Courts with regard to:

◆ Civil matters lies to the Supreme Court from any judgement, decree or final order in a civil proceeding of a High Court in the territory of India if the High Court certifies under article 134A (*a*) that the case involves a substantial question of law of general importance; and (*b*) that in the opinion of the High Court the said question needs to be decided by the Supreme Court. [Article 133(1)].

◆ Criminal matters lies to the Supreme Court from any judgment, final order or sentence in a criminal proceeding of a High Court in the territory of India if the High Court—

(a) has on appeal, reversed order of acquittal of an accused person sentenced him to death; or

(b) has withdrawn for trial before itself any case from any court subordinate to its authority and has in such trial, convicted the accused person and sentenced him to death; or

(c) certifies under article 134A that the case is a fit one for appeal to the Supreme Court.[see article 134(1)].

<table>
<tr><td>Certificate for appeal to the Supreme Court by High Court (Article 134A)

While passing or making a judgment, decree, final order, or sentence, the High Court (a) may, if it deems fit so to do, on its own motion; and (b) shall, if an oral application is made, by or on behalf of the party aggrieved, immediately after the passing or making of such judgment, decree, final order or sentence, has to determine, as soon as may be after such passing or making, the question whether a certificate of the nature referred to in clause (1) of article 132, or clause (1) of article 133 or, as the case may be, sub-clause (c) of clause (1) of article 134, may be given in respect of that case.</td></tr>
</table>

Advisory Jurisdiction

Under Advisory Jurisdiction of the Supreme Court, the President of India can seek the opinion of the Court if there is a question of law or fact has arisen, or is likely to arise, which is of such a nature and of such public importance that it is expedient to obtain the opinion of the Supreme Court upon it and the Court may, after such hearing as it thinks fit, report to the President its opinion thereon.

Power of Judicial Review–Article 13, articles 32, 226 and 227 provide a constitutional basis to judicial review in India.

Power of Supreme Court to grant Special leave to appeal–The Supreme Court under Article 136 of the constitution may, in its discretion, grant special leave to appeal from any judgment, decree, determination, sentence or order in any cause or matter passed or made by any court or tribunal in the territory of India. But this provision does not apply to any judgment, determination, sentence or order passed or made by any court or tribunal constituted by or under any law relating to the Armed Forces.

Review of judgments or orders by the Supreme Court–Subject to the provisions of any law made by Parliament or any rules made under article 145, the Supreme Court shall have power to review any judgment pronounced or order made by it. (Article 137 of the constitution).

Grounds of Review

A. Grounds mentioned in order XL VII Rule 1 of the Code of Civil Procedure:

Any person aggrieved : (a) by a decree or order from which an appeal is allowed, but from which no appeal has been preferred, (b) by a decree or order from which no appeal is allowed, or (c) by a decision on a reference from a Court of Small Causes, may apply for a review of judgment to the Court which passed the decree or made the order under following circumstances:

◆ On the discovery of new and important matter or evidence which, after the existence of due diligence, was not within his knowledge or could not be produced by him at the time when the decree was passed or order made, or

◆ On account of some mistake or error apparent on the face of the record, or

◆ For any other sufficient reason, desires to obtain a review of the decree passed or order made against him.

Case Laws

In *M/s Northern India Caterers (India) Ltd. v. Lt. Governor of Delhi (1978 AIR 1591)*, Supreme Court held that a party is not entitled to seek a review of a judgment delivered by the Supreme Court merely for the purpose of a re hearing and a fresh decision of the case.

In *Col. Avtar Singh Sekhon v. Union of India and Ors (1980 AIR 2041)*, Court held that review is not a routine procedure but an application for review could be entertained when material error manifest on the face of the earlier order undermines its soundness or results in miscarriage of justice.

Enlargement of the jurisdiction of the Supreme Court–The Supreme Court shall have such further jurisdiction and powers with respect to any of the matters in the Union List as Parliament may, by law confer. [Art 138 (1)]. The Supreme Court shall have such further jurisdiction and powers with respect to any matter as the Government of India and the Government of any State may by special agree-ment confer, if Parliament by law provides for the exercise of such jurisdiction and powers by the Supreme Court. [Art 138 (2)].

Supreme Court and Public Interest Litigation– Public interest litigation is the litigation initiated in the court of law and has been used as a tool to address and protect the matters of collective public interest of those who are socially or economically at disadvantaged position and are not able to approach the court on account of some disability. The beginning can be traced from the cases *Mumbai Kamgar Sabha v. Abdul Thai (AIR 1976 SC 1455)* and

Bharatiya Shoshit Karmachari Sangh (Railway) v. Union of India (AIR 1981 SC 298). The supreme court of India also liberalized the concept of locus standi as enunciated in the case of *Fertilizer Corporation Kamgar Union v. Union of India (AIR 1981 SC 344)*, where it is observed that "the rule of law must win the aggrieved person for the law court and wean him from the lawless street. In simple terms, locus standi must be liberalised to meet the challenges of the times. Ubi jus ibi remedium must be enlarged to embrace all interests of public-minded citizens or organisations with serious concern for conservation of public resources and the direction and correction of public power so as to promote justice in its triune facets."

> **Do you know?**
> *Ubi jus ibi remedium* is a Latin legal maxim which means 'where there is a right there is a remedy'. The basic principle contemplated in the maxim is that, when a person's right is violated or infrin-ged, the victim will have an equitable remedy under law which one has to enforce through law courts.

High Court

The High Court is the highest court in a state. Article 214 of the Constitution provides that there shall be a High Court for each State. However, Parliament may by law, establish a common High Court for two or more States and a Union territory (Article 231). The Constitution also provides that Parliament may by law, extend the jurisdiction of a High Court or excludes its jurisdiction from any Union Territory (under Artcle 230). Under the Government of India Act, 1935, the constitution and organisation of the High Court's was vested in the provincial legislature while in the Indian constitution the subject and organisation of the High Court's was included in entry 78 of the union list.

Each High Court comprises of a Chief Justice and such other judges as the President of India, appoints from time to time (Article 216). Article 223 provides that when the office of Chief Justice of a High Court is vacant or any Chief Justice, by reason of absence or otherwise, is unable to perform the duties of his office, such duty shall be performed by such one or the other Judges of the court as the President may appoint.

High Court as Court of record -Every High Court also like a Supreme Court, is the court of record and has all the powers of such a court including the power to punish for contempt of itself (article 215).

Jurisdiction of High Court–High Court can exercise both civil and criminal jurisdiction, general and special jurisdiction, ordinary as well as extra-ordinary jurisdiction under article 226 of the constitution. It can issue various writs and this power can also be exercised by any High Court exercising jurisdiction in relation to territories within which the cause of action, wholly or in part, arises for exercise of such power, notwithstanding that the seat of such government or authority or residence of such person is not within those territories. The High Court has original as well appellate jurisdiction.

High Court exercises original jurisdiction in respect of admiralty (maritime law), matrimonial matters, contempt of court and cases ordered to be transferred to High Court by lower court.

The appellate jurisdiction of the High Court's extends both in civil and criminal cases, in which the accused has been sentenced to four years imprisonment by the Sessions Judge or has been awarded death sentence by Sessions Judge, the death sentence is subject to the approval by the High Court.

The High Court also hears the cases that involves interpretation of the Constitution or Law, on income tax, sales tax etc., and the States High Courts like the Supreme Court has the power of Judicial Review. The High Court hears first appeal from the decision of the District Courts. Further, in accordance with the Section 100 of the Code of Civil Procedure, an appeal also lies to the High Court from every decree passed in appeal by any Court subordinate to the High Court, if the High Court is satisfied that the case involves a substantial question of law. Under this section, an appeal may lie from an appellate decree passed ex parte. When an appeal is made under this section, the memorandum of appeal shall precisely states that the substantial question of law is involved in the appeal; where the High Court is satisfied that a substantial question of law is involved in any case, High Court can formulate that question and the appeal shall be heard on the question so formulated and the respondent shall, at the hearing of the appeal, be allowed to argue that the case does not involve such question. But this section does not take away or abridge the power of the Court to hear, for reasons to be recorded, the appeal on any other substantial question of law, not formulated by it, if it is satisfied that the case involves such question.

The amount of pecuniary jurisdiction is different for all High Courts and the limit is decided by respective High Court Rules. In many states High court has no pecuniary jurisdiction. All civil suits go before District Courts, and only appeal lies before High Court.

Appointment and conditions of the office of a Judge of a High Court (Article 217)

Appointment - Every Judge of a High Court shall be appointed by the President by warrant under his hand and seal after consultation with the Chief Justice of India, the Governor of the State, and, in the case of appointment of a Judge other than the Chief Justice, the Chief Justice of the High court.

Qualification of Judge-A person be qualified for appointment as a Judge of a High Court must be–

- A citizen of India and
- Has for at least ten years held a judicial office in the territory of India; or
- Has for at least ten years been an advocate of a High Court or of two or more such Courts in succession.

(Explanation: For the purposes of this clause (a) in computing the period during which a person has held judicial office in the territory of India, there shall be included any period, after he has held any judicial office, during which the person has been an Advocate of a High Court or has held the office of a member of a tribunal or any post, under the Union or a State, requiring special knowledge of law; (aa) in computing the period during which a person has been an advocate of a High Court, there shall be included any period during which the person has held judicial office or the office of a member of a tribunal or any post, under the Union or a State, requiring special knowledge of law after he became an advocate; (b) in computing the period during which a person has held judicial office in the territory of India or been an advocate of High Court, there shall be included any period before the commencement of this Constitution during which he has held judicial office in any area which was comprised before the fifteenth day of August, 1947, within India as defined by the Government of India Act, 1935, or has been an advocate of any High Court in any such area, as the case may be)

Retirement and removal of Judges

i. High Court Judge retires upon attaining the age of 62 years.

ii. A Judge may, by writing under his hand addressed to the President, resign his office.

iii. A Judge may be removed from his office by the President in the manner provided in clause (4) of Article 124 for the removal of a Judge of the Supreme Court.

iv. The office of a Judge shall be vacated by his being appointed by the President to be a Judge of the Supreme Court or by his being transferred by the President to any other High Court within the territory of India.

Jurisdiction and powers of the High Court

◆ The original jurisdiction of High Court extends to matters of admiralty, matrimonial, contempt of court and cases ordered to be transferred to High Court by lower court. It also has power of judicial review of legislation.

◆ High Courts have been conferred the power to issue writs (Article 226 of constitution), notwithstanding anything in article 32, every High Court has the power, throughout the territories in relation to which it exercises jurisdiction, to issue to any person or authority, including in appropriate cases, any government, within those territories directions, orders or writs, including writs in the nature of habeas corpus, mandamus, prohibition, quo warranto and certiorari, or any of them, for the enforcement of any of the rights conferred by Part III and for any other purpose [Article 226 (1)].

◆ The power conferred by article 226 (1) upon High Courts to issue directions, orders or writs to any government, authority or person may also be exercised by any High Court exercising jurisdiction in relation to the territories within which the cause of action, wholly or in part, arises for the exercise of such power, notwithstanding that the seat of such government or authority or the residence of such person is not within those territories. [Article 226 (2)]

◆ The High Courts have superintendence over all the courts and tribunals throughout the territories in relation to which it exercises jurisdiction. Article 227 of the constitution. However, the High Court does not have powers of superintendence over any court or tribunal constituted by or under any law relating to the Armed Forces. [Article 227 (4)].

◆ The High Court, on satisfaction that a case pending in a court subordinate to it, involves a substantial question of law as to the interpretation of the Constitution the determination of which is necessary for the disposal of the case, it shall withdraw the case and may (a) either dispose of the case itself, or (b) determine the said question of law and return the case to the court from which the case has been so withdrawn together with a copy of its judgment on such question, and the said court shall on receipt thereof proceed to dispose of the case in conformity with such judgment. (Article 228).

Other Powers of High Court

◆ High Court has power to withdraw cases involving substantial question of law as to the interpretation of constitution from the subordinate courts (Article 228). it shall withdraw the case and may (a) either dispose of the case itself, or (b) determine the said question of law and return the case to the court from which the case has been so withdrawn together with a copy of its judgment on such question, and the said court shall on receipt thereof, proceed to dispose of the case in conformity with such judgment.

◆ It has administrative control over the staff of the High Court (article 229) and

◆ Has general power to regulate the subordinate judiciary (article 233-235).

Establishment of various High Courts–Let us look below the location and establishment of various High Courts in India.

S. No.	Name	Year and Act of Establishment	Territorial Jurisdiction	Seat and bench at present
1.	Allahabad	1866. For the North-Western Provinces at Agra by the High Court's Act, 1861. Name changed to Judicature at Allahabad from 11th March, 1919.	Uttar Pradesh	Allahabad (Bench at Lucknow)
2.	Andhra Pradesh	1956 by Andhra State Act, 1953	Andhra Pradesh	Hyderabad
3.	Bombay*	By Letter Patent on June 26, 1862 by virtue of Indian high court Act of 1861	Maharashtra, Goa, Dadra and Nagar Haveli and Daman and Diu	Bombay (Benches at Nagpur, Panaji and Aurangabad)
4.	Calcutta*	Letters Patent dated 14th May, 1862 by virtue of Indian high court Act of 1861	West Bengal, Andaman and Nicobar Islands.	Calcutta (Circuit Bench at Port Blair)
5.	Delhi	1966. Delhi High Court Act,1966	Delhi	New Delhi

6.	Guwahati	1948. Indian Provisional Constitution (Amendment) Order, 1948 by virtue of Government of India Act, 1935.	Assam, Nagaland, Mizoram and Arunachal Pradesh.	Guwahati. (Benches at Kohima, Aizwal & Itanagar.
7.	Gujarat	1960. Bombay Re organisation Act, 1960	Gujarat	Ahmedabad
8.	Himachal Pradesh	1971. State of Himachal Pradesh Act, 1970	Himachal Pradesh	Shimla
9.	Jammu & Kashmir	1928. By virtue of Order No. 1 dated 26.3.1928. The Letters Patent was conferred on 10.9.1943 by Maharaja.	Jammu & Kashmir	Srinagar & Jammu
10.	Karnataka	1884. Mysore High Court Act, 1884	Karnataka	Bangaluru. (Circuit Benches at Hubli-Dharwad & Gulbarga)
11.	Kerala	1956. States Reorganisation Act, 1956	Kerala & Lakshadweep	Ernakulam
12.	Madhya Pradesh	1936. Government of India Act, 1935	Madhya Pradesh	Jabalpur (Benches at Gwalior and Indore)
13.	Madras*	1862. Letters Patent granted by Her Majesty Queen Victoria on 26th June 1862 by virtue of Indian high court Act of 1861.	Tamil Nadu & Pondicherry	Madras (bench at Madurai)
14.	Orissa	1948. Orissa High Court Order,1948	Orissa	Cuttack
15.	Patna	1916. Government of India Act, 1915	Bihar	Patna
16.	Punjab & Haryana	The States Re-organisation Act, 1966**	Punjab, Haryana & Chandigarh	Chandigarh
17.	Rajasthan	1949. Rajasthan High Court Ordinance, 1949	Rajasthan	Jodhpur (Bench at Jaipur)
18.	Sikkim	1955. High Court of Judicature (Jurisdiction and Powers) Proclamation, 1955 ***	Sikkim	Gangtok
19.	Chhattisgarh	2000. Madhya Pradesh Reorganisation Act, 2000	Chhattisgarh	Bilaspur
20.	Jharkhand	2000. Bihar Reorganisation Act, 2000	Jharkhand	Ranchi
21.	Uttarakhand	2000. Uttar Pradesh Reorganisation Act, 2000	Uttarakhand	Nainital
22.	Manipur	2013. North-Eastern Areas (Reorganisation) and Other Related Laws (Amendment) Act, 2012	Manipur	Imphal
23.	Tripura	---do---------	Tripura	Agartala
24.	Meghalaya	---do---------	Meghalaya	Shillong

Sources: http://indiancourts.nic.in/ # and websites of various High Courts.

Notes:

*   The Indian High Court Act of 1861 itself did not create or establish the High Courts in India but vested in the Queen of England to issue Letters Patent to erect and establish High Court of Calcutta, Madras (now Chennai) and Bombay.

**   The East Punjab High Court of judicature was established at Shimla on August 15, 1947 by the Governor General's High Court (Punjab) Order 1947 issued under Section 9 of the Indian Independence Act, 1947.

*** The constitution (thirty-sixth amendment) act, 1975, article 371f(b)(i) provided that the High Court functioning as such immediately before the appointed day in the territories comprised in the State of Sikkim shall, on and from the appointed day, be deemed to be the High Court for the State of Sikkim.

Subordinate Courts

The Subordinate Courts, at the level of districts and lower levels of the judiciary plays a crucial role in delivery of justice. There are slight variations in structure of subordinate courts throughout the country with slight variation. The highest court in each district is that of the District and Sessions Judge. The District Court is subordinate to the High Court and is under the administrative control of the High Court of the State to which it belongs. Every Civil Court of a grade inferior to that of a District Court and every Court of small causes is subordinate to the High Court and District Court. (refer to section 3 CPC).

Appointment of District Judges

The District Judge is appointed   in any State by the Governor of the State in consultation with the High Court exercising jurisdiction in relation to such State. Further a person not already in the service of the Union or of the State shall only be eligible to be appointed as a district judge if he has been for not less than seven years, an advocate or a pleader and is recommended by the High Court for appointment. (Article 233).

The expression "**District Judge**" includes judge of a city Civil Court, Additional District Judge, Joint District Judge, Assistant District Judge, Chief Judge of a small cause court, Chief Presidency Magistrate, and Additional Chief Presidency Magistrate (Article 236(a). The District Judge possesses unlimited original jurisdiction, both civil and criminal and hears 1st appeals from the decision of Subordinate Judge and also from the Munsif Court unless they are transferred to a Subordinate Judge.

Further, the persons other than district judges are appointed to the judicial service of a State by the Governor of the State in accordance with rules made by him in that behalf after consultation with the State Public Service Commission and with the High Court exercising jurisdiction in relation to such State (Article 234).

Court Structure

The two branches of judicial system: civil and criminal are bifurcated in lowest judiciary and the subordinate courts deal with civil and criminal cases in accordance with their respective jurisdictions. On the civil side, the judges are designated as District Judge, Additional District Judge and Civil Judges. On the criminal side, the designations commonly used are Sessions Judge, Additional Sessions Judge, Chief Judicial Magistrate, Judicial Magistrate etc.

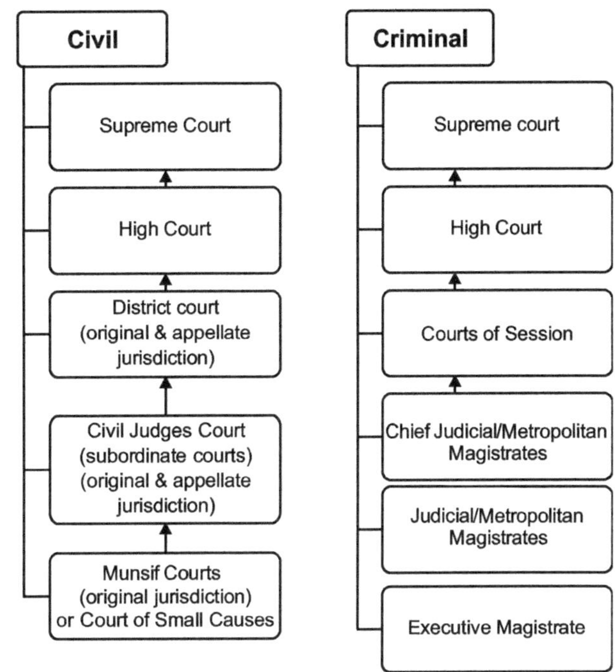

Subordinate Courts (at District and Subordinate level)

◆ The District Judges are appointed by the governor of the state in consultation with the corresponding High Court [Article 233(1)].

◆ As per (2) of Article 233, a person not already in the service of the Union or of the State shall only be eligible to be appointed a district judge, if he has been for not less than seven years, an advocate or a pleader and is recommended by the High Court for appointment.

◆ In case of recruitment of persons other than district judges to the judicial service of a State, the same is made by the Governor of the State in accordance with rules made by him in that behalf after consultation with the State Public Service Commission and with the High Court exercising jurisdiction in relation to such State.

◆ The jurisdiction and nomenclature of subordinate courts in the various States of the country are different and at present, there are three or more tiers of civil and criminal courts below the High Court and is represented below :

Civil Courts		
In Districts		**In Cities**
First grade	District Judge and Additional District Judge	Chief Judge and Additional Chief Judge
Second Grade	Assistant District Judge or Senior Civil Judge	Assistant Chief Judge or Senior Civil Judge
Third Grade	Munsif or Junior Civil Judge	Munsif or Junior Civil Judge
Criminal Courts		
In Districts		**In Cities**
Sessions Court (Sessions Judge, Addl. Sessions Judges and Asst. Sessions Judges)		Sessions Court (Sessions Judge, Addl. Sessions Judges and Asst. Sessions Judges)
Chief Judicial Magistrate's Court		Chief Metropolitan Magistrate's Court
Judicial Magistrates of First Class.		Metropolitan Magistrates' Courts
Judicial Magistrates of Second Class.		
Source: http://www.hrdiap.gov.in/		

Civil process and functioning of Civil Courts

The Civil Procedure Code, 1908 (C.P.C.) is a procedural law, an act to consolidate and amend the laws relating to the procedure of the Courts of Civil Judicature. It regulates the functioning of civil courts and lays down parameters and jurisdictions within which the civil courts should function and also lays down the procedure for filing a civil case; powers of court to pass various orders. The Civil Procedure Code is applicable to the whole of India except : (a) the State of Jammu and Kashmir; (b) the State of Nagaland and the tribal areas. The codes of civil procedure, 1908 has no retrospective operation. It contains 158 sections divided in to 11 parts that provides for substantive aspects of civil procedure. It has 5 schedules that deal with procedural aspects. The sections under CPC are fundamental in nature and cannot be amended except by the legislature. However, the First Schedule of the CPC, containing Orders and Rules can be amended by High Courts.

The courts have jurisdiction of three types :

1. **Jurisdiction as to subject matter**–Section 9 states that have jurisdiction to try all suits of a civil nature excepting suits of which their cognizance is either expressly or impliedly barred. This shows that civil courts are not empowered to deal with all cases before them and some cases like revenue, Income tax, Sales tax are heard by special forums/tribunals established for the purpose.

> **Subject matter of civil suits:** Disputes relating to property, for determination of any other right to or interest in immovable property, for compensation for wrongs committed, suit relating to Bills of Exchange, Hundis, Promissory Notes.

2. **Jurisdiction as to value of the suit or pecuniary jurisdiction**–The courts are competent to try the suits of the value as fixed by various orders and acts. Sec 6 CPC provides that save in so far as is otherwise expressly provided, nothing herein contained shall operate to give any Court jurisdiction over suits, the amount or value of the subject-matter of which exceeds the pecuniary limits (if any) of its ordinary jurisdiction.

3. **Jurisdiction as to place of suing or territorial jurisdiction**–The various sections of CPC specifies the place of suing. Every suit has to be instituted in the Court of the lowest grade which is competent to try it (Section 15 CPC). The civil suits can be instituted either in the Court within the local limits of whose jurisdiction, the property is situated, or in the Court within the local limits of whose jurisdiction the defendant actually and voluntarily resides, or carries on business, or personally works for gain or where cause of action wholly or in part, arises.

> **Illustrations:**
>
> A, residing in Delhi, publishes in Calcutta statements defamatory of B. B may sue A either in Calcutta or in Delhi.
>
> A is a tradesman in Calcutta; B carries on business in Delhi. B, by his agent in Calcutta, buys goods of A and requests A to deliver them to the East Indian Railway Company. A delivers the goods accordingly in Calcutta. A may sue B for the price of the goods either in Calcutta, where the cause of action has arisen or in Delhi, where B carries on business.

The Munsif Courts are the lowest civil courts and have pecuniary jurisdiction as notified by the State Government. Every suit has to be instituted before the court of lowest jurisdiction. The Munsif Court is the competent court to try the suit in case the value of the subject matter of the suit is worth rupees one lakh or below. If the value exceeds above rupees one lakh, the suit should be filed before the Subordinate Judge's Court (Sub Court). An appeal from the decision of the Munsif Court is filed before the District Court.

In metropolitan cities such as Delhi, Bombay, Calcutta, Madras, etc, the courts of small causes are at the lower end. Section 16 of the Provincial Small Causes Courts Act, 1887 provides for the exclusive jurisdiction of Courts of Small Causes, it provides that when a Court of Small Causes under the Provincial Small Causes Courts Act, 1887, has jurisdiction in any locality, ordinary, Civil Courts cannot try suits, which are cognizable by that court unless it is expressly provided otherwise by the aforesaid Act or any other enactment.

The next in hierarchy is the court of subordinate Civil Judge, class-I. In some states, these courts have unlimited pecuniary jurisdiction and are called courts of Civil Judge (senior division) and in some states, they are described as courts of subordinate judge. Immediately above are the courts of district and sessions judge which also include the courts of additional judge, joint judge or assistant judge. In some states there is a court of Civil and Sessions Judge.

The District Judge, Additional District Judge and Subordinate Judge of the 1st class have jurisdiction to hear suits without any limits as to their value. In the case of Subordinate Judges of a power class, however, jurisdiction depends, *inter alia*, on the value of the suit. The value of a suit for purposes of jurisdiction has to be calculated in accordance with the provisions of the Suits Valuation Act and the rules there under. Further, under certain enactments, Courts of Subordinate Judges have no jurisdiction at all to take cognizance of proceedings under those enactments like the Companies Act, 1956; the Indian Divorce Act, 1869. There are proceedings under certain other enactments of which subordinate Judges can take cognizance only if specifically empowered in that behalf as for *e.g.,* Section 4-A of the Guardians and Wards Act, 1890; Section 388 of the Indian Succession Act (see Jurisdiction-Delhi High Court).

Appeals from the decisions of the Sub Court are filed before the District Court in case the subject matter of the suit is valued up to rupees two lakhs, if the value is above rupees two lakhs, the appeal should be filed before the High Court and next to the Supreme Court.

<table><tr><td>Do you know?

The Kerala Civil Courts (Amendment) Act, 2012 had enhanced the pecuniary jurisdiction of Munsif Court to "seven lakh and fifty thousand rupees" and the appellate pecuniary jurisdiction of District Court to "twenty lakh rupees.</td></tr></table>

Decree, Judgement and Order

Definitions :

Section 2(2) of CPC defines "decree" as to mean the formal expression of an adjudication which so far regards, the court expressing it, conclusively determines the rights of the parties with regard to all or any of the matters in controversy in the suit and may be either preliminary or final. It shall be deemed to include the rejection of a plaint and the determination of any question within Section 144, but shall not include: (a) any adjudication from which an appeal lies as an appeal from an order, or (b) any order of dismissal for default.

Explanation : A decree is preliminary when further proceedings have to be taken before the suit can be completely disposed of. It is final when such adjudication completely disposes of the suit, it may be partly preliminary and partly final.

Section 2(9) of CPC defines a 'judgment' as the statement given by a judge of the grounds of a decree or order.

Section 2(14) of CPC defines an "order" to mean the formal expression of any decision of a Civil Court which is not a decree.

Decree and Judgement

Section 33 CPC further provides that the Court, after the case has been heard, shall pronounce judgment, and on such judgment a decree shall follow. Thus, a judge cannot pronounce decree without giving statement of reasons for arriving at a particular decision. Rule 4(2) of Order 20 of CPC states that apart from the judgment of Small Cause Courts, judgments of all other Courts shall contain a concise statement of the case; the points for determination; the decision thereon; and the reasons for such decision.

Decree and order–The decree and order are formal expressions of decision of civil court relating to any matter in controversy.

- An order may not conclusively determine the right of parties to the suit whereas a decree is an adjudication conclusively determining the rights of the parties with regard to all or any of the matters in controversy.

- Every decree is appealable, unless otherwise something contrary is expressly provided in the CPC or by the law for the time, being in force. But every order is not appealable. Only those orders are appealable as specified in section 104 and 0.43 RL.

- Decrees always originate from the suit commenced by presentation of a plaint. On the other hand, an order may not necessarily originate from the suit and may arise from a proceedings commenced on application.

- A decree may be preliminary or final, but there is no such distinction in case of an order.

The Criminal Process and Functioning of Criminal Courts – Investigation and Prosecution

The Code of Criminal Procedure, 1973 (Cr.P.C.) is an act to consolidate and amend the law relating to Criminal Procedure governing the powers and functions of the criminal courts except in the state of Jammu & Kashmir, providing further that the provisions of this code, other than those relating to Chapters VIII, X and XI thereof, shall not apply to the state of Nagaland, to the Tribal Areas in Assam. The Cr.P.C. contains 484 sections divided in to 37 (XXXVII) chapters and deals with the procedure for arrest, framing of charge and trial before a court. The code prescribes that all the offence under Indian penal code,1860 (substantive criminal law) shall be investigated, inquired into, tried unless it is otherwise dealt. The code does not affect any special law, local law or any special jurisdiction provided under any other law and there may also be other courts that are constituted under the laws other than the Cr.P.C. The Indian Evidence Act of 1872 in addition to Cr.P.C. guides the process of investigation and trial. It deals with the relevancy, admissibility, examination and proof of facts to know the existence and non existence of any fact or facts.

Classes of Criminal Courts

The Cr.P.C. provides that every State shall have following classes of criminal courts (see sec. 6 of Cr.P.C.):

   i. Courts of Session;

   ii. Judicial Magistrate of the first class and, in any Metropolitan area, Metropolitan Magistrate;

   iii. Judicial Magistrate of the second class; and

   iv. Executive Magistrate.

Territorial divisions–Every state consists of sessions divisions and every session division is a or consist of districts. The state government, in consultation with the high courtalters the limits or the numbers of such divisions and districts and may also divide any district into sub-divisions and may alter the limits or the number of such sub-divisions. (Sec 7 Cr.P.C.).

Metropolitan areas–The State Government, by notification, may declare any area in the State comprising a city or town whose population exceeds one million shall be a metropolitan area for the purposes of this Code and by notification, extend, reduce or alter the limits of a metropolitan area but the reduction or alteration shall not be so made as to reduce the population of such area to less than one million.

Court of Session

They are established under Section 9 of Cr.P.C. by the State Government for every session's division, presided over by a Judge appointed by the High Court of the state.

The Court of Sessions shall ordinarily hold its sitting at such place or places as the High Court may, by notification, specify; but, if, in any particular case, the Court of Session is of opinion that it will tend to the general convenience of the parties and witnesses to hold its sittings at any other place in the sessions division, it may, with the consent of the prosecution and the accused, sit at that place for the disposal of the case or the examination of any witness or witnesses therein.

The High Court may also appoint Additional Sessions Judges and Assistant Sessions Judges to exercise jurisdiction in a Court of Session.

Subordination of Assistant Sessions Judges–All Assistant Sessions Judges are subordinate to the Sessions Judge in whose Court they exercise jurisdiction. The Sessions Judge may also make provision for the disposal of any urgent application, in the event of his absence or inability to act, by an Additional or Assistant Sessions Judge, or, if there be no Additional or Assistant Sessions Judge, by the Chief Judicial Magistrate, and every such Judge or Magistrate shall be deemed to have jurisdiction to deal with any such application (section 10 Cr.P.C.).

Court of Judicial Magistrate of the first class and of the second class

Courts of Judicial Magistrates–Chief Judicial Magistrate; Additional Chief Judicial Magistrates, Sub-divisional Judicial Magistrates and Special Courts of Judicial Magistrate.

In every district (not being a metropolitan area), there shall be established *as many Courts of Judicial Magistrates of the first class and of the second class,* and at such places, as the State Government may specify by notification after consultation with the High Court.

However, the State Government after consultation with the High Court may establish, for any local area, one or more *Special Courts of Judicial Magistrate* of the first class or of the second class to try any particular case or particular class of cases. In case, where any such Special Court is established then no other Court of Magistrate in the local area shall have jurisdiction to try any case or class of cases for the trial of which such Special Court of Judicial Magistrate has been established. The presiding officers of such Courts are appointed by the High Courts.

The High Court, whenever, it appears to it to be expedient or necessary, may confer the powers of a Judicial Magistrate of the first class or of the second class, on any member of the Judicial Service of the State, functioning as a Judge in a Civil Court. (Section 11 Cr.P.C.)

In every district (not being a metropolitan area), the High Court shall appoint, a Judicial Magistrate of the first class to be the Chief Judicial Magistrate; additional chief judicial magistrates and subdivisional judicial magistrates. (Section 12 Cr.P.C.).

Subordination of Judicial Magistrates

Every Chief Judicial Magistrate shall be subordinate to the Sessions Judge and every other Judicial Magistrate shall, subject to the general control of the Sessions Judge, be subordinate to the Chief Judicial Magistrate. Further the Chief Judicial Magistrate may, from time to time, make rules or give special orders, consistent with this Code, as to the distribution of business among the Judicial Magistrates subordinate to him. (sec 15 Cr.P.C.).

Courts of Metropolitan Magistrates : Chief Metropolitan Magistrate, an Additional Chief Metropolitan Magistrate, Special Metropolitan Magistrates

The Courts of Metropolitan Magistrates shall be established in every metropolitan area at such places, as the State Government may specify by notification after consultation with the High Court. The presiding officers of such Courts are appointed by the High Court and the jurisdiction and powers of every Metropolitan Magistrate extends throughout the metropolitan area. (Sec 16 Cr.P.C.).

The High Court, in relation to every metropolitan area within its local jurisdiction shall appoint a:

i. Metropolitan Magistrate to be the Chief Metropolitan Magistrate;

ii. Metropolitan Magistrate to be an Additional Chief Metropolitan Magistrate having all or any of the powers of a Chief Metropolitan Magistrate under criminal procedure Code or under any other law for the time being in force as the High Court may direct (Sec 17 Cr.P.C.).

iii. Special Metropolitan Magistrates on the request by any Central or State Government for such term, not exceeding one year at a time. The High Court or the State Government, as the case may be, can empower any Special Metropolitan Magistrate to exercise, in any local area outside the metro-politan area, the powers of a Judicial Magistrate of the first class. (Sec 18 Cr.P.C.)

Subordination of Metropolitan Magistrates

The Chief Metropolitan Magistrate and every Additional Chief Metropolitan Magistrate shall be subordinate to the Sessions Judge.

- Every other Metropolitan Magistrate shall, subject to the general control of the Sessions Judge, be subordinate to the Chief Metropolitan Magistrate.

- The High Court may, for the purposes of this Code, define the extent of the subordination if any, of the Additional Chief Metropolitan Magistrates to the Chief Metropolitan Magistrate.

- The Chief Metropolitan Magistrate may, from time to time, make rules or give special orders, consistent with this Code, as to the distribution of business among the metropolitan Magistrates and as to the allocation of business to an Additional Chief Metropolitan Magistrate. (Sec 19 Cr.P.C.).

Executive Magistrates : Additional District Magistrate, Special Executive Magistrates.

In every district and in every metropolitan area, the State Government may appoint as many persons as it thinks fit to be Executive Magistrates and shall appoint one of them to be the District Magistrate.

Power of Courts to pass sentence from lowest to higher level

- The Judicial Magistrate of the Second Class, at the lowest level may pass a sentence of imprisonment for a term not exceeding one year, or with fine not exceeding five thousand rupees, or with both.

- The Judicial Magistrate of the first class may pass a sentence of imprisonment for a term not exceeding three years, or of fine not exceeding ten thousand rupees, or both.The Metropolitan Magistrate has the powers of the Court of a Magistrate of the first class.

- The Court of a Chief Judicial Magistrate may pass any sentence authorised by law except a sentence of death or of imprisonment for life or of imprisonment for a term exceeding seven years. The Court of a Chief Metropolitan Magistrate shall have the powers of the Court of a Chief Judicial Magistrate.

- An Assistant Sessions Judge may pass any sentence authorised by law except a sentence of death or of imprisonment for life or of imprisonment for a term exceeding ten years.

- A Sessions Judge or Additional Sessions Judge may pass any sentence authorised by law; but any sentence of death passed by any such Judge shall be subject to confirmation by the High Court.

- A High Court may pass any sentence authorised by law.

Reference: Sec 28 and 29 Cr.P.C.

The State Government may appoint any Executive Magistrate to be an Additional District Magistrate and such Magistrate shall have such of the powers of a District Magistrate under this Code or under any other law for the time being in force as may be directed by the State Government. (refer to Sec 20 Cr.P.C.).

The State Government may appoint, for such term as it may think fit, Executive Magistrates, to be known as *Special Executive Magistrates* for particular areas or for the performance of particular functions and confer on such Special Executive Magistrates, such of the powers as are conferrable under this Code on Executive Magistrate, as it may deem fit. (Sec 21 Cr.P.C.).

Subordination of Executive Magistrates

- All Executive Magistrates, other than the Additional District Magistrate, shall be subordinate to the District Magistrate and

- Every Executive Magistrate (other than the Sub-divisional Magistrate) exercising powers in a sub-division shall also be subordinate to the Sub-divisional Magistrate, subject, however, to the general control of the District Magistrate

- The District Magistrate may, from time to time, make rules or give special orders, consistent with this Code, as to the distribution of business among the Executive Magistrates subordinate to him and as to the allocation of business to an Additional District Magistrate. (Sec 23 Cr.P.C.).

Criminal Liability

The leading doctrine of criminal law liability is *actus non facit reum nisi men sit rea*. There are two necessary elements in crime, namely actus reus, an act of commission or omission, a physical act and secondly, a mental element 'mens rea' (guilty mind). According to Sec. 82 of Indian penal code, an act of a child under seven years is no offence and this immunity from criminal liability also extends to offences under any special or local law. However any act which would otherwise be criminal is not an offence if done by a child aged between 7 and 12 years, who has not attained sufficient maturity of understanding to judge the nature and consequences of the alleged conduct (Sec 83 IPC). Further, nothing is an offence which is done in the exercise of the right of private defence (Sec 96 IPC). Nothing is an offence, if it is also committed by the insane person, who by reason of his unsound mind, under section 84 IPC, is incapable of knowing the nature of the act, or that what he is doing is either wrong or contrary to law.

Criminal Justice Processes-Prosecution, Investigation, Inquiry and Trial

The criminal justice system is concerned with prevention and control of crime, to maintain peace and public order and protection of rights of victim as well as of accused. The administration of criminal justice can be divided into three stages: investigation, inquiry and trial.

Investigation- Sec 2(h) of Cr.P.C., provides that "investigation" includes all the proceedings under this Code for the collection of evidence conducted by a police officer or by any person (other than a Magistrate) who is authorised by a Magistrate in this behalf.

As per Sec 2(i) of Cr.P.C., "judicial proceeding" includes any proceeding in the course of which evidence is or may be legally taken on oath.

The investigation starts with the reporting or registration of crime and passes through the following:

- Inspection of the place where crime has been committed;

- Ascertaining facts and circumstances;

- Discovery and arrest of the suspected offender/accused;
- Interrogation of persons acquainted with facts and circumstances of the case;
- Search and seizure;
- Examination of witness;
- Collection of evidence;
- Bail and remand process and preparation and filing of charge sheet/final report to courts.

The police (any officer in-charge of a police station) are powered under section 156 Cr.P.C. to investigate cognizable offences suo moto without the order of magistrate (on the basis of police report or F.I.R lodged with the police) but they have no power to investigate non-cognizable offences on their own (private criminal offence may fall under this category). Such offences can be investigated by the police on the magistrate's order having jurisdiction.

> ### Cognizable and Non-cognizable offence
>
> "Cognizable offence" means an offence for which a police officer may, in accordance with the First Schedule or under any other law for the time being in force, *arrest without warrant* [Sec. 2 (c)]. As per the First Schedule of Cr.P.C., all offences punishable with imprisonment for not less than three years are taken as serious offences and are treated as cognizable offences.
>
> "Non-cognizable offence" means an offence for which a police officer *has no authority to arrest without warrant* [Sec 2 (l)].

> ### Function and Role of Police
>
> The Police Force is considered as an instrument for the prevention and detection of crime having paramount obligation and duty to function according to the requirements of the Constitution, law and the democratic aspirations of the people. The Police Act, 1861 is the basic statutory law governing the constitution and organisation of police forces in the states.
>
> In a state, the Director General of Police (DGP) is vested with power of overall administration of the police. In every district, the District Superintendent of Police is the head of the police force. The District Magistrate (usually the District Collector) is the chief executive officer of the district and he belongs to the Administrative Service. The police in the district functions under his general direction and control. For the Union Territories, the Police Act, 1949 provides for creation of police force on the pattern of the Police Act of 1861. Section 23 of the Police Act, 1861 provides for duties of police officer to obey and execute all orders and warrants lawfully issued to him by any competent authority; to collect and communicate intelligence affecting the public peace; to prevent the commission of offences and public nuisance; to detect and bring offenders to justice and to apprehend all persons whom he is legally authorised to apprehend, and for whose apprehension sufficient grounds exist.
>
> Under Cr.P.C., the police officers have been given power to arrest, search and seize offensive weapons. The basic duty of the police forces is to register cases, investigate them in accordance with the procedure laid down in Code of Criminal Procedure. Sec. 60A of the code provides that no arrest shall be made except in accordance with the provisions of this Code or any other law for the time, being in force providing for arrest.

Categories of offences	
Cognizable offence	**Non-cognizable offence**
<ul><li>Murder;</li><li>Attempt to murder</li><li>Causing death by rash or negligent act;</li><li>Dowry death;</li><li>Attempt to commit suicide;</li><li>Abetment of suicide;</li><li>Causing miscarriage without woman's consent;</li><li>Kidnapping or abduction;</li><li>Rape;</li><li>Theft.</li></ul>	<ul><li>Wrongfully restraining/confining any person;</li><li>Buying or disposing of person as a slave;</li><li>Intercourse by a man with wife not being under twelve years of age;</li><li>Dishonest misappropriation of property;</li><li>Cheating;</li><li>Causing miscarriage;</li><li>Mischief;</li><li>Forgery;</li><li>Offences relating to marriage (sec 493-498 IPC);</li><li>Criminal intimidation.</li></ul>

☞ **Reporting of cognizable offence and Investigation**

First Information Report–F.I.R, this is the information recorded by the police officer on duty under Section 154 Cr.P.C. given either by the aggrieved person or any other person about the commission of alleged cognizable offence within the area, jurisdiction of police station, where the offence has occurred. Information can be given either orally or in writing. The oral information has to be later reduced in writing by officer in charge police station or under his direction and be read over to the informant and shall be signed by the person providing such information. The substance thereof must be entered in record (station House diary) by the police officer in such form as the state government may prescribe in this behalf. A copy of such information shall be given to the informant forthwith, free of cost. [see Sec. 154(1) and (2)] FIR can be lodged in respect of cognizable offence.

By Criminal Law Amendment Act 2013, **in sub-section (I) 154 Cr.P.C., the following proviso has been inserted—**

If the information is given by the woman against whom an offence under section 326A, section 326B, section 354, section 354A, section 354B, section 354C, section 354D, section 376, section 376A, section 376B, section 376C, section 45 of 1860. 376D, section 376E or section 509 of the Indian Penal Code is alleged to have been committed or attempted, then such information shall be recorded, by a woman police officer or any woman officer:

Provided further that :

a. in the event that the person against whom an offence under section 354, section 354A, section 354B, section 354C, section 354D, section 376, section 376A, section 376B, section 376C, section 376D, section 376E or section 509 of the Indian. Penal Code is alleged to have been committed or attempted, is temporarily or permanently mentally or physically disabled, then such information shall be recorded by a police officer, at the residence of the person seeking to report such offence or at a convenient place of such person's choice, in the presence of an interpreter or a special educator, as the case may be;

b. the recording of such information shall be video graphed;

c. the police officer shall get the statement of the person recorded by a Judicial Magistrate under clause (a) of sub-section (5A) of section 164 as soon as possible."

Procedure for investigation

Once the F.I.R. is registered, the investigation in the case begins. Section 157 casts a duty upon the investigating officer to forthwith send the report of the cognizable offence to the concerned Magistrate and as per section 158 CrPC, every report sent to a Magistrate under section 157 shall, if the State Government so directs, be submitted through such superior officer of police as the State Government, by general or special order, appoints in that behalf. Such superior officer may give such instructions to the officer in charge of the police stationas he thinks fit, and shall, after recording such instructions on such report, transmit the same without delay to the Magistrate.

Case Laws

In Sheikh Hasib v. State of Bihar, AIR 1972 SC 283- court observed the following:

◆ The principal object of the first information report from the point of view of the informant is to set the criminal law in motion and from the point of view of the investigating authorities is to obtain information about the alleged criminal activity so as to be able to take suitable steps for tracing and bringing to book the guilty party.

◆ The first information report does not constitute substantive evidence though its importance as conveying the earliest information regarding the occurrence cannot be doubted.

◆ F.I.R, however, only be used as a previous statement for the purpose of either corroborating its maker under Section 157 of the Indian Evidence Act or for contradicting him Under Section 145 of that Act. It cannot be used for the purpose of corroborating or contradicting other witnesses.

In Lalita Kumari v. Govt. of U. P. & Ors (12 November, 2013)- the supreme court in this writ petition held the following:

◆ Registration of FIR is mandatory under Section 154 of the Code, if the information discloses commission of a cognizable offence and no preliminary inquiry is permissible in such a situation.

◆ If the information received does not disclose a cognizable offence but indicates the necessity for an inquiry, a preliminary inquiry may be conducted only to ascertain whether cognizable offence is disclosed or not.

◆ If the inquiry discloses the commission of a cognizable offence, the FIR must be registered. In cases where preliminary inquiry ends in closing the complaint, a copy of the entry of such closure must be supplied to the first informant forthwith and not later than one week. It must disclose reasons in brief for closing the complaint and not proceeding further.

◆ The police officer cannot avoid his duty of registering offence if cognizable offence is disclosed. Action must be taken against erring officers who do not register the FIR if information received by him discloses a cognizable offence.

◆ The scope of preliminary inquiry is not to verify the veracity or otherwise of the information received but only to ascertain whether the information reveals any cognizable offence.

Information as to non-cognizable cases and investigation of such cases. Section 155 Cr.P.C. provides that:

1. When information is given to an officer in charge of a police station of the commission within the limits of such station of a non-cognizable offence, he shall enter or cause to be entered the substance of the information in a book to be kept by such officer in such form as the State Government may prescribe in this behalf, and refer, the informant to the Magistrate.

2. No police officer shall investigate a non-cognizable case without the order of a Magistrate having power to try such case or commit the case for trial.

3. Any police officer receiving such order may exercise the same powers in respect of the investigation (except the power to arrest without warrant) as an officer in charge of a police station may exercise in a cognizable case.

However where a case relates to two or more offences of which at least one is cognizable, the case shall be deemed to be a cognizable case, notwithstanding that the other offences are non-cognizable [sec155(4)].

Investigation completes when the police report is submitted and matter is brought before the Magistrate or the concerned court. Generally non-cognizable offences are bailable and compoundable also.

Inquiry

Every offence shall ordinarily be inquired into and tried by a Court within whose local jurisdiction it was committed. Therefore, after investigation the inquiry is the second stage of the process wherein a Magistrate, either on receiving a police report or upon a complaint seeks to find out whether the accused should be committed to the Sessions or discharged. Sec 2(g) of Cr.P.C., defines the term "inquiry" to mean every inquiry, other than a trial, conducted under this Code by a Magistrate or Court. If upon consideration of the record of case and the documents submitted therewith and hearing the submission of accused and prosecution, court finds that prima facie case is not made out against the accused, the court dismisses the complaint or discharges the accused and records reasons for the same but where prima facie case is made out, the court frames the charge against the accused and proceed for trial.

Investigation	Inquiry
Is Conducted by police officer or by any person (other than a Magistrate) who is authorised by a Magistrate in this behalf.	Is Conducted by magistrate either on receiving a police report or upon a complaint.
Objective is to collect evidence, discovery and arrest of the suspected accused necessary for the prosecution .	Objective is to ascertain truth and falsity of allegations against accused to determine whether accused should be committed to the sessions or discharged.

Trial

Once the charge is framed against accused, the third and final stage of trial begins. Trial is judicial determination of a person's guilt or innocence. Indian system of criminal trial is adversary system based on the accusatorial method and the basic principle of criminal justice is the presumption of innocence, an individual is presumed to be innocent till proved guilty beyond reasonable doubt. Further no person can be accused and convicted of an offence for an act, which was not an offence under the law in force on the date when it was committed.

Inquiry	Trial
It is a judicial inquiry into the matter by magistrate or a court.	Trial is judicial determination of a person's guilt or innocence.
Inquiry results in either discharge or charge against the accused.	A trial invariably ends in acquittal or conviction of the accused.

Criminal Trial under Cr.P.C.

The criminal trial under Cr.P.C. can be categorised under three heads: warrants, summons and summary trials as discussed below:

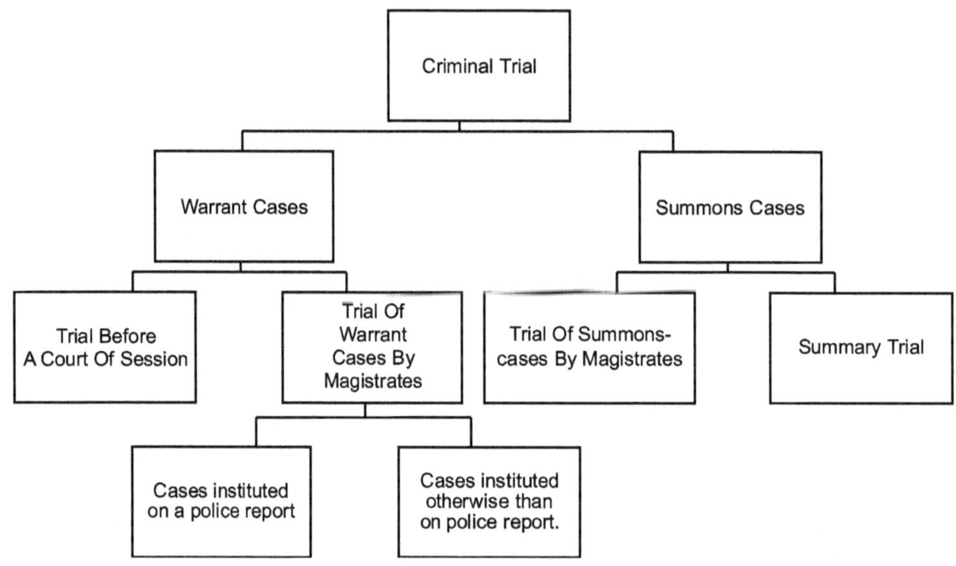

Warrants, Summons and Summary Trials

Warrant case

Section 2(x) of the Cr.P.C. defines "warrant-case" as a case relating to an offence punishable with death, imprisonment for life or imprisonment for a term exceeding two years. The Cr.P.C. lays down two procedures for trial of warrant cases by magistrates:

A-Cases instituted on a police report

In such cases, the accused appears or is brought before a Magistrate at the commencement of the trial. The magistrate, upon considering the police report and the documents sent with it and after making such examination, if any, of the accused as the Magistrate thinks necessary and after giving the prosecution and the accused an opportunity of being heard, considers that the charge against the accused is groundless, he shall discharge the accused, and record his reasons for so doing.(see sec 238-239 of Cr.P.C.).

B-Cases instituted otherwise than on police report

When, in any warrant case instituted otherwise than on a police report the accused appears or is brought before a Magistrate, the Magistrate shall proceed to hear the prosecution and take all such evidence as may be produced in support of the prosecution. The Magistrate on the application of the prosecution may also issue a summons to any of its witnesses directing him to attend or to produce any document or other thing. After taking in to consideration all such evidences, when no case against the accused has been made out, the magistrate, for reasons to be recorded, shall discharge the accused. Magistrate can also discharge the accused, if he considers the charge to be groundless at any previous stage of the case, for reasons to be recorded by such Magistrate. (see Sec 244-245 Cr.P.C.)

In both the above cases, if accused is not discharged, the magistrate (competent to try the offence) holds regular trial after framing charge.

C-Summons Case

Section 2(W) of the CrPC defines "summons-case" to mean a case relating to an offence, and not being a warrant case.The cases relating to offences punishable with imprisonment not exceeding two years are summons cases,where there is no need to frame a charge and the court gives "notice" to the accused (summons) for the attendance of the accused. Every summon issued by a Court under the Cr.P.C. shall be in writing, in duplicate, signed by the presiding officer of such Court or by such other officer as the High Court may, from time to time, by rule direct, and shall bear the seal of the Court (sec 61 Cr.P.C.).

The court under sec 87 Cr.P.C. has the power to issue warrant in lieu of, or in addition to, summons after recording its reasons in writing if :

(a) either before the issue of such summons, or after the issue of the same, but before the time fixed for his appearance, the Court sees reason to believe that he has absconded or will not obey the summons; or (b) at such time he fails to appear and the summons is proved to have been duly served in time to admit of his appearing in accordance therewith and no reasonable excuse is offered for such failure.

<table>
<tr><td>

Sec. 259 Cr.P.C. : Power of Court to convert summons cases into warrant cases

When in the course of the trial of a summons case relating to an offence punishable with imprison-ment for a term exceeding six months, it appears to the Magistrate that in the interests of justice, the offence should be tried in accordance with the procedure for the trial of warrant cases, such Magistrate may proceed to rehear the case in the manner provided by this Code for the trial of warrant cases and may recall any witness who may have been examined.

</td></tr>
</table>

D-Summary Trial

Section 260 of Cr.PC provides that : (a) any Chief Judicial Magistrate; (b) any Metropolitan Magistrate;

(c) any Magistrate of the first class shall have Power to try summarily certain offences, when specially empowered on this behalf by the High Court.

The Offences that can be tried summarily may fall under following categories:

i.   Offences not punishable with death, imprisonment for life or imprisonment for a *term exceeding two years*;

ii. Theft, under section 379, section 380 or section 381 of the Indian Penal Code, where the value of the property stolen does not exceed two hundred rupees;

iii. Receiving or retaining stolen property, under section 411 of the Indian Penal Code, where the value of the property does not exceed two hundred rupees;

iv. Assisting in the concealment or disposal of stolen property, under section 414 of the Indian Penal Code, where the value of such property does not exceed two hundred rupees;

v.   Offences under sections 454 and 456 of the Indian Penal Code (45 of 1860);

vi. Insult with intent to provoke a breach of the peace, under section 504 and [criminal intimidation punishable with imprisonment for a term which may extend to two years, or with fine, or with both], under section 506 of the Indian Penal Code;

vii. Abetment of any of the foregoing offences;

viii. An attempt to commit any of the foregoing offences, when such attempt is an offence;

ix. Any offence constituted by an act in respect of which a complaint may be made under section 20 of the Cattle-Trespass Act, 1871(1 of 1871).

<table>
<tr><td>

Do you know?

In the course of a summary trial, when it appears to the Magistrate that the nature of the case is such that it is undesirable to try it summarily, the Magistrate shall recall any witnesses who may have been examined and proceed to rehear, the case in the manner provided by this Code.

</td></tr>
</table>

Summary trial by magistrate of the second class

The High Court may also confer on any Magistrate having the powers of a Magistrate of the second class, the power to try summarily any offence which is punishable only with fine or with imprison-ment for a term not exceeding six months with or without fine, and any abetment of or attempt to commit any such offence (sec 261 Cr.P.C.).

Procedure of summary trial

In a summary trial, no sentence of imprisonment for a term exceeding three months can be passed in any conviction (sec 262 Cr.P.C.). The particulars of the summary trial are entered in the record of the court in such form as the State Government may direct (sec 263 Cr.P.C.).

In every case tried summarily in which the accused does not plead guilty, the Magistrate records the substance of the evidence and a judgment containing a brief statement of the reasons for the finding (sec 264 Cr.P.C.).

Let us now discuss in brief the common features of the criminal trial under distinct stages :

Framing of charge or issuance of notice

The trial begins after the charges are framed and notice is issued to accused. At this stage, the judge has to carefully examine and to assess the reliability and probative value of evidence for the purpose of finding out whether or not a prima facie case against the accused has been made out or not.

Recording of prosecution evidence

In every trial before a Court of Session, the prosecution shall be conducted by a Public Prosecutor. The Public Prosecutor or Assistant Public Prosecutor in charge of a case may appear and plead without any written authority before any Court in which that case is under inquiry, trial or appeal (section 301 Cr.P.C.).

After the charge is framed, on the date so fixed, the Judge proceeds to take all such evidence as may be produced in support of the prosecution. Then there is examination in chief of the witnesses before the court where the prosecution is asked to examine the witness and the statement of witnesses is taken under an oath. The accused is also given an opportunity to cross-examine all the witnesses presented by the prosecution.

Statement of accused

The court has powers to examine the accused at any stage of inquiry or trial for the purpose of revealing information against incriminating circumstances appearing before it. After examining the evidence of the prosecution, if it incriminates the accused, it is mandatory for the court to question the accused to provide him the reasonable opportunity to explain the incriminating facts and circumstances in the case and such examination is without oath and before the accused enters a defence.

Defence evidence

The defence is also given chance to put up its case. If after taking the evidence for the prosecution, examining the accused and hearing the prosecution and defence, the judge considers that there is no evidence that the accused has committed the offence, the judge is required to record the order of acquittal (see sec 232).

In case the accused is not acquitted, he shall be called upon to enter on his defence and adduce evidence he may have in support thereof.

Arguments

This is the final stage of the trial. The provisions of the Cr.P.C. provide that when examination of the witnesses, if any for the defence, is complete, the prosecutor shall sum up the prosecution case and the accused or his pleader is entitled to reply provided that where any point of law is raised by the accused or his pleader, the prosecution may, with the permission of the Judge, make his submissions with regard to such point of law (sec 234 Cr.P.C.). The arguments can be done orally or can be submitted in writing.

Judgment - Acquittal or conviction

The judgement is given by the judge after hearing arguments and points of law (if any). The judgment is written in the language of the Court. If after hearing the prosecution and the defence, the judge finds there is no evidence to indicate that the accused has committed the offence or finds the accused not guilt with which charged, the judge can record an order of acquittal. According to sec 53 of IPC, the following punishments can be awarded by the respective courts: Death sentence, imprisonment for life, imprisonment for specified period, forfeiture of the property and fine.

Rights of accused/arrested persons

The criminal justice system should be just, fair and reasonable. There are two fundamental principles of natural justice as discussed below which are required to be followed in all trials.

Procedural safeguards as provided under Cr.P.C. and other Acts

I. **Protection against double jeopardy**–Pursuant to the principle enshrined in Article 20(2) of the constitution that no person shall be prosecuted and punished for the same offence more than once, the provision is also laid down in section 300 of Cr.P.C., which provides that :

◆ A person who has once been tried by a Court of competent jurisdiction for an offence and convicted or acquitted of such offence shall, while such conviction or acquittal remains in force, not be liable to be tried again for the same offence, nor on the same facts for any other offence for which a different charge from the one made against him might have been made.

◆ A person acquitted or convicted of any offence may be afterwards tried, with the consent of the State Government for any distinct offence for which a separate charge might have been made against him at the former trial under sub-section (1) of section 220.

◆ Further, a person convicted of any offence constituted by any act causing consequences which, together with such act, constituted a different offence from that of which he was convicted, may be afterwards tried for such last mentioned offence (different offence), if the consequences had not happened or were not known to the Court to have happened, at the time when he was convicted.

◆ A person acquitted or convicted of any offence constituted by any acts may, notwithstanding such acquittal or conviction be subsequently charged with, and tried for, any other offence constituted by the same acts which he may have committed if the Court by which he was first tried was not competent to try the offence with which he is subsequently charged.

◆ A person discharged under section 258 shall not be tried again for the same offence except with the consent of the Court by which he was discharged or of any other Court to which the first mentioned Court is subordinate.

Explanation–the dismissal of a complaint, or the discharge of the accused, is not an acquittal for the purposes of this section.

II. Rights of accused at the time of arrest

Arrest is restraint on liberty of person. Section 41 of Cr.P.C. deals with the situations when Police may arrest any person for a cognizable offence without an order from a Magistrate or without warrant and Section 42 specifies the situation where a police officer can arrest a person without an order from a Magistrate **on refusal to give name and residence, in case of** non-cognizable offence. Section 43 provides for when an arrest can be made by a private person and the procedure to be followed on such arrest. Section 44 deals with arrest by a magistrate. Section 45 protects the members of the Armed Forces from being arrested under sections 41 to 44.

Procedure for arrest

Sec 46 of Cr.P.C. lays down the procedure to be followed to affect the arrest. Clause (1) provides: in making an arrest the police officer or other person making the same shall actually touch or confine the body of the person to be arrested, unless there be a submission to the custody by word or action but in case provided that where a woman is to be arrested, unless the circumstances indicate to the contrary, her submission to custody on an oral intimation of arrest shall be presumed and, unless the circumstances otherwise require or unless the police officer is a female, the police officer shall not touch the person of the woman for making her arrest. The police officer or other person may use all means necessary to effect the arrest in a case person to be arrested forcibly resists the endeavour to arrest but this does not give police a right to cause the death of a person who is not accused of an offence punishable with death or with imprisonment for life Sec 46(2) and (3). Sec 46(4) provides that 'Save in exceptional circumstances, no women shall be arrested after sunset and before sunrise, and where such exceptional circumstances exist, the woman police officer shall, by making a written report, obtain the prior permission of the Judicial Magistrate of the first class within whose local jurisdiction the offence is committed or the arrest is to be made'.

Further, section 49 of the Cr.P.C. provides that the person arrested shall not be subjected to more restraint than is necessary to prevent his escape. Section 44 of the police act, 1861 requires the arresting officer to maintain diary recording all the particulars of arrest, including the articles seized at the time of arrest and subsequent to it.

Right to know ground of arrest– section 50 (1) of Cr.P.C. corresponds to clause (1) of Article 22 of the Constitution and states that : Every police officer or other person arresting any person without warrant shall forthwith communicate to him full particulars of the offence for which he is arrested or other grounds for such arrest.

In *D. K. Basu v. State of West Bengal* (AIR1997 SC610). The Supreme Court had issued certain directions/ requirements to be followed in all cases of arrest or detention, till legal provisions are made in that behalf, as preventive measures. According to court the requirements, referred below flow from Articles 21 and 22(1) of the Constitution and need to be strictly followed by police and other governmental agencies in addition to the constitutional and statutory safeguards.

- The police personnel carrying out the arrest and handling the interrogation of the arrestee should bear accurate, visible and clear identification and name tags with their designations. The particulars of all such police personnel who handle interrogation of the arrestee must be recorded in a register.

- That the police officer carrying out the arrest of the arrestee shall prepare a memo of arrest at the time of arrest and such memo shall be attested by at least one witness, who may be either a member of the family of the arrestee or a respectable person of the locality from where the arrest is made. It shall also be countersigned by the arrestee and shall contain the time and date of arrest.

- A person who has been arrested or detained and is being held in custody in a police station or interrogation center or other lock-up, shall be entitled to have one friend or relative or other person known to him or having interest in his welfare being informed, as soon as practicable, that he has been arrested and is being detained at the particular place unless the attesting witness of the memo of arrest is himself such a friend or a relative of the arrestee.

- The time, place of arrest and venue of custody of an arrestee must be notified by the police where the next friend or relative of the arrestee lives outside the district or town through the Legal Aid Organisation in the District and the police station of the area concerned telegraphically within a period of 8 to 12 hours after the arrest.

- The person arrested must be made aware of this right to have someone informed of his arrest or detention as soon as he is put under arrest or is detained.

- An entry must be made in the diary at the place of detention regarding the arrest of the person which shall also disclose the name of the next friend of the person who has been informed of the arrest and the names and particulars of the police officials in whose custody the arrestee is.

- The arrestee should, where he so requests, be also examined at the time of his arrest and major and minor injuries, if any, present on his/her body, must be recorded at that time. The "Inspection Memo" must be signed both by the arrestee and the police officer effecting the arrest and its copy provided to the arrestee.

- The arrestee should be subjected to medical examination by a trained doctor every 48 hours during his detention in custody by a doctor on the panel of approved doctors appointed by Director, Health Services of the concerned State or Union Territory, Director, Health Services should prepare such a panel for all Tehsils and Districts as well.

- Copies of all the documents including the memo of arrest, referred to above, should be sent to the Ilaqa Magistrate for his record.

- The arrestee may be permitted to meet his lawyer during interrogation, though not throughout the interrogation.

- A police control room should be provided at all district and State headquarters, where information regarding the arrest and the place of custody of the arrestee shall be communicated by the officer causing the arrest, within 12 hours of effecting the arrest and at the police control room it should be displayed on a conspicuous police board.

Failure to comply with the requirements herein above mentioned shall apart from rendering the concerned official liable for departmental action, also renders him liable to be punished for contempt of Court and the proceedings for contempt of Court may be instituted in any High Court of the country, having territorial jurisdiction over the matter.

Section 50A inserted by the code of criminal procedure (amendment) act, 2005, puts an obligation on person making arrest to inform about the arrest, etc., to a nominated person:

1. Every police officer or other person making any arrest under this Code shall forthwith give the information regarding such arrest and place where the arrested person is being held to any of his friends; relatives or such other persons as may be disclosed or nominated by the arrested person for the purpose of giving such information.

2. The police officer shall inform the arrested person of his rights under subsection (1) as soon as he is brought to the police station.

3. An entry of the fact as to who has been informed of the arrest of such person shall be made in a book to be kept in the police station in such form as may be prescribed on this behalf by the State Government.

4. It shall be the duty of the Magistrate before whom such arrested person is produced, to satisfy himself that the requirements of sub-section (2) and sub-section (3) have been complied with in respect of such arrested person.

III. Right to Bail

The term bail has not been defined in criminal procedure code. The purpose is to procure the release of a person from legal custody, by undertaking that he/she shall appear at the time and place designated and submit him to the jurisdiction and judgment of the court. For the purpose of bail, the offences have been classified in two categories "bailable" and "non-bailable" offences. Chapter XXXIII of CrPC provides for provisions as to bail and bonds. "**bailable offence**" means an offence which is shown as bailable in the First Schedule, or which is made bailable by any other law for the time being in force and "**non-bailable offence**" means any other offence. [sec 2(a) CrPC]. The offences punishable with imprisonment for three years or more have been considered as non bailable offences. The right to bail cannot be nullified by imposing a very high amount for bail. Section 440(1) specifically provides that the amount of bail cannot be excessive.

When Bail is taken: bailable offences

As per section 436(1) CrPC : A person is entitled to be released on bail if;

- He is accused of bailable offence (other than a non-bailable offence);
- He is arrested or detained without warrant by an officer in charge of a police station, or appears or is brought before a Court;
- He is prepared at any time while in the custody of such officer or at any stage of the proceeding before such Court to give bail.

Proviso to section 436(1) that such officer or Court, if he or it thinks fit, may, instead of taking bail from such person, discharge him on his executing a bond without sureties for his appearance.

The police officer has no discretion to refuse bail if the accused is prepared to give bail or execute bond.

The terms of bond or bail bond executed under this section should be in accordance with Form 45 of schedule II.

Source: Section 436A CrPC. It was aready discussed.

There has been an amendment of the Code of Criminal Procedure in 2005. Insertion of new section

436A.- After section 436 of the principal Act, the following section shall be inserted, namely:-"436A", maximum period for which an undertrial prisoner can be detained. Where a person has, during the period of investigation, inquiry or trial under this Code of an offence under any law (not being an offence for which the punishment of death has been specified as one of the punishments under that law) undergone detention for a period extending up to one-half of the maximum period of imprisonment specified for that offence under that law, he shall be released by the Court on his personal bond with or without sureties :

Provided that the Court may, after hearing the Public Prosecutor and for reasons to be recorded by it in writing, order the continued detention of such person for a period longer than one-half of the said period or release him on bail instead of the personal bond with or without sureties provided further that no such person shall in any case be detained during the period of investigation, inquiry or trial for more than the maximum period of imprisonment provided for the said offence under that law.

Explanation–In computing the period of detention under this section for granting bail, the period of detention passed due to delay in proceeding caused by the accused shall be excluded.

Sec 50 (2) of the CrPC provides that in case, where a police officer arrests without warrant any person other than a person accused of a non-bailable offence, he shall inform the person arrested that he is entitled to be released on bail and that he may arrange for sureties on his behalf.

Bail to under trial prisoners

Under Section 436A of the Criminal Procedure Code as inserted by criminal procedure amendment act 2005, in cases other than those attracting death sentence, once the prisoner during the period of investigations, inquiry or trial has undergone detention up to half of the maximum period of imprisonment specified for that offence under the law, he should be released by the court on his personal bond with or without sureties subject to expectations as may be recorded for reasons in writing by the court.

The proviso to the section provides that : the Court may, after hearing the Public Prosecutor and for reasons to be recorded by it in writing, order the continued detention of such person for a period longer than one half of the said period or release him on bail instead of the personal bond with or without sureties.

Provided further that no such person shall in any case be detained during the period of investigation, inquiry or trial for more than the maximum period of imprisonment provided for the said offence under that law.

Explanation–In computing the period of detention under this section for granting bail, the period of detention passed due to delay in proceeding caused by the accused shall be excluded.

When Bail be taken in case of non bailable offences- section 437 CrPC

1. When any person accused of, or suspected of, the commission of any non-bailable offence is arrested or detained without warrant by an officer in charge of a police station or appears or is brought before a court other than the High Court or Court of Session, he may also be released on bail *(bail here is matter of judicial discretion)*.

   A person accused of non-bailable offence shall not be so released under following conditions:

   i. if there appear reasonable grounds for believing that he has been guilty of an offence punishable with death or imprisonment for life;

   ii. if such offence is a cognizable offence and he had been previously convicted of an offence punishable with death, imprisonment for life or imprisonment for seven years or more, or he had been previously convicted on two or more occasions of a non-bailable and cognizable offence.

   ◆ Proviso to the section provides that in both the above cases referred in clause (i) or clause (ii), the court may direct that a person be released on bail, if such person is under the age of sixteen years or is a woman or is sick or infirm.

   ◆ Provided further that the court may also direct that a person referred to in clause (ii) be released on bail if it is satisfied that it is just and proper to do so for any other special reason.

   ◆ Provided also that the mere fact that an accused person may be required for being identified by witnesses during investigation shall not be sufficient ground for refusing to grant bail if he is otherwise entitled to be released on bail and gives an undertaking that he shall comply with such directions as may be given by the court.

2. If it appears to such officer or court at any stage of the investigation, inquiry or trial as the case may be, that there are not reasonable grounds for believing that the accused has committed a non-bailable offence, but that there are sufficient grounds for further inquiry into his guilt, the accused shall, subject to the provisions of section 446A and pending such inquiry, be released on bail, or, at the discretion of such officer or court on the execution by him of a bond without sureties for his appearance as hereinafter provided.

3. When a person accused or suspected of the commission of an offence punishable with imprisonment which may extend to seven years or more or of an offence under Chapter VI, Chapter XVI or Chapter XVII of the Indian Penal Code (45 of 1860) or abetment of, or conspiracy or attempt to commit, any such offence, *is released on bail* under sub-section (1) the *Court may impose any condition which the Court considers necessary* :

   i. in order to ensure that such person shall attend in accordance with the conditions of the bond executed under this Chapter, or

   ii. in order to ensure that such person shall not commit an offence similar to the offence of which he is accused or of the commission of which he is suspected, or

   (c) otherwise in the interests of justice.

4. An officer or a court releasing any person on bail under sub-section (1), or sub-section (2), shall record in writing his or its reasons or special reasons for so doing.

5. *Any Court which has released a person* on bail under sub-section (1), or sub-section (2), may, if it considers it necessary so to do, direct that such person be arrested and commit him to custody. (*Court's power to cancel bail*)

6. If, in any case triable by a Magistrate, the trial of a person accused of any non-bailable offence is not concluded within a period of sixty days from the first date fixed for taking evidence in the case, such person shall, if he is in custody during the whole of the said period, be released on bail to the satisfaction of the Magistrate, unless for reasons to be recorded in writing, the Magistrate otherwise directs.

7. If, at any time, after the conclusion of the trial of a person accused of a non-bailable offence and before judgment is delivered, the Court is of the opinion that there are reasonable grounds for believing that the accused is not guilty of any such offence, it shall release the accused, if he is

in custody, on the execution by him of a bond without sureties for his appearance to hear judgment delivered.

Section 437A of Cr.P.C. provides that before conclusion of the trial and before disposal of the appeal, the Court trying the offence or the Appellate Court, as the case may be, shall require the accused to execute bail bonds with sureties, to appear before the higher Court as and when such Court issues notice in respect of any appeal or petition filed against the judgment of the respective Court and such bail bonds shall be in force for six months and in case such accused fails to appear, the bond stand forfeited and the procedure under section 446 shall apply.

Anticipatory Bail: Direction for grant of bail to person apprehending arrest- Section 438 Cr.P.C. provides for the following:

1. When any person has reason to believe that he may be arrested on an accusation of having committed a non-bailable offence, he may apply to the *High Court or the Court of Session* for direction under this section; and that Court may, if it thinks fit, direct that in the event of such arrest, he shall be released on bail.

2. When the High Court or the Court of Session makes a direction under sub-section (1), it may include such conditions in such directions in the light of the facts of the particular case, as it may thinks fit, including :

   i. a condition that the person shall make himself available for interrogation by a police officer as and when required;

   ii. a condition that the person shall not, directly or indirectly, make any inducement, threat or promise to any person acquainted with the facts of the case so as to dissuade him from disclosing such facts to the Court or to any police officer;

   iii. a condition that the person shall not leave India without the previous permission of the Court;

   iv. such other condition as may be imposed under sub-section (3) of section 437, as if the bail were granted under that section.

3. If such person is thereafter arrested without warrant by an officer in charge of a police station on such accusation, and is prepared either at the time of arrest or at any time while in the custody of such officer to give bail, he shall be released on bail, and if a Magistrate taking cognizance of such offence decides that a warrant should be issued in the first instance against that person, he shall issue a bailable warrant in conformity with the direction of the Court under sub-section (1).

Special powers of High Court or Court of Session regarding bail- section 439 Cr.P.C.

1. A High Court or Court of Session may direct:

   i. that any person accused of an offence and in custody be released on bail, and if the offence is of the nature specified in sub-section (3) of section 437, may impose any condition which it considers necessary for the purposes mentioned in that sub-section;

   ii. that any condition imposed by a Magistrate when releasing any person on bail be set aside or modified:

   Provided that the High Court or the Court of Session shall, before granting bail to a person who is accused of an offence which is triable exclusively by the Court of Session or which, though not so triable, is punishable with imprisonment for life, give notice of the application for bail to the Public Prosecutor unless it is, for reasons to be recorded in writing, of opinion that it is not practicable to give such notice.

(2) A High Court or Court of Session may direct that any person who has been released on bail under this Chapter be arrested and commit him to custody (cancel bail).

IV. Safeguard against search of the person, property or belongings of the accused

The search procedure is laid down in section 51, 93, 94, 97, 100(4) to (8) and section 165 CrPC. Section 51 provides for search of arrested person while section 52 empowers the police officer to seize offensive weapons from the arrested person. Sec 51 (2) lays down that whenever it is necessary to cause a female to be searched, the search shall be made by another female with strict regard to decency. Section 44 of the police act 1861 requires that the police officer has to search a person in presence of witness and mention the full particulars of the search in a police diary.

V. Right against illegal detention and to be produced before magistrate

Section 56 and 57 of the CrPC corresponds to clause (2) of Article 22 of the Constitution, provides that the person arrested shall not be kept in the custody of a police officer for a longer period than is reasonable and that in any event, such period shall not exceed 24 hours exclusive of the time necessary for the journey from the place of arrest to the magistrate's court. However, by special order of a Magistrate under section 167, the police officer can keep such person in his custody beyond the period of 24 hours.

Section 58 casts an obligation upon the officers in charge of police station to report to the specified authorities of arrests made without warrant within their jurisdiction and of the fact whether such persons have been admitted to bail or not.

VI. Right against torture

Indian penal code contains some provisions which seek to punish violation of right to life. Section 220 IPC provides that, whoever, being in any office which gives legal authority to commit persons for trial or to confinement, or to keep persons in confinement, corruptly or maliciously commits any person for trial or to confinement, or keeps any person in confinement, in the exercise of that authority knowing that in so doing, he is acting contrary to law, shall be punished with imprisonment of either description for a term which may extend to seven years, or with fine, or with both. Section 330 IPC and section 331 IPC provides for punishment for those who inflict injury or grievous hurt on a person to extort confession or information in regard to commission of offence.

Illustrations:

i. A, a police-officer, tortures Z in order to induce Z to confess that he committed a crime. A is guilty of an offence under section 330 IPC.

ii. A, a police-officer, tortures B to induce him to point out where certain stolen property is deposited. A is guilty of an offence under section 330 IPC.

Section 25 Evidence Act also provides that no confession made to a police officer shall, be proved, as against a person accused of any offence.

VII. Right to know of the accusation

The essential requirement of trial is to give accused opportunity to defend himself. Sections 228, 240, 246 and 251 deal with the same. When the accused is brought before the court for trial, the particulars of offence of which he is accused shall be stated to him. When charge is framed by the Judge, the same has to read and explained to the accused and the accused shall be asked whether he pleads guilty of the offence charged or claims to be tried.

VIII. Evidence to be taken in presence of accused

Section 273 of the code provides that except as otherwise expressly provided, all evidence taken in the course of the trial or other proceeding shall be taken in the presence of the accused or, when his personal attendance is dispensed with, in the presence of his pleader but in case, where the evidence of a woman below the age of eighteen years who is alleged to have been subjected to rape or any other sexual offence, is to be recorded, the court may take appropriate measures to ensure that such woman is not confronted by the accused while at the same time ensuring the right of cross-examination of the accused[1].

---

1 Inserted by Criminal Law (Amendment) Act, 2013

Procedure when investigation cannot be completed in twenty-four hour (section 167 CrPC)

(1) Whenever any person is arrested and detained in custody, and it appears that the investigation cannot be completed within the period of twenty-four hours fixed by section 57, and there are grounds for believing that the accusation or information is well-founded, the officer in charge of the police station or the police officer making the investigation, if he is not below the rank of sub-inspector, shall forthwith transmit to the nearest Judicial Magistrate, a copy of the entries in the diary hereinafter prescribed relating to the case, and shall at the same time forward the accused to such Magistrate.

(2) The Magistrate to whom an accused person is forwarded under this section may, whether he has or has not jurisdiction to try the case, from time to time, authorise the detention of the accused in such custody as such Magistrate thinks fit, a term not exceeding fifteen days in the whole; and if he has no jurisdiction to try the case or commit it for trial, and considers further detention unnecessary, he may order the accused to be forwarded to a Magistrate having such jurisdiction:
Provided that-

(a) the Magistrate may authorise the detention of the accused person, otherwise than in the custody of the police, beyond the period of fifteen days; if he is satisfied that adequate grounds exist for doing so, but no Magistrate shall authorise the detention of the accused person in custody under this paragraph for a total period exceeding,- (i) ninety days, where the investigation relates to an offence punishable with death, imprisonment for life or imprisonment for a term of not less than ten years; (ii) sixty days, where the investigation relates to any other offence, and, on the expiry of the said period of ninety days, or sixty days, as the case may be, the accused person shall be released on bail if he is prepared to and does furnish bail, and every person released on bail under this sub- section shall be deemed to be so released under the provisions of Chapter XXXIII for the purposes of that Chapter;

(b) no Magistrate shall authorise detention of the accused in custody of the police under this section unless the accused is produced before him in person for the first time and subsequently every time till the accused remains in the custody of the police, but the Magistrate may extend further detention in judicial custody on production of the accused either in person or through the medium of electronic video linkage;

(c) no Magistrate of the second class, not specially empowered in this behalf by the High Court, shall authorise detention in the custody of the police.

Explanation I.- For the avoidance of doubts, it is hereby declared that, notwithstanding the expiry of the period specified in paragraph (a), the accused shall be detained in custody so long as he does not furnish bail;.

Explanation II.- If any question arises whether an accused person was produced before the Magistrate as required under clause (b), the production of the accused person may be proved by his signature on the order authorising detention or by the order certified by the Magistrate as to production of the accused person through the medium of electronic video linkage, as the case may be.

Provided further that in case of a woman under eighteen years of age, the detention shall be authorised to be in the custody of a remand home or recognised social institution.

This right is supplemented by section 278 which inter alia provides that wherever law requires the evidence of witness be read over to him after its completion, the reading shall be made in the presence of the accused, if in attendance, or of his pleader, if he appears by pleader, and shall, if necessary, be corrected. Evidence shall be interpreted to accused or his pleader in open Court in a language understood by accused or his pleader as the case may be (sec 279 CrPC). Besides section 138 of Evidence act gives the accused right to test the evidence by cross examination.

IX. Right to medical examination

Section 54 CrPC as amended by act 5 of 2009 provides that when any person is arrested, he shall be examined by medical officer in the service of Central or State Government or registered medical practitioner soon after the arrest and where arrested person is female, the examination of her body shall be made only by a female medical officer or registered female medical practitioner.

X. Right to health and safety

It shall be the duty of the person having the custody of an accused to take reasonable care of the health and safety of the accused. (Sec 55A)

Other Courts

We have discussed above the civil and criminal courts structure, powers and functions of such courts, apart from these courts, there are a number of special courts and tribunals established in India to govern specific areas of law to provide speedy justice to the litigants. For Example: Central Administrative Tribunals; Income Tax Appellate Tribunal (ITAT); the Motor Accidents Claims Tribunal (MACT), Appellant Tribunal for Electricity; Rent Control Tribunal; Debt Recovery Tribunal; Railway Claims Tribunal, (DRT); Central Excise and Service Tax Appellate Tribunal (CESTAT); Intellectual Property Appellate Tribunal (IPAT); National Green Tribunal (NGT), Family Courts, Central Government Industrial Tribunal-cum-Labour Courts.

Family Court

◆ Family Court deals with matrimonial matters.

◆ It is constituted as per Family Courts Act, 1984.

◆ It was established for speedy disposal of disputes relating to family and matrimonial matter.

◆ The order of Family Court can be challenged before High Court. The appeal should be heard by the bench consisting of two judges.

Central Administrative Tribunals (CAT)-The Central Administrative Tribunal has been established for adjudication of disputes with respect to recruitment and conditions of service of persons appointed to public services and posts in connection with the affairs of the Union or other local authorities within the territory of India or under the control of Government of India and for matters connected therewith or incidental thereto. This was done in pursuance of the amendment of Constitution of India by Articles 323A. The Administrative Tribunals were established under the Administrative Tribunals Act, 1985 at Delhi, Mumbai, Calcutta and Allahabad. Today, there are 17 Benches of the Tribunal located throughout the country wherever the seat of a High Court is located, with 33 Division Benches. In addition, circuit sittings are held at Nagpur, Goa, Aurangabad, Jammu, Shimla, Indore, Gwalior, Bilaspur, Ranchi, Pondicherry, Gangtok, Port Blair, Shillong, Agartala, Kohima, Imphal, Itanagar, Aizwal and Nainital. In addition to Central Government employees, the Government of India has notified 45 other organisations to bring them within the jurisdiction of the Central Administrative Tribunal. The provisions of the Administrative Tribunals Act, 1985 do not, however, apply to members of para-military forces, armed forces of the Union, officers or employees of the Supreme Court, or to persons appointed to the Secretariat Staff of either House of Parliament or the Secretariat staff of State/Union Territory Legislatures. The Central Administrative Tribunal is empowered to prescribe its own rules of practice for discharging its functions subject to the Administrative Tribunals Act, 1985 and Rules made there under. (cgat.gov.in)

Central Government Industrial Tribunal-cum-Labour Courts (CGIT-cum-LCs) are set up under the provisions of Industrial Disputes Act, 1947 for adjudication of industrial disputes arising in Central Sphere. The CGIT-cum-LCs have been set up with the objective of maintaining peace and harmony in the industrial sector by quick and timely disposal of industrial disputes through adjudication so that industrial growth does not suffer on account of any widespread industrial unrest. (labour.nic.in).

LET US SUM UP

⇨ The Legislature, Executive, and the Judiciary are the three organs of state and are substantiated by the doctrine of the separation of powers that implies separate and distinct powers and functions of each of these organs with no single agency having complete authority.

➪ In the present judicial system, for the administration of justice is pyramidal in nature with the Supreme Court is established as an apex court followed by the 24 High Courts, subordinate courts at the district level : civil and criminal courts, family courts and specialised tribunals.

➪ Judiciary, as separated from legislative and an executive organ of government is independent with power to have judicial review of the legislation enacted by the Parliament. Judicial review is one of the most potent weapons in the armoury of law.

➪ The heart of judicial independence is judicial individualism. The judiciary is not a disembodied abstraction. It is composed of individual men and women who work primarily on their own.

➪ Supreme Court is the court of record and the judgments of the court have authoritative value and are binding on Lower Courts.

➪ Supreme Court has the jurisdiction which can be categorised as original, appellate and advisory.

➪ The Supreme Court under article 136 of the constitution may, in its discretion, grant special leave to appeal from any judgment, decree, determination, sentence or order in any cause or matter passed or made by any court or tribunal in the territory of India except for any judgment, determination, sentence or order passed or made by any court or tribunal constituted by or under any law relating to the Armed Forces.

➪ The Apex Court has power to review its judgment and order as mentioned in Part VIII order XL of the Supreme Court 'Rules, 1966.

➪ Every High Court also like a Supreme Court is the court of record and has all the powers of such a court including the power to punish for contempt of itself.

➪ The Supreme Court shall have such further jurisdiction and powers with respect to any matter as the Government of India and the Government of any State may, by special agreement confer, if Parliament by law provides for the exercise of such jurisdiction and powers by the Supreme Court.

➪ Public interest litigation is the litigation initiated in the court of law for the protection of the public interest.

➪ Article 214 of the Constitution provides that there shall be a High Court for each State. However Parliament may by law, establish a common High Court for two or more States and a Union territory.

➪ High Court can exercise both civil and criminal jurisdiction, general and special jurisdiction, ordinary as well as extraordinary jurisdiction under article 226 of the constitution.

➪ High court exercises original jurisdiction in respect of admiralty (maritime law), matrimonial matters, contempt of court and cases ordered to be transferred to High Court by lower court.

➪ Under ss. 122 and 125 of the Code, the High Courts are conferred the power to make rules regulating their own procedure and the procedure of the civil courts and they can by such rules annul, alter or add to all or any of the rules in the first schedule to the Code.

➪ Article 227 of constitution gives power to the High Courts to have superintendence over all the courts and tribunals throughout the territories in relation to which it exercises jurisdiction except if any court or tribunal is constituted by or under any law relating to the Armed Forces.

➪ High Court has power to withdraw cases involving substantial question of law as to the interpretation of constitution from the subordinate courts (Article 228).

➪ The subordinate courts, at the level of districts and lower levels of the judiciary plays a crucial role in delivery of justice.

➪ The District Judge is appointed in any State by the Governor of the State in consultation with the High Court exercising jurisdiction in relation to such State.

➪ The expression "district judge" includes judge of a city civil court, additional district judge, joint district judge, and assistant district judge, chief judge of a small cause court, chief presidency magistrate, and additional chief presidency magistrate.

➪ The two branches of judicial system civil and criminal are bifurcated in lowest judiciary and the subordinate courts deal with civil and criminal cases in accordance with their respective jurisdictions.

➪ On the civil side, the judges are designated as District Judge, Additional District Judge and Civil Judges. On the criminal side, the designations commonly used are Sessions Judge, Additional Sessions Judge, Chief Judicial Magistrate, Judicial Magistrate etc.

➪ The Civil Procedure Code, 1908 (C.P.C.) is a procedural law regulates the functioning of civil courts and laying down parameters and jurisdictions within which the civil courts should function.

➪ The civil courts have three types of jurisdiction: Jurisdiction as to subject matter, pecuniary jurisdiction and territorial jurisdiction.

➪ Every suit has to be instituted before the court of lowest jurisdiction. *The Munsifs Courts* are the lowest civil courts and have pecuniary jurisdiction as notified by the State Government. In metropolitan cities such as Delhi, Bombay, Calcutta, Madras, etc., the courts of small causes are at the lower end.

➪ The next in hierarchy is the court of subordinate civil judge, class-I and immediately above are the courts of district and sessions judge which also include the courts of additional judge, joint judge or assistant judge. In some states there is a court of civil and sessions judge.

➪ "Decree" is the formal expression of an adjudication which so far regards, the court expressing it, conclusively determines the rights of the parties with regard to all or any of the matters in controversy in the suit and may be either preliminary or final.

➪ 'Judgment' is the statement given by a judge of the grounds of a decree or order.

➪ An order may not necessarily originate from the suit and may arise from proceedings commenced on application.

➪ The Code of Criminal Procedure, 1973 (Cr.P.C.) is an act to consolidate and amend the law relating to Criminal Procedure and deals with the procedure for arrest, framing of charge and trial before a court.

➪ The Cr.PC provides for following classes of criminal courts: Courts of Session; Judicial Magistrate of the first class and, in any Metropolitan area, Metropolitan Magistrate; Judicial Magistrate of the second class; and Executive Magistrate.

Courts	Power to pass sentence
Judicial Magistrate of the Second Class	One year imprisonment or fine (not exceed-ing Rs. 5,000) or both.
Judicial Magistrate of the first class / Metropolitan Magistrate	Three year imprisonment or fine (not exceed-ing Rs. 10,000) or both.
Chief Judicial Magistrate / Chief Metropolitan Magistrate	Any sentence authorised by law, except death sentence or life imprisonment or imprisonment for a term exceeding 7 years.
Assistant Sessions Judge	Any sentence authorised by law, except death sentence or life imprisonment or imprisonment for a term exceeding 10 years.
Sessions Judge / Additional Sessions Judge	Any sentence authorised by law but death sentence, death sentence passed shall be subject to confirmation by the High Court.
High Court	Any sentence authorised by law.

➪ Court of Session are presided over by a Judge appointed by the High Court of the state and are established by the State Government for every session's division.

➪ In every district (not being a metropolitan area), there shall be established as many Courts of Judicial Magistrates of the first class and of the second class, and at such places, as the State Government may specify by notification after consultation with the High Court. There can be Chief Judicial Magistrate; additional chief judicial magistrates, sub-divisional judicial magistrates and Special Courts of Judicial Magistrate.

➪ Every Chief Judicial Magistrate shall be subordinate to the Sessions Judge and every other Judicial Magistrate shall, subject to the general control of the Sessions Judge, be subordinate to the Chief Judicial Magistrate.

➪ The Courts of Metropolitan Magistrates shall be established in every metropolitan area at such places, as the State Government may specify by notification after consultation with the High

⇨ Court. The presiding officers of such Courts are appointed by the High Court and the jurisdiction and powers of every Metropolitan Magistrate extends throughout the metropolitan area.

⇨ The Chief Metropolitan Magistrate and every Additional Chief Metropolitan Magistrate shall be subordinate to the Sessions Judge.

⇨ In every district and in every metropolitan area, the State Government may appoint as many persons as it thinks fit to be Executive Magistrates and shall appoint one of them to be the District Magistrate. The State Government can appoint Additional District Magistrate, Special Executive Magistrates.

⇨ All Executive Magistrates, other than the Additional District Magistrate, shall be subordinate to the District Magistrate and every Executive Magistrate (other than the Sub-divisional Magistrate) exercising powers in a sub-division shall also be subordinate to the Sub-divisional Magistrate, subject, however, to the general control of the District Magistrate.

⇨ The criminal liability starts at the age of 7 years but any act which would otherwise be criminal is not an offence if done by a child aged between 7 and 12 years, who has not attained sufficient maturity of understanding to judge the nature and consequences of the alleged conduct.

⇨ The administration of criminal justice can be divided into three stages: investigation, inquiry and trial.

⇨ "Investigation" includes all the proceedings for the collection of evidence conducted by a police officer or by any person (other than a Magistrate) who is authorised by a Magistrate in this behalf under the criminal procedure code.

⇨ The police officer in charge of a police station is powered under section 156 CrPC to investigate cognizable offences suo moto without the order of magistrate on the basis of police report or F.I.R lodged with the police.

⇨ The police officer in charge of a police station, has no power to investigate non-cognizable offences on his own (private criminal offence). Such offences can be investigated by the police on the magistrate's order having jurisdiction.

⇨ The basic duty of the police forces is to register cases, investigate them in accordance with the procedure laid down in Code of Criminal Procedure.

⇨ All offences punishable with imprisonment for not less than three years are taken as serious offences and are treated as cognizable offences for which a police officer arrests without warrant.

⇨ In Non cognizable offence, a police officer has no authority to arrest without warrant.

⇨ First Information Report is the information recorded by the police officer on duty under Section 154 CrPC given either by the aggrieved person or any other person about the commission of alleged cognizable offence within the area, jurisdiction of police station.

⇨ If the officer in charge refuses to register the First Information Report, any person, aggrieved by such refusal may send the substance of information in writing and by post, to the Superintendent of Police concerned who, on satisfaction that such information discloses the commission of a cognizable offence, shall either investigate the case himself or direct an investigation to be made by any police officer subordinate to him.

⇨ Every offence shall ordinarily be inquired into and tried by a Court within whose local jurisdiction it was committed.

⇨ Trial is judicial determination of a person's guilt or innocence. Once the charge is framed against accused, the final stage of trial begins.

⇨ The criminal trial under CrPC can be categorized under three heads: warrants, summons and summary trials.

⇨ On the basis of the materials placed before the court that discloses the commission of a particular offence if the Judge is of opinion that there is ground for presuming that the accused has committed an offence, the court frames the charge in writing against the accused and proceeds with the trial.

⇨ Where the Judge frames any charge, it has to be read and explained to the accused.

⇨ In every trial before a Court of Session, the prosecution shall be conducted by a Public prosecutor.

⇨ The Public Prosecutor or Assistant Public Prosecutor in charge of a case may appear and plead without any written authority before any Court in which that case is under inquiry, trial or appeal.

⇨ With the consent of court, public prosecutor can also withdraw prosecution against any person.

⇨ After the charge is framed, the Judge proceeds to take all such evidence as may be produced in support of the prosecution. Then there is examination-in-chief of the witnesses and the statement of witnesses is taken under an oath. The accused is also given an opportunity to cross-examine all the witnesses presented by the prosecution.

⇨ The court has powers to examine the accused at any stage of inquiry or trial for the purpose of revealing information against incriminating circumstances appearing before it.

⇨ Any person accused of an offence before a Criminal Court, or against whom proceedings are instituted under this Code, may of right be defended by a pleader of his choice.

⇨ The defence is also given chance to put up its case, the accused can also apply for the issue of any process for compelling the attendance of any witness or the production of any document or thing and the Judge shall issue such process, unless for reasons to be recorded, judge considers that such application should be refused on the ground that it is made for the purpose of vexation or delay or for defeating the ends of justice.

⇨ When examination of the witnesses, if any for the defence, is complete, the prosecutor shall sum up the prosecution case and the accused or his pleader is entitled to reply. The arguments can be done orally or can be submitted in writing.

⇨ The judgement is given by the judge after hearing arguments and points of law (if any). The judgement is written in the language of the Court.

⇨ If after hearing the prosecution and the defence, the judge considers finds there is no evidence to indicate that the accused has committed the offence or finds the accused not guilty with which charged, the judge can record an order of acquittal.

⇨ If the Magistrate finds the accused guilty, he shall, after hearing,the accused on the question of sentence, pass sentence upon him according to law in cases of offences exclusively traible by session's judge or in offences traible by magistrates in warrant cases on the other hand in summon cases traible by magistrate, if he finds the accused guilty, magistrate, can pass sentence upon accused according to law.

⇨ The accused persons have many constitutional rights and procedural safeguards are also laid down in Cr.P.C., Indian penal code and Evidence Act as given below:

i. Right against Ex-post facto operation of laws.

ii. Protection against double jeopardy.

iii. Right against Self-incrimination.

iv. Right to fair trial.

v. Right to free legal aid and to be defended by lawyer.

vi. Right to speedy trial.

vii. Right to be informed of grounds of arrest.

viii. Right against illegal detention and to be produced before magistrate.

ix. Right to bail.

x. Right against torture.

xi. Right to know of the accusation.

xii. Evidence to be taken in presence of accused.

xiii. Right to medical examination.

ivx. Right to health and safety.

⇨ Apart from the civil and criminal courts at subordinate level, there are a number of special courts and tribunals established in India to govern specific areas of law to provide speedy justice to the litigants.

⇨ Example of other tribunals/courts : Central Administrative Tribunals; Income Tax Appellate Tribunal (ITAT); the Motor Accidents Claims Tribunal (MACT), Rent Control Tribunal; Debt Recovery Tribunal; Railway Claims Tribunal, (DRT); Central Excise and Service Tax Appellate Tribunal (CESTAT); Intellectual Property Appellate Tribunal (IPAT); National Green Tribunal (NGT), Family Courts, Central Government Industrial Tribunal-cum-Labour Courts.

Terminal Questions

1. Outline the Classifications and hierarchy of courts under Indian Legal system.

2. Write a note on judicial independence and impartiality in India.

3. Discuss in brief the original, appellate and advisory jurisdiction of Supreme Court.

4. What are the grounds under which Supreme Court can review its judgments or orders?

5. Discuss the High Court practice and procedure in exercise of its jurisdiction as laid down in the constitution of India.

6. Write a note on jurisdiction of civil courts.

7. Distinguish between the following:
   (a) Decree and order
   (b) Cognizable and non-cognizable offences.
   (c) Bailable and non bailable offences.

8. Trace the role of police in the administration of criminal justice.

9. Discuss in brief the stages involved in the criminal justice administration procedure.

10. Write short notes on the following:
   (a) First Information Report
   (b) Bail and Anticipatory bail
   (c) Rights of the accused.

●●

Family Law in India

India is a land of cultural diversity and Indian family law has been complex due to plurality of forms that vary with class, ethnicity and religion with each religion adhering to its own specific laws. Family law or personal law consists of family or personal matters like marriage, divorce, adoption, guardianship, maintenance, gifts, succession, inheritance, wills and so on. In India separate and distinct law govern Hindus, Muslims, Christians and followers of other religions. The Hindus, Sikhs, Jains and Buddhists follow Hindu family law though in Sikhs ceremonies for valid marriage are different but they are covered under Hindu law for the family matters and the Hindu law is also applicable to any other person who is not a Muslim, Christian, Parsi or Jew by religion. Under the Hindu Marriage Act, 1955, Buddhists, Jains and Sikhs are all considered Hindus. So even if the customs of all these faiths are different, the laws relating to marriage, divorce, adoption, maintenance and custody of children remain the same. The Muslims, Christians, Parsi's and Jews have their own laws and the traditional communities and tribal groups follow their own customary practices or customary laws. The Parsi, Christians have codified law but the law of marriage and divorce of Jews and Muslims are not codified in India. Even today they are governed by their religious laws; the Muslim law is based on the Sharia derived from the principles of the Islamic religious text Quran and from the teachings and example laid down by the Islamic prophet Muhammad.However in the state of Goa, a uniform civil code is applicable to all religious communities. To create a legal right a civil registration of marriages is required in Goa under the Code of Civil Registration. The Chapter VII prescribes that the registration of the marriages shall be made in accordance with the Decree Law No. 1, dated 25th December, 1910.

There are various types of problems that the Indian family system is facing, though the Government of India has taken several useful legislative measures for preventing violence against women and child; empowering women by granting her right in the property; marriage and dissolution of marri-age; abolition of child marriage, however there is no family policy per so far. Since the process of family formation and dissolution has become relatively faster now, it is important to know family law and justice system exiting in India.

Family Law in Medieval India (8th to 18th century CE)

In the preceding chapters we have discussed legal system in ancient India. In medieval period, the laws that were prescribed were not codified and the Hindu law was based on the *dharamshastra, shrutis, smriti, and other religious texts*. The Mitakshara and Daya-bhaga are the two major schools of personal laws that have been followed in medieval India. The *Mitakshara* is an eleventh or twelfth century digest and the *commentary on* the code of Yajnavalkya by Vijnaneshvara.The Mitakshara is the orthodox school; widely followed throughout India particularly in south and north India except in the State of Bengal and Assam. It was considered as an authority on the issues of family law in Hindus. It had four sub-schools, the Benaras (Northern and North-west), the Bombay (Western), the Mithila (Bihar), and, the Dravida or Madras school (South India). The *Dayabhaga* was the thirteenth or fourteenth-century digest; a reformist school of Hindu Law based on the commentary on the code of yagnavalkya written by Jimutavahana and was prevalent in the region of Bengal.

The major difference between two schools was related to inheritance :

Under Mitakshara School :–

◆ The ownership of property starts from the birth and the sons have equal rights along with the father in the ancestral property even during the life time of the father.

◆ It provides for inheritance through survivorship where living males can inherit property.

◆ Males/coparceners can institute a suit of partition against the Father.

On the other hand in Dayabagha School :

◆ Their is ownership or right in the ancestral property or joint family property by birth.

◆ It provides for inheritance by the way of succession where the heirs of deceased can inherit property.

The Muslims follows their personal laws called Muslim Law or Mohammedan Law based on Quran (divine law), Sunna (hadith), Sahabah, Ijma and Qiyas.

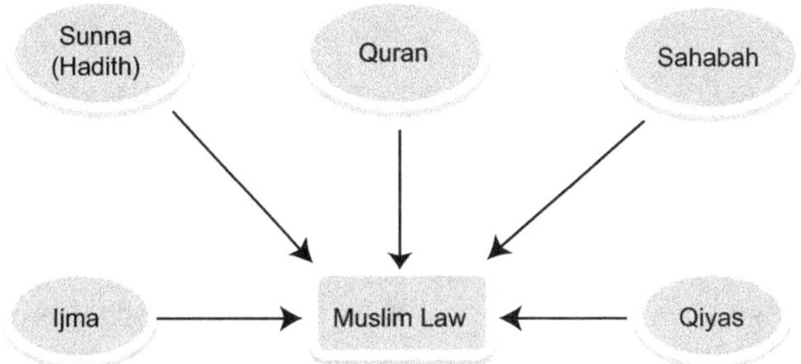

The two major denominations of Islam are Sunni and Shia and the majority of them are Sunni's. There are four schools (Madhhab) of Sunni Islam: Hanafi/Hanafiyya (founded by Persian scholor Abu Hanifa (699-767 AD). Maliki/Malikiyya (founded by Malik ibn Anas (d. 795 AD), Shaf'i/Shafiyya (founded by Muhammad ibn Idris al-Shafi'i (d. 819/820 AD) and Hanbali/Hanbaliyya (founded by Ahmad Hanbal (d. 855AD).

The Jafaryia or the "Twelvers," is the major school of thought of shia Islam headed by Imam Ja'far ibn Muhammad al-Sadiq (83H to 148H). The other minor schools of thought are known as the "Seveners" or the "Fivers" and refer to the number of imams (spiritual leader Shia Muslims recognise after the death of Muhammad.

Both the sects sunni's and shia's share common religious beliefs but they differ on interpretation of Hadith and sharia law. The shia's do not agree with the traditions (*hadith*) and religious practices narrated by the companions of Prophet, the Abu Bakr and Umar Ibn Al Khattab about the Prophet's life and religious and spiritual practices and supported the view that after the death of Prophet Muhammad's leadership should have passed directly to Ali Bin Abu Talib, his son-in-law. The Sunni Muslims, on the other hand are of firm opinion that the leader should be elected from among the companions of the Prophet Muhammad for example Abu Bakr.

Between the 16th and18th centuries under the Mughal Era in the India, the Hindus and Muslims were largely governed by their own personal laws and customs.

Family Law during the British period

In the beginning of British period, personal laws of the communities were followed. The Bengal Regulation of 1772 provided that in suits regarding inheritance, marriage, caste, and all religious usages and institutions, the judges should apply the laws of the Quran with regard to Mohammedan Laws and Shastra's with respect to the Hindu Laws as the general rule. The native law officers called pandits and kazis were also attached to the courts till 1860 to advise the courts on the questions pertaining to Hindu and Muslim law respectively. In *Skinner v. Orde* and others ((1871-73) LR 4 PC 60; [1871] UKPC 66) the Privy Council had observed with regard to the application of different personal laws that :

"While Brahmin and Buddhist, Christian and Mohammedan, Parsee and Sikh are one nation, enjoying equal political rights and having perfect equality before the tribunals, they co-exist as separate and very distinct communities, having distinct laws affecting every relation of life. The law of husband and wife, parent and child, the descent, devolution and disposition of property are all different, depending in each case, on the body to which the individual is deemed to belong; and the difference of religion pervades and governs all domestic usages and social relations."

The Courts in British era had relied on the translated texts on digests and manuals for example the Hedaya, an Arabic compilation of Sharia, translated by Charles Hamilton as per the directions of Warren Hastings. It was published by H. Allen and Company, 13, Waterloo Place London. The second edition was published in 1870 and reads as *A Commentary of the mussalman laws*. Gradually the precedents were developed and followed by the courts and judges, the whole court system was rationalised and the native law officers were abolished.

The family laws pertaining to various religious communities were also codified by legislation during British period.

The Hindu law pertaining to religious endowment, marriage, inheritance were enacted the Hindu Widow's Remarriage Act of 1856. The Act was passed when Lord Dalhousie was the Governor General of India, (repealed by Hindu Widow's Remarriage (repeal) Act of 1983; Social reformer Iswarchandra Vidyasagar was instrumental in the passing of the Act by the British Government. The Hindu disposition of property Act 1916; The Hindu Inheritance (Removal of Disabilities) Act of 1928; The Hindu Law of Inheritance (Amendment) Act of 1929;

The Child Marriage Restraint Act of 1929; The Hindu Married Women's Right to Separate Residence and Maintenance Act of 1944 (repealed by the Hindu Adoptions and Maintenance Act of 1958). The Hindu Marriage Disabilities removal Act 1946 (repealed by section 30 of the Hindu marriage act,1955). The Jains and Sikhs were included under Hindus, although in certain areas of practices these communities are governed by their customs, The Anand marriage Act 1909 was passed to remove doubts as to validity of the marriage ceremonies among Sikhs. By the Anand Marriage (Amendment) act 2012, Sikhs can now register their marriages under the Anand Marriage Act instead of the Hindu Marriage Act *w.e.f.* 1-11-2013. Section 6(1) provides that for the purposes of facilitation of proof of marriage ceremony (commonly known as Anand Karaj) customary among the Sikhs, the State Government shall, without prejudice to anything contained in the Hindu Marriage Act, 1955 or any other law for the time being in force, make rules providing that the parties to any such marriage [whether solemnised before or after the commencement of the Anand Marriage (Amendment) Act, 2012], may have the particulars relating to their marriage entered, in such manner and subject to such conditions as may be provided in the said rules, in a Marriage Register kept by such officer of the State Government or of a local authority authorised by the State Government, by notification in the Official Gazette, in this behalf. Further sec 6(3) provides that the validity of any Anand Marriage solemnised shall in no way be affected by the omission to make an entry in the Marriage Register and by virtue of Section 6(5), the parties to the marriage, whose marriage has been registered under this act, shall not be required to get their marriage registered under any other law for the time being in force (including State Act).

The Native Convert's Marriage Dissolution Act of 1866; the Indian Divorce Act 1869 and the Indian Christian Marriage Act, 1872 governs the Christians. For Parsi's, Parsi Marriage and Divorce Act 1937 was passed.

The Registration of Mohammedan Marriages and Divorces Act 1876 made registration of Muslim marriages, *nikah-nama*, voluntary or good enough if records are kept with the Qazi (judge) in the *masjid* or mosque precinct, etc. The Muslim Personal Law (Shariat) Application Act, 1937, an British enactment provides that notwithstanding any customs or usage to the contrary, in all questions (save questions relating to agricultural land) regarding intestate succession, special property of females, including personal property inherited or obtained under contract or gift or any other provision of personal law, marriage, dissolution of marriage, including talaq, ila, zihar, lian, khula and mubaraat, maintenance, dowry, guardianship, gifts, trusts and trust properties, and wakfs (other than charities and charitable institutions and charitable and religion endowments) the rule of decision in cases where the parties are Muslims shall be the Muslim Personal Law (Shariat). But as a reformative step Muslim Dissolution of Marriage Act, 1939 was passed that granted women the right to dissolution of marriage.

Family Law in India : Post Independence

The Constitution of India came in to force in 1950. The Parliament while making laws for its citizens has refrained itself from interfering with the personal laws of religious minorities; Articles 25 of the Constitution provides for freedom of conscience and the right to profess, practice and propagate religion to all persons and freedom to manage religious affairs under Article 26. The preamble to the constitution provides for justice, liberty, equality, and fraternity assuring the dignity to all. The constitution strongly provides for equality before law for every person (Article 14), prohibits discriminations based on religion, race, caste, sex or place of birth (Article15), and provides equality of opportunity in matters of public employment (Article 16).

The gender equity in all religious communities can only be achieved by uniform civil code but this is often viewed as contradiction to established social norms and traditional,cultural, customary practices followed by Hindus, Muslims or other communities.

> **Do you know?**
>
> The term Hindu has been defined to include other religious communities like the Jains, Buddhists and Sikhs.

Family law and Gender equality

Family law lays down the rights and responsibilities between spouses, parents and children and also among children's but it is seen that traditionally the male is given more rights in case of inheritance, adoption and guardianship and women rights under family laws varies from place to place that tends to put women at a disadvantage in comparison to other members, the gender disparities also exist in the context of access to education, health care, political representation, employment. The code of Manu, under ancient law provides for the code of conduct and status of women in a society leading to unequal treatment, where the women cannot be independent and is always be the subject to males in family, her father, husband and sons; she has to be chaste and lawful to her husband even after his death. The code also provides for punishments based on gender as well as caste.

In Hindu laws some reforms have been introduced by codification of four major legislations to govern the family and personal law of the Hindu's:- Hindu Marriage Act (1955), Hindu Succession Act (1956), Hindu Minority and Guardianship Act (1956), and Hindu Adoptions and Maintenance Act (1956).

The Hindu Marriage Act, 1955

The Hindu Marriage Act, 1955 is such an act that deals with matters pertaining to marriage among Hindus and provides for the conditions for a valid Hindu marriage and ground for dissolution of marriage to both men and women. The practice of polygamy among Hindus have been abolished, the act provides that a marriage between a man and a woman is invalid in case either of them has a spouse living. The child marriage is not allowed and minimum age for marriage is fixed to be 18 years for girls and 21 for boys.

The Hindu Succession Act, 1956

The Hindu Succession Act, 1956, codifies the uniform system of inheritance relating to intestate or unwilled succession, among Hindus abrogating all the customary laws but preserved dual mode of devolution of property by survivorship and by succession. Section 4(a) abrogates all those customs so far as those are inconsistent with the provisions of the Act, unless expressly saved.

The Act has based its rule of inheritance on Mitakshara principle of preference of heirs and retained earlier that the females cannot inherit in ancestral property as their male counterparts do and the female heir before 2005 was not allowed to request partition until the male heir chooses to divide their respective shares and the daughter of the deceased has the right to reside in the home if she is unmarried, divorced or widowed. The law by excluding the daughter from participating in the coparcenary ownership not only contributes to her discrimination on the ground of gender but also has led to oppression and negation of her fundamental right of equality guaranteed by the Constitution having regard to the need to render social justice to women and therefore by Amendment Act 2005, the difference between the female and male inheritor has been abolished and section 6 of the Act provides that now even female inheritor [daughter] can also claim partition of the ancestral property.

The Hindu Adoption and Maintenance Act, 1956

The Hindu Adoption and Maintenance Act, 1956, marked a radical departure from old Hindu law that recognises adoption of son for spiritual benefits but the act lays down that no religious ceremony is required for adoption and even one can adopt daughter, an illegitimate or orphan child or sister's son but married women still cannot adopt and adoption has to be made by husband with consent of wife unless the marriage has been dissolved or if the husband is dead or has renounced the world or has ceased to be a Hindu or has been declared to be of unsound mind.

The Hindu Minority and Guardianship Act, 1956

The Hindu minority and guardianship Act, 1956, attempts towards advancing status of women by giving them right to be appointed as guardian and the custody of minor child who has not attained the age of five years ordinarily resides with mother.

The reforms have been also introduced through other legislations: Indian Divorce (Amendment Act) 2001; Indian Succession Amendment Act, 2002; Marriage Laws (Amendment) Act, 2001.

The Indian Divorce Act, 1869 was amended by Acts 49 and 51 of 2001 to amend the law relating to Divorce and Matrimonial Causes and to introduce uniformity of matrimonial laws. The word Indian has been omitted by Act 51 of 2001 and the act may be called - DIVORCE ACT, 1869. The provision for dissolution of marriage by mutual consent has been added and grounds for dissolution have been further widened on the lines of the Hindu Marriage Act, 1955 and the Special Marriage Act, 1954; Section 7 - Court to act on principles of English Divorce Court was repealed; under section 36,wife was given rights to apply for expenses of proceedings and alimony pending suit and the provision for disposal of application within sixty days of service of such petition on the husband has been made.

The Indian Succession (Amendment) Act, 2002- The section 32 of the principal Act was discriminatory to widows and as such the provison to section 32 was omitted to remove discrimination in this regard. Section 213 was also amended by this amending Act to make Christians at par with other communities. The Marriage Laws (amendment) Act, 2001 (act no. 49 of 2001) was an act passed to amend the Indian Divorce Act, 1869, the Parsi Marriage and Divorce Act, 1936, the Special Marriage Act, 1954 and the Hindu Marriage Act, 1955 making provisions for disposal of application of wife for maintenance and education of the minor children, pending the proceeding as far as possible, within sixty days from the date of service of notice on the respondent.

Let us see the difference in Section 6 of Hindu Succession Act, 1956 and the Amendment in 2005

Section 6 of The Hindu Succession Act, 1956 : Devolution of interest in coparcenary property.

When a male Hindu dies after the commencement of this Act, having at the time of his death an interest in a Mitakshara coparcenary property, his interest in the property shall devolve by survivorship upon the surviving members of the coparcenary and not in accordance with this Act.

Provided that, if the deceased had left him surviving a female relative specified in class I of the Schedule or a male relative specified in that class who claims through such female relative, the interest of the deceased in the Mitakshara coparcenary property shall devolve by testamentary or intestate succession, as the case may be, under this Act and not by survivorship.

Explanation 1–For the purposes of this section, the interest of a Hindu Mitakshara coparcener shall be deemed to be the share in the property that would have been allotted to him if a partition of the property had taken place immediately before his death, irrespective of whether he was entitled to claim partition or not.

Explanation 2–Nothing contained in the proviso to this section shall be construed as enabling a person who has separated himself from the coparcenary before the death of the deceased or any of his heirs to claim on intestacy a share in the interest referred to therein.

Section 6 as amended 2005: Devolution of interest in coparcenary property.

(1) On and from the commencement of the Hindu Succession (Amendment) Act, 2005, in a Joint Hindu family governed by the Mitakshara law, the daughter of a coparcener shall :

(a) by birth become a coparcener in her own right in the same manner as the son;

(b) have the same rights in the coparcenary property as she would have had if she had been a son;

(c) be subject to the same liabilities in respect of the said coparcenary property as that of a son,and any reference to a Hindu Mitakshara coparcener shall be deemed to include a reference to a daughter of a coparcener:

Provided that nothing contained in this sub-section shall affect or invalidate any disposition or alienation including any partition or testamentary disposition of property which had taken place before the 20th day of December, 2004.

(2) Any property to which a female Hindu becomes entitled by virtue of sub-section (1) shall be held by her with the incidents of coparcenary ownership and shall be regarded, notwithstanding anything contained in this Act or any other law for the time being in force in, as property capable of being disposed of by her by testamentary disposition.

(3) Where a Hindu dies after the commencement of the Hindu Succession (Amendment) Act, 2005, his interest in the property of a Joint Hindu family governed by the Mitakshara law, shall devolve by testamentary or intestate succession, as the case may be, under this Act and not by survivorship, and the coparcenary property shall be deemed to have been divided as if a partition had taken place and the

(a) daughter is allotted the same share as is allotted to a son;

(b) share of the predeceased son or a predeceased daughter, as they would have got had they been alive at the time of partition, shall be allotted to the surviving child of such predeceased son or of such predeceased daughter; and

(c) share of the predeceased child of a predeceased son or of a predeceased daughter, as such child would have got had he or she been alive at the time of the partition, shall be allotted to the child of such predeceased child of the predeceased son or a predeceased daughter, as the case may be.

Explanation–For the purposes of this sub-section, the interest of a Hindu Mitakshara coparcener shall be deemed to be the share in the property that would have been allotted to him if a partition of the property had taken place immediately before his death, irrespective of whether he was entitled to claim partition or not.

(4) After the commencement of the Hindu Succession (Amendment) Act, 2005, no court shall recognise any right to proceed against a son, grandson or great-grandson for the recovery of any debt due from his father, grandfather or great-grandfather solely on the ground of the pious obligation under the Hindu law, of such son, grandson or great-grandson to discharge any such debt:

Provided that in the case of any debt contracted before the commencement of the Hindu Succession (Amendment) Act, 2005, nothing contained in this sub-section shall affect—

(a) the right of any creditor to proceed against the son, grandson or great-grandson, as the case may be; or

(b) any alienation made in respect of or in satisfaction of, any such debt, and any such right or alienation shall be enforceable under the rule of pious obligation in the same manner and to the same extent as it would have been enforceable as if the Hindu Succession (Amendment) Act, 2005 had not been enacted.

Explanation–For the purposes of clause (a), the expression "son", "grandson" or "great-grandson" shall be deemed to refer to the son, grandson or great-grandson, as the case may be, who was born or adopted prior to the commencement of the Hindu Succession (Amendment) Act, 2005

(5) Nothing contained in this section shall apply to a partition, which has been effected before the 20th day of December, 2004.

Explanation–For the purposes of this section "partition" means any partition made by execution of a deed of partition duly registered under the Registration Act, 1908 (16 of 1908) or partition effected by a decree of a court.

However in comparison, the Muslim Personal Law in India has not been reformed and has remained by and large unchanged, the various practices leading to gender inequality is still practiced *viz.*, practice of polygamy and divorce by triple talaq; Muslim women is not allowed to marry non-Muslim men; divorced women is entitled to maintenance only during the iddat period of three months. However the gender inequality still exists in some forms in Hindu laws, for example, different prescribed marriageable age for girls and boys; different methods of succession of property in case male and female dies intestates; Under Hindu Minority and Guardianship Act, mother can act as a child's natural guardian in case father is dead or otherwise disqualified . Further under Hindu Adoptions and Maintenance Act, mother cannot give her child in adoption unless the father is dead or otherwise disqualified.

Though the attempts have been made by the government to codify and unify the diverse practices followed under various communities to provide equal rights to the women in accordance with the constitution but still there is no secular law of adoption in India. Muslims do not recognise adoption except in case if there is valid custom of adoption or/and under Hanafi law where a man may adopt in absence of living relative and the escheat to the state or the religious community can be avoided. The Christians, Parsis and Jews also do not have adoption laws. They can have only a guardianship rights under the Guardians and Wards Act, 1890 and the adopted child under this Act does not get the inheritance and other rights.

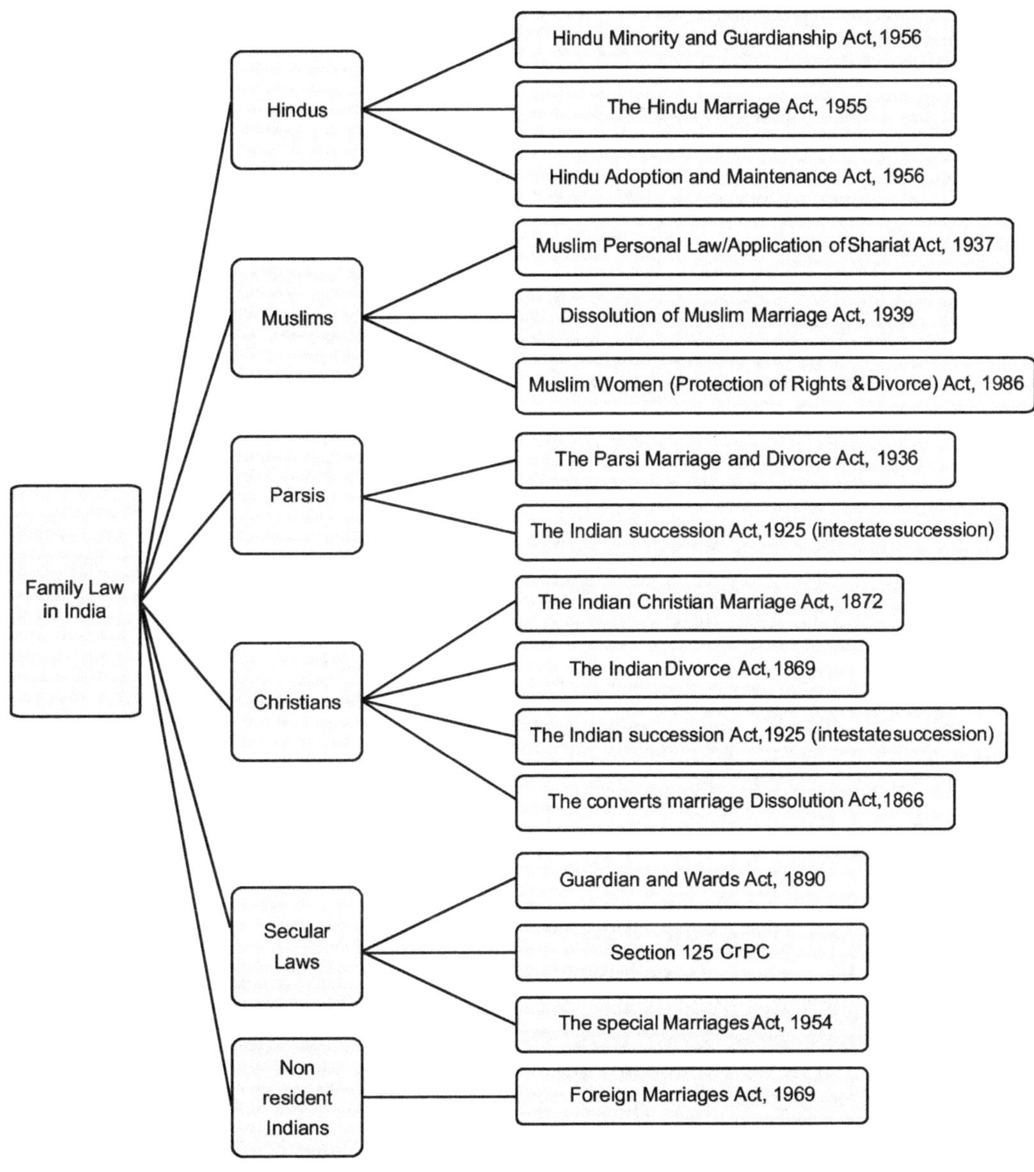

Family Laws presently governing different communities in India and may fall within purview of family courts.

Institutional Framework - Family Courts

The Family Courts Act ,1984 was enacted on 14 September, 1984 to provide for the family courts with a view to promote conciliation and secure speedy settlement of disputes relating to marriage and family affairs.

- **Establishment of family courts and their powers**–According to Section 2 (d) of the act, "Family Court" means a family court established under section 3 of the act which provides that the State Government after consultation with the High Court and by notification shall establish a Family Court for every area of the state consisting of a city or town whose population exceeds ten lakhs and for other areas in the state as it may deem necessary.

- The Act had laid down the broad guidelines and it was left to the State Government to frame the rules of procedure but most state governments have not taken any step towards framing of rules and for set up of family courts.

- Family courts are subordinate to the High Court, which has power to transfer the case from one family court to the other.

- The family courts have the power and jurisdiction under section 7 (1) of the Family Courts Act as exercisable by any District Court or subordinate civil court under any law for the time being in force in suits and proceedings of the nature referred to in the Explanation to sub-section (1) of section 7, of the Family Courts Act.

- The remedies provided by Family Courts in India are civil in nature.

- Under the provisions of the Family Courts Act, 1984, lawyers are not required to redress the grievances. The aggrieved parties can themselves address their grievances in the Family Courts.

Need for Family Courts and role of women in creation of Family Courts.

The need to establish the Family Courts was first emphasised by late Smt. Durgabai Deshmukh, social worker from Maharashtra after her visit to China in the year 1953, where she had the opportunity of studying the working of Family Courts. She discussed the subject and matter of establishment of the Family Courts with Hon'ble Justices M.C. Chagla and P. B. Gajendragadkar of Bombay High Court and also with the then Prime Minister Pandit Jawahar Lal Nehru. The Law Commission in its 59th report (1974) had stressed upon that in dealing with disputes relating to family, courts must resort to human rights approach an approach radically different from that adopted in ordinary civil proceedings and make efforts for settlement in matrimonial disputes before the commencement of trial and in due course state should think of establishing family courts. All India Family Court Conference was held in 1982 and need was felt for family courts to address the specified problems of matrimonial home, custody of children, speedy disposal of cases, informal procedure where the lawyers should be prohibited from arguing matters before the family courts in absence of specific permission of the court. Finally the Family Court Act was passed in 1984 and the Family Courts were established as special courts due to pressure from various Women's associations, welfare organisations and individuals to provide a forum that can resolve family disputes without resorting to adversial system of trial with the aim to promote conciliation between estranged family members and for speedy disposal of family matters.

Rajasthan and Karnataka were the first two states to set up family courts. The Act was implemented in Delhi only on 15.05.2009 with first family court in Dwarka District Court Complex, thereafter more Family Courts were established, four at the District Courts Complex, Rohini on 10.02.2010, the sixth Family Court at District Court Complex, Dwarka on 08.03.2011 and two more courts have also been set up at Saket in May 2011. To implement the Family Courts Act, 1984, Hon'ble Mr. Justice Vijender Jain, Hon'ble Mr. Justice Badar Durrez Ahmad and Hon'ble Mr. Justice Pradeep Nandrajog, Hon'ble Mr. Justice Muralidhar and Hon'ble Mr. Justice Manmohan and Hon'ble Mr. Justice A. K. Pathak Judges of Delhi High Court had played an effective role.

Types of Suits and proceedings under the act (act here referred is Family Courts Act)

Explanation to sub-section (1) of section 7 of the act provides that the *suits and proceedings referred to in this sub-section* are suits and proceedings of the following nature:

- a suit or proceeding between the parties to a marriage or a decree of nullity of marriage (declaring the marriage to be null and void or, as the case may be, annulling the marriage) or restitution of conjugal rights or judicial separation or dissolution of marriage;

♦ a suit or proceeding for a declaration as to the validity of a marriage or as to the matrimonial status of any person;

♦ a suit or proceeding between the parties to a marriage with respect to *the property* of the parties or of either of them.

♦ a suit or proceeding for an *order or injunction* in circumstances arising out of a *martial relationship*;

♦ a suit or proceeding for a *declaration as to the legitimacy* of any person;

♦ a suit or proceeding for *maintenance*;

♦ a suit or proceeding in relation to the *guardianship* of the person or the custody of, or access to, any minor.

➢ Section 7 (2) of the act provides that subject to the other provisions of this Act, a Family Court shall also have and exercise-

i. The jurisdiction exercisable by a Magistrate of the first class under Chapter IX (relating to order for maintenance of wife, children and parents) of the Code of Criminal Procedure, 1973; and

ii. The family courts may have such other jurisdiction as may be conferred on it by any other enactment.

♦ Section 8 of the act contains the provisions to exclude jurisdiction of other courts (the district Court or any subordinate civil court and also Magistrates powers under Chapter IX of the Code of Criminal Procedure, 1973) in respect of matters for which the family court has been conferred jurisdiction.

Procedure followed by Family Courts in deciding cases

Chapter IV of the Family Courts Act 1984 deals with the procedure of the family court in deciding cases before it (sec. 9).

♦ **Duty of family court to make effort for settlement between parties-**The family courts have to see that the parties are assisted and persuaded to come to a settlement and for this purpose they have been authorised to follow the procedure specified by the High Court by means of rules to be made by it.

If there is a possibility of settlement between the parties and there is some delay in arriving at such a settlement, the family court is empowered to adjourn the proceedings until the settlement is reached.

♦ **Family Courts as Deemed Civil Court-**Subject to the other provisions of this Act (Family Courts Act) and the rules, a Family Court is deemed to be a civil court and have all the powers of such court and the provisions of the Code of Civil Procedure, 1908 (5 of 1908) and of any other law for the time being in force shall apply to the suits and proceedings other than the proceedings under Chapter IX of the Code of Criminal Procedure, 1973 (2 of 1974)

Further subject to the other provisions of this Act and the rules, the provisions of the Code of Criminal Procedure, 1973 (2 of 1974.) or the rules made there under, shall apply to the proceedings under Chapter IX of *that Code* before a Family Court.

♦ **Power to lay down procedure-**The Family Court can also lay down its own procedure with a view to arrive at a settlement in respect of the subject-matter of the suit or proceedings or at the truth of the facts alleged by the one Party and denied by the other. (Section 10).

♦ **Provision for in camera proceedings-**The proceedings may also be held in camera if it is desired by the family court or by either party (Section 11 of the Family Court Act).

♦ **Assistance of legal and welfare experts-**The family court has also been given the power to obtain assistance of legal and welfare experts preferably women. (Section 12)

Role of Lawyers in Family Courts

The Act under section 13 restricts the role of lawyers and the party before a Family Court is not entitled as of right to be represented by a legal practitioner as opposed to the practice of the other courts in an adversarial system of adjudication. However, the court may, in the interest of justice, provide assistance of a legal expert as amicus curiae.

Thus the role of the lawyers has been limited to legal experts or 'amicus curiae' with the aim to encourage conciliation and prevent corruption, manipulation, long and bitter court litigation and excessive litigation costs but no mechanism has been framed which can ensure the availability of amicus curiae or legal experts as required by the courts further there may be certain cases and court procedures in which the counselors may not have the required expertise and there may be need of lawyers to help the client.

Role of counselors and gender sensitivity

♦ There exists wide disparity in practice followed by different states in relation to appointment of the counselors, their role, qualifications and remuneration.

♦ The Change in family counselors within three months in certain states leads to lack of continuity of discussion that had already taken place and requires re-explanation and examination of matrimonial disputes.

♦ The role and task of counselors is needed to be clearly defined so that their role may not become superficial and limited to ascertain whether the dispute can be reconciled or not.

♦ There is also need to train counsellors with gender-sensitivity so that they may play a role of neutral person taking into account unequal power relationships between men and women in reconciliation and settlement processes.

Do you know?

Family Courts Rules in Maharashtra and role of counsellors

In 1987, the Family Courts Rules in Maharashtra were framed dealing elaborately with the function and role of marriage counsellors in family courts. The powers that have been given to the marriage counsellors are to make home visits, to ascertain the standard of living of the spouses and the relationship with children, seek infomation from the employer, etc.

However this power has been used very rarely by the sensitive marriage counsellor in the interest of women and more often these powers are used against the women in the interest of the family since it is imbibed into the minds of such counsellors that their primary commitment is to preserve the institution of marriage.

Further, the reports prepared by marriage counsellors based on their investigation, are not binding on the judges. The report of the marriage counsellor is kept confidential, and not made a subject of cross-examination. After the preliminary meeting with the marriage counsellor, the case would proceed as per the rules of the Code of Civil Procedure. The rules do not simplify procedures but merely reproduce the Code of Civil Procedure with the minor addition that parties should be present in person. (*Family Courts: Report on Working of Family Courts and Model Family Courts. National Commission for Women.2002:4*)

Rule for evidence–Evidence may be given by affidavit also and it is open to the family court to summon and examine any person as to the facts contained in the affidavit. (Section 16).

Points to remember :

Family Courts

♦ Are subordinate to the High Court.

♦ High Courts have power to make rules for the procedure to be followed by the Family Courts.

♦ Family Court is deemed to be a Civil Court.

♦ Family Court have all powers of Civil Courts.

♦ Family Court have the power and jurisdiction as exercis-able by any District Court or Subordinate Civil Court.

♦ The provisions of code of Civil Procedure apply to the matters other than listed under Chapter IX of the Code of Criminal Procedure.

♦ The provisions of the Code of Criminal Procedure, 1973 (2 of 1974) or the rules made there under apply to the proceedings under Chapter IX of that Code: relating to order for maintenance of wives, children and parents.

♦ Both civil and criminal jurisdiction have been placed under one roof to promote conciliation and secure speedy settlement of matrimonial disputes and for the matters connected there with.

♦ Can also lay down its own procedure for settlement of family dispute.

♦ Have power to obtain assistance of legal and welfare experts preferably women.

♦ Has duty to make effort for settlement between parties.

However it is to be noted that

♦ The term family has not been defined under the act.

♦ Testamentary matters are not included.

♦ Need for legal experts and gender sensitised counsellors cannot be ignored.

♦ Need of aligning Family Courts with non-governmental organisations working in matters related to women's or gender issues.

♦ Need for establishing monitoring mechanisms at state level to review the functioning and outcome of the cases.

Judgement and decree of Family Court–The judgement of the family court contains a concise statement of case, the point for determination, the decision there on and the reason for the same (Section 17). The decree of the Family Court can be executed in accordance with the provisions of the Code of Civil Procedure or Code of Criminal Procedure as the case may be (Section 18).

An appeal against judgement or order of family court not being an interlocutory order lies to the High Court. However, no appeal lies from any decree or order passed by family courts with the consent of parties. (Section 19)

Power of High court to frame rules–The Act gives power to each of the High Courts to make rules for the procedure to be followed by the family courts in arriving at settlements and other matters. (Section 20).

The different High Courts have specified different rules of procedure for the determination and settlement of disputes by the family courts. For example in the rules made by the Madhya Pradesh High Court-the family court judge is also involved in the settlement, and if a settlement cannot be reached then a regular trial follows.

Power of central and state government–The Central Government has been given the power to make rules prescribing additional qualifications for appointment of a Judge of the family court. (Section 21). The State Government has also been empowered to make rules providing for, inter alia, the salaries of family court judges, terms and conditions of association of counsellors and the term and conditions of service of the officers and other employees. (Section 22).

The Act had laid down the broad guidelines and it was left to the State Government to frame the rules of procedure but most State Governments have not taken any step towards framing of rules and set up of family courts may be because of financial and other constraints.

Marriage and Divorce

Concept of marriage

Marriage is the most important social institutions in a human society. As per the oxford dictionary, 'it is the formal union of a man and a woman, typically as recognised by law, by which they become husband and wife'. It is a social and legal union between spouses creating a family, Kinship consisting of members related by blood, marriage, or adoption having mutual rights and duties towards each other. Marriage imposes on both the spouses the obligation to live together, to cohabit and entitles both the spouses conjugal rights and companionship. As a social institution, marriage provides for social functions relating to co-habitation, sexual relations, reproduction, rearing and protection of children and socialisation. It is also a legal union and leads to certain legal consequences that arise due to marriage

viz., provides the status of husband and wife to the couples; confer legitimacy on children born after marriage; create rights to maintenance and inheritance of property on husband, wife and children. If either spouse deserts or withdraws from the society of the other spouse without any reasonable cause, the aggrieved party can approach court for the relief of restitution of conjugal rights.

Societal norms and different forms of marriage

There are certain societal norms that govern the concept of marriage for example, one norm as followed universally is **Incest taboo** that prohibits sexual relationship and marriage with close kin i.e between father and daughter; mother and son; Brother and sister extendable to other close relatives such as cousins, uncles, aunts, nieces, nephews in some societies. In many societies marriage norms/rules are defined with respect to endogamy and exogamy. **Endogamy** requires people to find marriage partners within their own tribe, group, family or social unit based on caste, village, class, and lineage (within extended families) generally to keep their cultural values intact. On the other hand, **exogamy** provides for rule that marriage is not permitted between same tribe, gotra, pravara or sapindas and therefore partners should be identified outside their own group or social unit *i.e.*, between non blood relatives. Under Hindu law the term sapinda is generally used in a relation connected with the same body or through funeral oblations of food.

Monogamy is a recognised form of marriage in most of the societies that provides for the marriage and union of one woman to one man for a lifetime, this is the strict form of monogamy but the serial monogamy allows the spouses to marry to more than one person but not at the same time. In **polygamy and polyandry form of marriages**, the marriage between multiple partners is allowed. The **Polygamy (Polygyny)**permits a person to have multiple wives at the same time and may consist of sororal polygyny, where man's wives are sisters. The other form of polygamy is **Levirate marriage** which is followed as of custom of marrying a widow to her late husband's brother and was common among the ancient Hebrews. Polygamy has been a prerogative in many countries like Arabia, ancient India, Iran, Egypt and Babylon and is considered as strategic means to put all the women under the care of man and for increasing the population size. It is legal in countries like Afghanistan, Algeria, Bahrain, Indonesia, Iran and Bangladesh.

On the other hand, **Polyandry** means having two or more husbands at one time, though it is not widely prevalent form of marriage but is practiced as a *fraternal polyandry* in Himalayan areas of Nepal, Sri Lanka and Tibbet to pool the resources, where brothers may work together and have common wife in order to sustain one household and to lead the comfortable lives. But it can also be *non-fraternal* polyandry, where husbands are not related with each other. The practice of polyandry is seen among the Tibetan society (though outlawed today); Today, the pastoral tribe; Sherpa; Hephtalites, the tribe originated from northern China and lived in Persia during 400-500AD; The Marquesas of Polynesia, ancient Celtic societies and among certain hill tribes in India and earlier in Nayars of Kerala.

The other form of marriage includes: **Polygynandry**, a group marriage involving multiple men married to multiple women simultaneously, the group may be based on caste, class, ethnicity, common culture or be a religious group; **preferential marriages** which includes levirate and sororate marriages. Sororate marriage is where a widower marries his deceased (or barren) wife's sister; **Hypergyny**, a marriage of a woman with a husband belonging to a family having higher social status or rank; **Hypogyny**, a marriage of a woman to a husband of lower social status, rank or age. In recent years, the concept of same Sex marriage or gay marriage has emerged which is a marriage between two people of the same biological sex or gender. It has got legal recognition in few countries like Denmark, Argentina, France, Iceland, Mexico and Netherland.

Conditions of a valid marriage and ceremonies

Marriages are solemnised in every religion by performance of certain ceremonies and are considered valid subject to certain conditions required to be fulfilled by the parties to the marriage which may differ from religion to religion.

Hindu Law

The marriages under Hindu law are considered as a Holy sacrament or sanskars and consider husband and wife as one and permanent union. Earlier eight forms of marriage were recognised by Hindu dharma (Brahma, Daiva, Arsha, prajapatya or kaya, Aura, Gandharba, Rakshasa and Paisacha, out of which four were considered Dharmya or regular form of marriage and the rest were adharma or irregular forms of marriage and the polygamy was also permitted. The Kanyadan (formal donation of bride to groom by her father), Panigrahan, Vivahahoma and saptpadi (circumambulation of holy fire by bride and the groom) were important religious/shastric ceremonies of Hindu marriage. The Brahma is the only form of marriage that now prevails. With the codification of Hindu marriage laws contained in Hindu Marriage Act, 1955, the rule of monogamy of marriage has been made law among Hindus.

Section 5 of the act provides for conditions of valid Hindu marriage as given below. *A marriage may be solemnised between any two Hindus, if the following conditions are fulfilled, namely:-*

1. **Monogamy**–neither party has a spouse living at the time of the marriage

2. **Capacity to marriage**–at the time of the marriage,

     i.   neither party is incapable of giving a valid consent to marriage in consequence of unsoundness of mind; or

     ii. neither party, though capable of giving a valid consent, has been suffering from mental disorder of such a kind or to such an extent as to be unfit for marriage and the procreation of children; or

     iii. neither party has been subject to recurrent attacks of insanity or epilepsy;

3. **Age of marriage**–the bridegroom has completed the age of 21 years and the bride has completed the age of 18 years at the time of the marriage;

4. **Prohibited relationship**–the parties are not within the degrees of prohibited relationship unless the custom or usage governing each of them permits of a marriage between the two;

5. **Sapinda relationship**–the parties are not sapindas of each other, unless the custom or usage governing each of them permits of a marriage between the two.

Section 7 of the act laid down Ceremonies for a Hindu marriage as follows:

1. A Hindu marriage may be solemnised in accordance with the customary rites and ceremonies of either party thereto.

2. Where such rites and ceremonies include the saptapadi (that is, the taking of seven steps by the bridegroom and the bride jointly before the sacred fire), the marriage becomes complete and binding when the seventh step is taken.

For Hindus registration of marriage will be made compulsory. The registration of births and deaths (amendment) bill, 2012 has been introduced in Rajya

Sabha to include registration of marriages so that marriages can be registered in a specified procedural manner that will help in maintaining proper records and statistics of marriage. In Delhi, the Delhi (compulsory registration of marriage) order, 2014 has been passed that provides that any marriage solemnised in Delhi between a man having completed 21 years and a woman of at least 18 years of age on the date of solemnisation of the marriage and of which at least one of the party is an Indian citizen, will have to be compulsorily registered irrespective of caste, creed and religion professed by any party or parties to such marriage but if the marriage is already registered under any existing law, the same shall not be required to register under this law. (http://www.delhi.gov.in)

In Sikhs solemnisation of marriage took place by Anandkaraj ceremony where four hymns of Laav are performed during the four nuptial rounds. In Buddhism marriage rituals, the family bride and groom and the guests assembled in front of the shrine of Lord Buddha all set up with candles and flowers and recite the Tisarana, Pancasila and the Vandana in either English or Pali. Then the couple lights the candles and incense sticks and offer flowers to the image of Buddha and around it. After this the bride and the groom recites in turn, the vows as prescribed for each of them in the Sigilovdda Sutta (Digha Nikilya) and in the end, only the parents or the assembly recites the Mangala Sutta and Jayamangala gatha to offer their blessings for the couple.

Parsi Law

Parsi's also recognise monogamy and are governed by *The Parsi Marriage and Divorce Act, 1936,* an act to amend the law relating to marriage and divorce among Parsi's.

Monogamy–Section 4 (1) of the act provides that no Parsi, whether such Parsi has changed his or her religion or domicile or not, shall contract any marriage during the lifetime of his or her wife or husband, except in case of lawful divorce, dissolution or declaration of marriage as null and void.

Section 3 provides for requisites for validity of Parsi marriages as follows :

Prohibited relationship–Section 3 (1)(a) provides that no marriage shall be valid if, the contracting parties are related to each other in any of the degrees of consanguinity (certain blood relations) or affinity (certain persons with whom relationship has arisen due to marriage);

Ceremonies of marriage–as per section 3 (1)(b), no marriage shall be valid if, such marriage is not solemnised according to the *Parsi form of ceremony called" Ashirvad"* by a priest in the presence of two Parsi witnesses other than such priest;

Age of marriage–in the case of any parsi (whether such Parsi has changed his or her religion or domicile or not) who, if a male, has not completed twenty-one years of age, and if a female, has not completed eighteen years of age, no marriage shall be valid. Section 3 (1)(c).

Christian Law

The concept of marriage and the status of partners in Christian are reflected in the leading case of *Hyde v. Hyde and Woodmansee (1866) LR 1 P&D 130):*

"Marriage has been well said to be something more than a contract, either religious or civil – to be an Institution. It creates mutual rights and obligations, as all contracts do, but beyond that it confers a status. The position or status of 'husband' and 'wife' is a recognised one throughout Christendom the laws of all Christian nations throw about that status a variety of legal incidents during the lives of the parties, and induce definite lights upon their offspring…that marriage, as understood in Christendom, may for this purpose be defined as the voluntary union for life of one man and one woman, to the exclusion of all others."

The Indian Christian Marriage Act, 1872 deals with the law relating to the solemnisation of the marriages *of Christians in India* and recognises monogamy form of marriage between persons, one or both of whom is [or are] a Christian or Christians *i.e.,* the marriages between a Christian and non-Christian can be solemnised.

Section 5 deals with solemnisation of Christian Marriages in India by the following persons:

1. any person who has received Episcopal ordination, provided that the marriage be solemnised according to the rules, rites, ceremonies and customs of the Church of which he is a Minister;

2. any Clergyman of the Church of Scotland, provided that such marriage be solemnised according to the rules, rites, ceremonies and customs of the Church of Scotland;

3. any Minister of Religion licensed under this Act to solemnise marriages;

4. or in the presence of, a Marriage Registrar appointed under this Act;

5. any person licensed under this Act to grant certificates of marriage between [Indian] Christians.

Section 60 lays down the conditions on which the marriages of Indian Christians may be certified as given below:

1. **Age of marriage**–the age of the man intending to be married shall not be under twenty-one years, and the age of the woman intending to be married shall not be under eighteen years;

2. **Monogamy**–neither of the persons intending to be married shall have a wife or a husband still living;

3. **Ceremonies of marriage**–In the presence of a person licensed under section 9 of the act   and of at least two credible witnesses other than such person, each of the parties shall say to the other–

"I call upon these persons here present to witness that. 1, A. B., in the presence of Almighty God, and in the name of   our Lord Jesus Christ, do take thee, C. D., to be my lawful wedded wife [or husband]" or words to the like effect.

Muslim Law

In Muslim law marriage (Nikah) is considered as civil contract with the object of procreation and legitimisation of children though it is solemnised generally with recitation of certain verses from Quran but no religious ceremony is essential.

Essentials of the valid Muslim marriage:

1. Both the parties to marriage should be of sound mind and had obtained puberty (generally presumption is 15 years but it can be earlier).

2. There should be proposal by one of the parties and acceptance by other (*i.e.,* Consent of both parties at one and same meeting).

3. Two male witnesses or one male and two female witnesses, who must be Muslim of sound mind and major, however in Hanafi law, the witnesses are not required.

4. Mahr, a gift from the groom to his bride.

Special Marriage Act

The marriage between any two persons may be solemnised under the special marriage act on the similar conditions under section 4 as provided under Hindu marriage. However, it did not lay down any specific condition dealing with sapinda relationship.

Section 11 of SMA provides for declaration by the parties and three witnesses in the presence of the Marriage Officer before the marriage is solemnised, in the form specified in the Third Schedule of the act and the declaration is countersigned by the Marriage Officer.

Section 12 deals with place and form of solemnisation of marriage:

♦   The marriage may be solemnised at the office of the Marriage Officer or at such other place within a reasonable distance there from as the parties may desire, and upon such conditions and the payment of such additional fees as may be prescribed. [Section 12(1)]

♦   The marriage may be solemnised in any form which the parties may choose to adopt: Provided that it shall not be complete and binding on the parties, unless each party says to the other in the presence of the Marriage Officer and the three witnesses and in any language understood by the parties.-" I, (A), take thee (B), to be my lawful wife (or husband)." [Section 12 (2)]

Section 494 of Indian penal code (IPC) makes a bigamous marriage an offence punishable with imprisonment of either description for a term which may extend to seven years, and shall also be liable to fine.   This will apply if first marriage is perfectly valid and not void or voidable and the second marriage is duly solemnised with proper ceremonies either shastric or customary.

Concept of void and voidable marriage

In general there are two bars or impediments to marriage, absolute or relative. If absolute bar exists, Marriage is void and when relative bar exists, a marriage is voidable *i.e.,* when all the conditions of valid marriage prescribed by the personal laws as discussed above are fulfilled, then there is no legal impediment but if any of the essential condition is not fulfilled, marriage may void or voidable subject to the nature of the conditions so violated.

In void marriage, the parties to the marriage though had undergone the ceremonies of marriage but since lack absolute capacity to marry, marriage is deemed to be not in existence from the very beginning (void ab initio). Further no legal consequence flows from such marriage .

In voidable marriage, the marriage is perfectly valid marriage untill annulled by the court on the petition of any of the party.

The Sunni sect under Muslim law classifies marriage into three categories: valid (sahih); void (batil) and irregular/fasid (which is capable of becoming valid marriage by remedying the prohibition, for example: a person can marry fifth wife by divorcing any of the four wives). The unlawful conjunction by consanguinity, affinity or fosterage; marriage of Muslim Major without his/her consent; marriage with idolatress or fire worshiper; absence of improper witness (only under sunni law as shia do not require witness); marriage with women undergoing iddat (period of seclusion), all such marriages are irregular under sunni law(relative bars). But the

Shia sect do not recognise the distinction between irregular and void marriage and the marriage which are irregular under sunni are void under shia law. However shia law recognises that shia male (but not the shia woman) can contract any number of muta or temporary marriage with kitabia woman professing Muslim, Christian, Jewish religion and even with fire worshiper but not with women following any other religion

The Parsi and Christian law does not recognise any distinction between void and voidable marriages and the act provides only some grounds where marriage may be declared as null and void or dissolved.

Grounds of void/voidable marriage under various personal laws					
S. No.	**Grounds**	**Hindu Marriage Act (HMA)**	**Special Marriage Act (SMA)**	**Indian Christian Marriage Act (ICMA) and Divorce act (DA)**	**Parsi Marriage and Divorce Act (PMDA)**
1.	Bigamous marriage-i.e at the time of marriage, either party has the spouse living	Void u/s11 penal offence u/s 17 for both male and female u/Ss 494 and 495 IPC.	Void u/s 24	decree of nullity u/s18 DA	Void u/s 4 (2) unless there is lawful divorce or 1st marriage is declared null and void or dissolved
2.	Parties are sapindas to each other	Void u/s11			
3.	Parties are within prohibited degrees of relationship	Void u/s11		Non-Valid u/s88 ICMA- null u/s18 DA (consanguinity and affinity)	
4.	Improper marriage ceremonies	Void			
5.	Any party if, incapable of giving valid consent.	Voidable (unsoundness of mind)	Void u/s24	null u/s18 DA (lunatic /idiot)	
6.	Suffering from mental disorder, unfit for marriage and the procreation of children.	Voidable	Void u/s24		
7.	Either of party subject to recurrent attacks of insanity	Voidable (includes epilepsy)	Void u/s24		
8.	Less than the age of marriage.	Neither void nor voidable -Panel punishment is specified u/s 18	Void u/s24		
9.	Impotency	Voidable	Void u/s24	Null u/s18 DA	
10.	consummation of the marriage impossible due to natural causes				null and void u/s 30
11.	Willful non consummation of marriage.		Voidable		
12.	Wife pregnant by some other person	Voidable (Husband ignorant of the fact at the time of marriage)	Voidable	Ground for divorce	
13.	Consent obtained by fraud /coercion/force.	Voidable within 1yr of discovery of fraud or cessation of force & no marital intercourse with consent after discovery of ground	Voidable within 1yr of discovery of fraud or cessation of force & no marital intercourse with consent after discovery of ground	Null u/s19 DA	

Prohibited Relationships

Under Hindu law two persons are sapindas to each other if one is lineal ascendant of the other within the limit of sapinda relationship (5 degrees inline of ascent through father and three degree in line of descent through mother) or if both are sapinda to common ancestor. The sapinda relationship is always traced upward *i.e.*, ascent.[sec3(f) HMA]

Prohibited relationship includes as per sec 3 (g) of HMA

1. If one is lineal ascendant of the other (marriage prohibited between ancestors). There is no degree of limit.

2. If one was wife or husband of lineal ascendant. Again there is no degree of limit.

3. One cannot marry wives of a) brother b) of the father's or mother's brother c) of the grand-father's or grandmother's brother.

4. if the two are brother and sister, uncle and niece, aunt and nephew, or children of brother and sister or of two brothers or of two sisters.

Explanation to section provides that for the purposes of clauses (f) and (g), relationship includes-

i. Relationship by half or uterine blood as well as by full blood;

ii. Illegitimate blood relationship as well as legitimate;

iii. Relationship by adoption as well as by blood; and all terms of relationship in those clauses shall be construed accordingly.

Under the Special Marriage Act, the list of prohibited relationships is the same as provided by the HMA.

Under Christian law, the relationship of kindred or affinity or other lawful hindrance are diriment impediments to marriage that invalidates an attempted marriage (see sec 42 of ICMA). Section 88 of the act is titled as non-validation of marriages within prohibited degrees and provides that nothing in this Act shall be deemed to validate any marriage which the personal law applicable to either of the parties forbids him or her to enter into.

The Kindred or consanguinity (lineal or collateral) is the connection or relation of persons descended from the same stock or common ancestor (see sec 27 & 28 of the Indian succession act)

Prohibited degrees of consanguinity and affinity under Parsi law–The schedule 1 of the PMDA list the relationships to which man and women cannot marry and is given in the table below:

A man shall not marry the following:	A woman shall not marry the following:
1. Paternal grand-father's mother.	1. Paternal grand father's father.
2. Paternal grand-mother's mother.	2. Paternal grand-mother's father.
3. Maternal grand-father's mother.	3. Maternal grand-father's father.
4. Maternal grand-mother's mother.	4. Maternal grand-mother's father.
5. Paternal grand-mother.	5. Paternal grand-father.
6. Paternal grand-father's wife.	6. Paternal grand-mother's husband.
7. Maternal grand-mother.	7. Maternal grand-father.
8. Maternal grand-father's wife.	8. Maternal grand-mother's husband.
9. Mother or step-mother.	9. Father or step-father.
10. Father's sister or step-sister.	10. Father's brother or step-brother.
11. Mother's-sister or step-sister.	11. Mother's brother or step-brother.
12. Sister or step-sister.	12. Brother or step-brother.
13. Brother's daughter or step-brother's daughter, or any direct lineal descendant of a brother or step-brother.	13. Brother's son or step-.brother's son, or any direct lineal descendant of a brother or step-brother.
14. Sister's daughter or step-sister's daughter, or any direct lineal descendant of a sister or step-sister.	14. Sister's son or step-sister's son, or any direct lineal descendant of sister or step-sister.
15. Daughter or step-daughter, or any direct lineal descendant of either.	15. Son, or step-son, or any direct lineal descendant of either.
16. Son's daughter or step-son's daughter, or any direct lineal descendant of a son or step-son.	16. Daughter's son or step-daughter's son, or any direct lineal descendant of a daughter or step-daughter.
17. Wife of son or step-son, or of any direct lineal descendant of a son or step-son.	17. Husband of daughter or of step-daughter, or of any direct lineal descendant of a daughter or step-daughter.

18. Wife of daughter's son or of step-daughter's son, or of any direct lineal descendant of a daughter or stepdaughter.	18. Husband of son's daughter or of step-son's daughter, or of any direct lineal descendant of a son or step-son.
19. Mother of daughter's husband.	19. Father of daughter's husband.
20. Mother of son's wife.	20. Father of son's wife.
21. Mother of wife's paternal grand-father.	21. Father of husband's paternal grand-father.
22. Mother of wife's paternal grand-mother.	22. Father of husband's paternal grand-mother.
23. Mother of wife's maternal grand-father.	23. Father of husband's maternal grand-father.
24. Mother of wife's maternal grand-mother.	24. Father of husband's maternal grand-mother.
25. Wife's paternal grand-mother.	25. Husband's paternal grand-father.
26. Wife's maternal grand-mother.	26. Husband's maternal grand-father.
27. Wife's mother or step-mother.	27. Husband's father or step-father.
28. Wife's father's sister.	28. Brother of husband's father.
29. Wife's mother's sister.	29. Brother of husband's mother.
30. Father's brother's wife.	30. Husband's brother' son, or his direct lineal descendant.
31. Mother's brother's wife.	31. Husband's sister's son, or his direct lineal descendant.
32. Brother's son's wife.	32. Brother's daughter's husband.
33. Sister's son's wife.	33. Sister's daughter's husband.
The words "brother" and "sister" denote brother and sister of the whole as well as half blood.	
The relationship by step means relationship by marriages.	

Absolute bars under Muslim Laws

1. Prohibition on ground of Consanguinity–*i.e.,* Muslim law prohibits marrying with certain persons of blood relations. For example, a Muslim cannot marry his mother, grandmother, daughter, grand-daughter, sister (full, half or uterine), niece, grand niece paternal and maternal uncles and aunts etc.

2. Prohibition on ground of Affinity– *i.e.,* prohibition of marrying certain persons with whom relationship has arisen on account of marriage. For example, a Muslim cannot marry ascendants and descendants of wife: wife's mother or grand-mother, wife's daughter (from another husband) or granddaughter-prohibition arises here if the marriage is consummated; wife of ascendant/descendent. The rule is also applicable to women.

3. Prohibition on ground of Fosterage– *i.e.,* when a woman, other than the mother of the child suckled a child under the age of two years, she becomes the foster mother of the child. A man cannot marry his foster-mother, foster sister or her foster mothers daughter.

4. Prohibition on marrying another's wife whose husband is alive and has not divorced her.

Matrimonial Rights and Obligations

Marriage imposes certain marital rights and obligations on both the spouses like right of Husband and wife to society and comfort of each other called conjugal rights, rights of maintenance and inheritance. Let us discuss them in brief

Conjugal Rights

Marriage confers conjugal rights on the both the spouses to marriage, the mutual right and privileges of companionship and cohabitation or consortium. It includes enjoyment of association or alliance, sympathy, confidence and an emotional and physical intimate relationship. If any of the spouses infringes this marital obligation, the remedy is suit for restitution of conjugal rights, a legal right of one spouse to have company and comfort with the other.

Section 9 of HMA provides decree for restitution of conjugal rights to the aggrieved party, when either the husband or the wife has, without reasonable excuse, withdrawn from the society of the other and the court is satisfied of the truth of the statements made in such petition and there is no legal bar for not granting the application.The burden of proving reasonable excuse is on the person who has withdrawn from the society.

The similar provisions are available to either spouse for restitution of conjugal rights under section 22 of the Special Marriage Act, 1954; To Christians under section 32 of the Indian Divorce Act, 1869; To Parsi's under section 36 of the Parsi Marriage and Divorce Act, 1936 the right is also available under Muslim law by way of civil suit which in general has been used by the husbands.

The non-restitution of conjugal rights between the parties to the marriage for a period of one year or upwards after the passing of a decree for restitution of conjugal rights in a proceeding to which they were parties gives right to either party to a marriage to present a petition for the dissolution of the marriage by a decree of divorce [see sec 131A (ii), HMA; Section 27(2) (ii), SMA; Section 32A, PMDA].

The decree of restitution of conjugal rights can be enforced by the attachment of property and in case of further non-compliance; The court can punish for contempt of court but cannot force the erring spouse to consummate marriage.

Maintenance and Alimony

The marriage confers on husband an obligation to provide wife means of support or livelihood out of his earnings and even the divorced women have right to maintenance under section 125 of the Code of Criminal Procedure code, a secular law. Section 125 or of the Code of Criminal Procedure is a quasi-criminal procedure meaning that on default of payment of the amount of maintenance by the earning husband to the dependent wife, it can lead to sentencing for civil prison. Section 125 deals with every form of dependent including mother, father, wife, children.

The maintenance of wife, children and parents and to provide them food, clothing and shelter, when they are unable to maintain themselves is considered as natural duties of a man. Under Hindu Law, the wife has an absolute right to claim maintenance from her husband. The right of maintenance is codified under Hindu marriage act (HMA), 1955 and in the Hindu Adoptions and Maintenance Act (HA&MA), 1956.

Section 24 of HMA provides for maintenance Pendente lite and expenses of proceeding for divorce, restitution of conjugal rights or judicial separation etc., as an ancillary relief, on the application of the wife or the husband, if it appears to the court that either the wife or the husband, as the case may be, has no independent income sufficient for her or his support and the necessary expenses of the proceeding, it may, order the respondent to pay to the petitioner the expenses of the proceeding and, monthly during the proceeding such sum as it may seem to the court to be reasonable. While assessing such amount court will take in to account the petitioner' s own income and the income of the respondent.

Section 25(1) provides for Permanent alimony and maintenance on the application made to it for the purpose by *either the wife or the husband*, court at the time of passing any decree or at any time subsequent thereto, can order that the respondent shall pay to the

applicant for her or his maintenance and support such gross sum or such monthly or periodical sum for a term not exceeding the life of the applicant.

The court while assessing amount of maintenance, takes into account various factors like income and other property of the respondent and applicant, the conduct of the parties and other circumstances of the case (for *e.g.* liability of non-claimant to maintain other dependents *viz.*, parents, brothers and sisters). Further if it seems to the court to be just and necessary, any such payment may be secured by a charge on the immovable property of the respondent.

However incase of change in the circumstances of either party at any time after it has made an order, the court may vary, modify or rescind any such order in such manner as the court may deem just at the instance of either party [under section 25(2)]. Further, the court at the instance of the other party may vary, modify or rescind any such order in such manner as the court may deem just on the satisfaction that the party in whose favour an order has been made under this section has remarried or, if such party is the wife, that she has not remained chaste, or, if such party is the husband, that he has had sexual intercourse with any woman outside wedlock.

The special marriage act section 36 and 37 of the act and the Parsi Marriage and Divorce Act, 1936 under section 39 and 40 of the act respectively recognises the right of husband as well as of the wife to claim maintenance pendent lite (to be paid weekly or monthly) as well as permanent alimony and maintenance in parity with Hindu law. Similar provisions for maintenance, both alimony pendent lite and permanent alimony are also available in Christian law codified under the Indian Divorce Act, 1869 under section 36 and section 37 of the act. Section 36 however also provides that alimony pending the suit shall in no case exceed one-fifth of the husband's average net income for the three years next preceding the date of the order, and shall continue, in case of a decree for dissolution of marriage or of nullity of marriage, until the decree is made absolute or is confirmed, as the case may be. However, the Hindu wife has also the right to claim maintenance under Hindu Adoptions and Maintenance Act (HA&MA) which is independent of the right to maintenance by both the Hindu spouses under section 24 of HMA.

Section 3 (b) of HA & MA defines the term "maintenance" to include; (i) in all cases, provision for food, clothing, residence, education and medical attendance and treatment; (ii) in the case of an unmarried daughter, also the reasonable expenses of and incidents to her marriage.

The Hindu Adoptions and Maintenance Act provides for maintenance of wife by her husband during her lifetime [section 18(2)]. A Hindu wife is entitled to live separately from her husband without forfeiting her claim to maintenance where husband is (a) guilty of desertion; (b) has treated her with cruelty; (c) is suffering from a virulent form of leprosy; (d) has any other wife living; (e) keeps a concubine in the same house in which his wife is living or habitually resides with a concubine elsewhere; (f) has converted to another religion; and (g) if there is any other cause justifying her living separately [section 18(2)] but Hindu wife's claim for separate residence and maintenance from her husband is forfeited, if she is unchaste or ceases to be a Hindu by conversion to another religion. [section 18(3)]

Under the Muslim Law, the dissolution of Muslim marriage act 1939 provides that a women married under Muslim law is entitled to obtain divorce from the husband on the ground of failure on the part of the husband to pay maintenance to wife for the period of two years. The Muslim Women (Protection of Rights on Divorce) Act, 1986 lays down under that Mahr or other properties of Muslim woman is to be given to her at the time of divorce (section 3), a reasonable and fair provision and maintenance is to be made and paid to Muslim divorced women within *the iddat* period by her former husband [section 3 (a)]. where a Magistrate is satisfied that a divorced woman has not remarried and is not able to maintain herself after the iddat period, he may make an order directing such of her relatives as would be entitled to inherit her property on her death according to Muslim law to pay such reasonable and fair maintenance to her as he may determine fit and proper [section 4(1)] and in case she has no relatives as mentioned or such relatives or any one of them have not enough means to pay the maintenance, court can order state Waqf Board to pay maintenance. [section 4 (2)].

Right of Inheritance

The law of succession deals with testamentary and intestate succession. The rules relating to devolution of the property of a person on relatives as well as others is testamentary succession as per the will of testator. The inheritance consists of rules which determine the mode of devolution of the property of the deceased on heirs solely on the basis of their relationship to the deceased (intestate succession). When two persons get married, they get mutual rights of inheritance. There are different laws of succession governing persons belonging to different religions. The rules relating to devolution of property of a Hindu male or female intestate i.e dying without making a will is prescribed in the Hindu Succession Act, 1956. Under the Act, both husband and wife are included in the category of class I heirs (who are entitled to inherit property after the death of intestate) and are also called preferential heirs and simultaneous heirs but for the purpose of succession the property of Hindu female, source of the property matters; in case female dying intestate has obtained property by inheritance or any other sources under section 15(1), property will firstly devolves on husband as simultaneous heir; under section 15(2) (a), any property inherited by a female Hindu from her father or mother shall devolve to son, daughter son and daughter of predeceased son or daughter. In this category husband is not included. In absence of such heirs, the property will devolve on heirs of father; under section 15(2) (b), any property inherited by a female Hindu from her husband or from her father-in-law shall devolve, in the absence of any son or daughter of the deceased (including the children of any pre-deceased son or daughter) upon the heirs of the husband. Further both husband and wife enjoy full freedom of bequeathing their separate properties by way of will but the ancestral property has to be disposed off in accordance with the Hindu Succession Act, 1956. The act does not apply to Hindu who is married to non Hindu under special marriage act, 1954; Succession to the property of such person is regulated by the provisions of the Indian Succession Act. However if two persons who are Hindus get married under the Special Marriage Act, this provision will not apply and they are governed by the Hindu Succession Act.

The Christians and Parsi's are governed by Indian succession act, 1925 that recognises three types of heirs; The spouse, the lineal descendants, and the kindred. Chapter II provides for rules in cases of Intestates other than Parsis (section 30 to 49). Where intestate has left a widow and (a) any lineal descendants- widow will get 1/3 of his property and the remaining 2/3 shall go to his lineal descendants; (b) has no lineal descendant, but has left persons who are of kindred to him widow will get 1/2 of his property and the other half goes to those who are kindred to him; (c) none who are of kindred to him, the whole of his property shall belong to his widow (see section 35 of the act). A husband surviving his wife has the same rights in respect of her property, if she dies intestate, as a widow has in respect of her husband's property, if he dies intestate. (Section 35 of the act). Chapter III deals with Special Rules for Parsi Intestates (section 50 to 56). The property of which a Parsi dies intestate shall be divided in the case - (a) where such Parsi dies leaving a widow or widower and children- all have equal shares; (b) where such Parsi dies leaving children, but no widow or widower- among the children in equal shares (Section 51 of the act).

Under Muslim law, there is no distinction between ancestral or self-acquired property and the right of an heir comes in to existence on death of ancestor. The Muslim cannot dispose off more than 1/3 of his property by a will. The primary heirs under muslin law are father, mother, son, daughter, Husband and wife. On the death of wife, the share of husband is 1/4 of the property when there is a child or son's child, how low so ever; but he takes–when there is no child or son's. Incase of the death of the husband, the share of the wife is 1/8 when there is a child or son's child, how low so ever; But when there are no such children, then her share becomes 1/4.

Matrimonial Property

The property rights of the woman in India depend upon her marital status and the religion to which she belongs. In Hindu law there is a concept of 'stridhan' and any property or gifts given to wife by her parents and in-laws and by relatives and friends, is the absolute property of women. Section 27 of the Hindu Marriage Act empowers the Court that while deciding a matrimonial dispute, court can also pass a decree in respect of property which may jointly belong to both the husband and the wife." However the Section would apply to such property only (a) which has been "presented at or about the time of marriage" and (b) "may belong jointly to both the husband and the wife".

The concept of 'dower' under Muslim law is also an example of the absolute property of wife. Dower is a sum of money or other property which the wife is entitled to receive from the husband in consideration of marriage. Under shia's the amount of dower is fixed at the time of marriage or may also be fixed before or after the marriage. However a Muslim woman is not entitled to dower if separation takes place without consummation of marriage.

Minor Custody and Guardianship

The law relating to minority and guardianship amongst Hindus can be found through old Hindu law as laid down by the smritis, shrutis and the commentaries and as recognised by the Courts of law. Presently the law relating to Custody and

Guardianship is governed by Hindu *Marriage Act 1956 and the Hindu Minority and Guardianship Act 1956 (HM&GA)* and is also governed by other statutes: Indian Majority Act of 1875; *Guardians and Wards Act 1890. Section 4* (a) of the *Hindu Minority and Guardianship Act 1956 defines* "minor" means a person who has not completed the age of eighteen years; (b) "major" means a person having the care of the person of a minor or of his property or of both his person and property, and includes (i) a natural guardian, (ii) a guardian appointed by the will of the minor's father or mother, (iii) a guardian appointed or declared by a court, and (iv) a person empowered to act as such by or under any enactment relating to any court of wards.

Do you know?

♦ The guardian means a person having the care of the person of a minor or his property. The law recognised the de facto and de jure guardian of a minor.

♦ Guardian-de-fact, is one who has taken upon himself the guardianship of a minor.

♦ Guardian de-jure is a legal guardian, having legal right to guardianship of a person or the property or both as the case may be. This concept of legal guardian includes a natural guardian, a testamentary guardian or a guardian appointed or declared by Court of law.

The natural guardians–The natural guardians of a Hindu minor in respect of the minor's person as well as in respect of the minor's property (excluding his or her undivided interest in joint family property) as per section 6 of the Hindu Minority and Guardianship Act 1956 are-

   i. **in the case of a boy or an unmarried girl**- the father, and after him, the mother provided that the custody of a minor who has not completed the age of five years shall ordinarily be with the mother;

   ii. **in the case of an illegitimate boy or an illegitimate unmarried girl**- the mother, and after her, the father;

   iii. **in the case of a married girl**-the husband;

The expressions 'father' and 'mother' here do not include a step-father and a step-mother. Further no person is entitled to act as the natural guardian of a minor under the provisions of section 6, (a) if he has ceased to be a Hindu, or (b) if he has completely and finally renounced the world by becoming a hermit (vanaprastha) or an ascetic (yati or sanyasi).

In *Gita Hariharan v. Reserve Bank of India* AIR 1999 SUPREME COURT 1149 *(1999)*, Supreme Court held that a Hindu woman is the natural guardian of her children as much as the father. The court observed that:

"Section 6(a) itself recognises that both the father and the mother ought to be treated as natural guardians and the expression 'after' therefore shall have to be read and interpreted in a manner so as not to defeat the true intent of the legislature."

"In our opinion the word 'after' shall have to be given a meaning which would sub-serve the need of the situation viz., welfare of the minor and having due regard to the factum that law courts endeavour to retain the legislation rather than declaring it to be a void, we do feel it expedient to record that the word `after' does not necessarily mean after the death of the father, on the contrary, it depicts an intent so as to ascribe the meaning thereto as 'in the absence of ' - be it temporary or otherwise or total apathy of the father towards the child or even inability of the father by reason of ailment or otherwise and it is only in the event of such a meaning being ascribed to the word `after' as used in Section 6 then and in that event the same would be in accordance with the intent of the legislation viz. welfare of the child."

As per section 6 of the Hindu Minority and Guardianship, husband is the guardian of married girl. The earlier Hindu law also recognizes the guardian of a minor widow by affinity. In *Alagumperumal v. Vinayagathammal* (AIR 1929 Mad 110), Devadoss and Mackay, J.J., held that the husband is the legal guardian of his minor wife and, if he happens to die during her minority, his nearest sapinda will be her guardian and not her paternal relations. *In Mst. Ganga Devi v. Narshtng Das, AIR 1935 Lah 25*, Beckett, J., has observed that "under Hindu Law, the father of a minor girl ceases to be the guardian of her person as soon as she is married. On the death of her husband, this right does not revive in favour of the father, but devolves upon the husband's relations." The same view was reiterated in *Paras Ram And Ors. v. State AIR 1960 All 479, 1960 CriLJ 1054.*

Testamentary guardianship–Section 9(1) of the *HM&GA* confers testamentary power on Father in respect of legitimate children. In respect of illegitimate children, Section 9(4) confers such power on the mother.

The Guardians and Wards Act, 1890-It is the non-religious, secular law regarding the guardianship of a child and is applicable to **Christians** and **Parsis**.

Court to makeorders as to guardianship–The Act gives power to the Court to make orders as to guardianship consistently with the law to which the minor is subject (called certificated guardian) - see section 17 of the act. The basis of appointing such guardian is satisfaction of the court that appears on the circumstances to be for the welfare of the minor. The legal guardian can also be a close relative of the child or parent.

However the Court cannot appoint or declare a guardian under the act in the following cases (Section 19):

♦ of the property of a minor whose property is under the superintendence of a Court of Wards;

♦ of the person of a minor who is married female and whose husband is not, in the opinion of Court, unfit to be guardian of her person.

♦ of a minor whose father is living and is not in the opinion of the Court, unfit to be guardian of the person of the minor.

♦ of a minor whose property is under the superintendence of a Court of Wards competent to appoint a guardian of the person of the minor.

A guardian of the person of a ward is charged with the custody of the ward and must look to his support, health and education, and such other matters as the law to which the ward is subject requires (See Section 24)

Custody of child in marital dispute–In a marital dispute and in any proceeding under the Hindu marriage act, the Child custody can only be granted to one or both parents of the child by the court.

The court from time to time can pass such interim orders and make such provisions in the decree as it may deem just and proper with respect to the custody, maintenance and education of **minor children**, consistently with their wishes. The court may after final decree upon application by petitioner, revoke, suspend or vary any such orders and provisions with respect to the custody, maintenance and education of such children (*Section 26 of HMA*). Similar provisions are available under Section 38 of the SMA; Section 41 of DA; Section 49 of PMDA (in place of minor term used is children below 18 years).

In Muslims, there is no codified law for custody and guardianship. The concept of guardianship is distinct from the concept of custody under Muslim law. The concept of the custody (hizanat) of children varies from school/sects to which Muslims belong but generally it is with mother irrespective of the fact whether the child is legitimate or illegitimate, up to certain age of child keeping in view welfare of child but this right of mother is not absolute and she can be deprived of custody of child in case of her own misconduct; Subsequent marriage of Hazina with a person not related to the child; Neglect of child; Abjuration of Islam. On attaining puberty or such age that would permit consummation of marriage, the custody of girl lies with the Husband.

child's father. She can also appoint an executor in respect of her own property that will devolve after her death on her children.

In absence of natural guardians and testamentary guardians, the kazi were entrusted with the power of appointment of guardian of a Muslim minor. Guardian can also be appointed by the Court as per the provisions of the Guardians and Wards Act, 1890.

School	Custody of son is with mother till he attains	Custody of daughter is with mother till she
Hanafi School	7 yrs	attains Puberty.
Shafiis and hanabalis	–do–	gets married.
Maliki	Puberty	gets married.
Shias	2 years	

Guardianship – under both the Sunnis and the Shias, the father is recognised as the sole guardian of the person and property of the minor children (legitimate) and mother is not recognised as a guardian, natural or otherwise, even after the death of the father.

In Sunnis, after the death of the father, the guardianship passes on to the executor appointed as guardian by father (testamentary guardian) and no other person can be a legal guardian. In absence of the father and his executor, the grandfather has the power of appointing a testamentary guardian. But in case of shia's, after the death of father, the guardianship belongs to the grandfather, even though father has appointed an executor. In absence of the grandfather, the executor of the father or the executor of grandfather as the case maybe, becomes the guardian.

The testamentary guardians can be appointed either orally or by will in writing but the acceptance of the same express or implied is necessary.

The mother can also be appointed as a testamentary guardian or executrix by the father or by the grandfather but if mother is non-Muslim, she can be validly appointed as testamentary guardian under Sunni law. Under the Malikis and the Shafii law also a non-muslim can be a validly appointed as a testamentary guardian of the property of the minor, but not of the person of the minor. But the Shias did not allow the appointment of non-Muslim testamentary guardian.

The mother under Muslim law cannot appoint a testamentary guardian of her children but she can appoint a testamentary guardian, executor, of property of her minor children where she has been appointed as a general executrix by the will of the

Dissolution of Marriage and Theories of Divorce

In the Indian society, a marriage is dissolved either by the death of either of the spouse or either by divorce through court. Divorce results in termination of a marital union and status of being Husband and wife, it ceases right of inheritance and cohabitation. The various theories of divorce explains that marriage is a special contract that becomes dissoluble when one of the spouse is guilty or their relationship is irretrievably broken or by their mutual consent. Let us discuss them in brief:

Offence or guilt theory/fault theory

This theory provides that if any party is guilty of and has rendered him or herself unworthy of consortium, then as the mode of punishment innocent party can get divorce from the party who has committed marital offence but if the innocent party condones the act of guilty party, no divorce can be granted. The common grounds of guilty theory are adultery (sexual intercourse outside wedlock), cruelty (may be physical and mental) and desertion (is total repudiation of obligations of marriage–it may be actual, constructive or willful neglect) but a person cannot take advantage of his/her own wrong act.

Later on recognition of, insanity and epilepsy as grounds of divorce led to renaming of the guilty theory as **fault theory**. If one of the parties to marriage has some fault in him or her, the marriage could be dissolved, whether that fault is his or her conscious act or providential.

The major draw back of the fault theory is the presumption of one innocent party and one guilty party for divorce but there may be circumstances when husband and wife are not able to live together harmoniously and there may not be fault of either of them.

Consent Theory

The theory of *divorce by mutual consent* provides for recognition of the dissolution of marriage by mutual consent of both the husband and the wife in case they are not able to live together by decree of the court. The main criticism of the theory is that:

- It will lead to easy and hasty divorce.
- May promote ill-considered divorces.
- May lead to dissolution of marriages in cases of slight incompatibility of temperament.

Irretrievable breakdown of marriage

The Divorce on the ground of ir-retrievable breakdown of marriage represents modern view of divorce that if a marriage has broken down beyond possibilities of repair *i.e.,* irretrievably with no reasonable possibility of spouses to live together, then it should be dissolved without looking into causes of breakdown and the fault of either of the party. The Law Commission in its Seventy-First Report (1978) had strongly recommended introducing breakdown of marriage as a ground for divorce in addition to fault grounds in the divorce law and has suggested period of three years separation as criterion of breakdown.

Till date however, this ground has not been specifically included in the Hindu Marriage Act, 1955, but the Supreme Court in the past has granted divorce based on irretrievable breakdown of marriage as in the case of *Naveen Kohli v. Neelu Kohli, AIR 2006 SC 1675, the* three-judge Bench has observed:

"We have been principally impressed by the consideration that once the marriage has broken down beyond, repair, it would be unrealistic for the law not to take notice of that fact, and it would be harmful to society and injurious to the interests of the parties. Where there has been a long period of continuous separation, it may fairly be surmised that the matrimonial bond is beyond repair. The marriage becomes a fiction, though supported by a legal tie. By refusing to sever that tie the law in such cases does not serve the sanctity of marriage; on the contrary, it shows scant regard for the feelings and emotions of the parties. Public interest demands not only that the married status should, as far as possible, as long as possible, and whenever possible, be maintained, but where a marriage has been wrecked beyond the hope of salvage, public interest lies in the recognition of that fact. Since there is no acceptable way in which a spouse can be compelled to resume life with the consort, nothing is gained by trying to keep the parties tied for ever to a marriage that in fact has ceased to exist.."

In Rishikesh Sharma v. Saroj Sharma, Civil Appeal, (5129) of 2006, Supreme Court gave a decision in favour of irretrievable breakdown of marriage. But it was an exceptional case where the spouses were old persons and were litigating for a long time. But in recent case of *Vishnu Dutt Sharma v. Manju Dutt Sharma* (2009) 6 SCC 379, two-judge Bench, refused to grant divorce on the ground of irretrievable breakdown of marriage and held that a bare reading of Section 13 of the Act, it is crystal clear that no such ground of irretrievable breakdown of the marriage is provided by the legislature for granting a decree of divorce. This Court cannot add such a ground to Section 13 of the Act as that would be amending the Act, which is a function of the legislature.

The Indian Parliament has introduced the Marriage Laws (Amendment) Bill, 2010 to further amend the Hindu Marriage Act, 1955 and the Special Marriage Act, 1954, to provide there in irretrievable break down of marriage as a ground of divorce in the Hindu Marriage Act, 1955.

Grounds for Divorce

Different laws of divorce govern people belonging to different religions. The Hindu Marriage Act, 1955, governs divorce among Hindus. The Parsi Marriage and Divorce Act, 1936 governs the divorce among Parsis. The Indian Divorce Act, 1869, governs divorce among Christians. Muslims do not have a codified law for marriage and divorce; they are governed by their religious texts.

The Hindu marriage act, 1955 and Special Marriage Act, 1954 provides for grounds of divorce based on theories of divorce as discussed above fault/guilty and mutual consent.

The act on Parsi's and Christian marriage also provides for certain ground of dissolution of marriage including divorce by mutual consent.

Both the husband and wife are entitled to file petition for dissolution of marriage on the grounds discussed below, but the wives were also given some special grounds of divorce.

In divorce by mutual consent both the parties can file a joint petition for divorce under the relevant acts on the ground that they are living separately for a period of one year or more and are not able to live together and have mutually agreed that marriage should be dissolved. Then, after the filing of petition, the parties are required to wait for period of six months but not more than 18 months and then move second motion in the court for the grant of divorce. The district court on being satisfied, after hearing the parties and after making such inquiry as it thinks fit, that a marriage has been solemnised under this Act and that the averments in the petition are true, pass a decree declaring the marriage to be dissolved with effect from the date of the decree. The decree of divorce by mutual consent can be granted by court by waiving the statutory period of 6 months. The Parsi marriage act however do not provide for waiting period of six months from filing of petition for divorce but lays down specifically that no suit under section 32B(1) of the act shall be filed unless at the date of the filing of the suit one year has lapsed since the date of the marriage.

Grounds for dissolution of marriage/divorce				
Grounds	**HMA**	**SMA**	**PMDA**	**DA**
Adultery	U/s13(1)(i)	U/s27(1)(a)	U/s32 (d)-also includes fornication; the suit be filed within 2 yrs after the know-ledge of the fact.	U/s10
Cruelty	U/s13(1)(i-a)	U/s27(1)(d)	U/s32(dd)- court may grant decree of judicial separation.	U/s10
Desertion for a continuous period of not less than 2 years	U/s13(1)(i-b)	U/s27(1)(b)	U/s32(g)	U/s10
Conversion to another religion	U/s13(1)(ii) court may grant decree of judicial separation		U/s32(j) - the suit be filed within 2 yrs after the know-ledge of the fact	U/s10
Incurably of unsound mind /insane/mental disorder to such an extent that the petitioner cannot reasonably be expected to live with the respondent.	U/s13(1)(iii)	U/s27(1)(e)	U/s32(b) - at the time of marriage or for a period of two years or more preceding suit	U/s10
Suffering from a virulent and incurable from of leprosy	U/s13(1)(iv)	U/s27(1)(g)		U/s10 (for a period not less than 2 yrs)
Suffering from venereal disease in a communicable from	U/s13(1)(v)	U/s27(1)(f)		U/s10 (for a period not less than 2 yrs)
Renunciation of the world by entering any religious order	U/s13(1)(vi) -court may grant decree of judicial separation			
Not been heard of as being alive for a period of seven years or more	U/s13(1)(vii)- court may grant decree of judicial separation	U/s27(1)(h)	U/s31 (term used is continuously absent instead alive)	U/s10
Willful refusal to consummate marriage	-		U/s 32(a) - within one year after solemnisation of marriage	U/s10
Wife pregnant by some other person	-		U/s 32(c)-plaintiff must be ignorant of the fact at the time of marriage; the suit filed within 2y of the date of marriage and no marital intercourse after the know-ledge of the fact	
Bigamy	Special ground to wife U/s13(2) (i)		U/s32(d)	
Rape or unnatural offence (sodomy or bestiality	Special ground to wife U/s13(2) (ii)	Special ground to wife U/s27 (1A)(i)		Special ground to wife U/s10

			U/s32(e)	
voluntarily causing grievous hurt/infected the plaintiff with venereal disease/ husband compelled the wife to submit herself to prostitution.			U/s32(e)	
Undergoing imprisonment for 7 years or more for offence U/Indian penal code (IPC).		U/s27(1)(c)	U/s32 (f) - the defendant prior to the filing of the suit must have under-gone at least one year imprisonment.	
No marital intercourse for one year or more since passing of decree or order against defendant for maintenance.	Special ground to wife U/s13 (2)(iii)	Special ground to wife U/s27 (1A)(ii)	U/s32(h)	
Repudiation of marriage after attaining age of 15 years and before attaining the age of 18 years irrespective of consum-mation of marriage.	Special ground to wife U/s13 (2)(iv)			
Non-resumption of cohabitation or restitution of conjugal rights within one year in pursuance of a decree to be ground for divorce.	U/s13(1A)	U/s27(2) clause (i)&(ii)	U/s32(A)	U/s10 (for a period of 2 yrs or up-wards)
Divorce by mutual consent.	U/s13(B)	U/s28	U/s32(B)	U/s10A

Concept of divorce under Muslim Law

Under Muslim law, Muslim of sound mind can divorce his wife effected orally or by a written talak nama. Among sunnis talak may be express, implied, contingent, constructive (for example illa-vow of continence; Zihar-unlawful comparison) or delegated to wife or third person. Delegation of power to divorce may be made before or after the marriage and is irrevocable. In *Badu Mia v. Badrannessa, 40 Ind Cas 803 (AIR 1919 Cal 511 (2)*, it was held that Muslim wife can divorce her husband, under his delegated power in the event of his taking a second wife. A marriage can be dissolved by decree of divorce by court but there is no requirement of such decree under Muslim law. The Muslim husband generally enjoys special privileges in the area of divorce but Muslim law also recognizes divorce at the wife's instance called khula (to put off), here the offer is from the wife to compensate husband by voluntarily giving away something of monetary value to him, in lieu of his acceptance to release her from marital ties. The divorce by mutual consent –Mubara'at is also recognized under Muslim law.

The dissolution of Muslim marriage act, 1939 gives corresponding right to Muslim women and lays down grounds under which women can obtain decree of dissolution of marriage. The ground for decree for dissolution of marriage as provided under section (2) of the act includes the following:

i. the whereabouts of the husband not been known for a period of four years-In this case, a decree shall not take effect for a period of six months from the date of such decree, and if the husband appears either in person or through an autho-rized agent within that period and satisfied the Court that he is prepared to perform his conjugal duties, the Court shall set aside the said decree.

ii. Husband has neglected or failed to provide maintenance for a period of two years to his wife.

iii. Husband has been sentenced to imprisonment for a period of seven years or upwards - however no decree shall be passed on this ground until the sentence has become final.

iv. The husband has failed to perform, without reasonable cause, his marital obligations for a period of three years.

v. Impotency of husband at the time of the marriage and continuation of same–in this case, before passing a decree on this ground, the Court shall, on application by the husband, issue an order requiring the husband to satisfy the Court within a period of one year from the date of such order that he has ceased to be impotent, and if the husband so satisfies the Court within such period, no decree shall be passed on the said ground.

vi. Insanity of the husband for a period of two years or husband suffering from leprosy or a virulent venereal disease;

vii. that she, having been given in marriage by her father or other guardian before she attained the age of fifteen years, repudiated the marriage before attaining the age of eighteen years (provided that the marriage has not been consummated)

viii. cruelty by the husband- The act of cruelty by husband includes : (a) habitual assaults, making the life of wife miserable by cruelty of conduct even if such conduct does not amount to physical ill-treatment; (b) association with women of evil repute or leading an infamous life; (c) attempts to force her to lead an immoral life; (d) disposes of her property or prevents her exercising her legal rights over it; (e) obstructs her in the observance of her religious profession or practice; (f) if he has more wives than one, does not treat her equitably in accordance with the injunctions of the Quran.

ix. On any other ground which is recognized as valid for the dissolution of marriages under Muslim law.

Children

As per the United Nation Convention on the Rights of the Child 1989, Article 1, 'Child' means a human being below the age of 18 years unless under the Law applicable to the child, majority is attained earlier. The Indian Majority Act, 1875, defines a minor as a person who is below 18 years of age and in case where a minor is under superintendence of the Courts of Wards, the age of majority is 21 yrs. Under the Hindu, Mohammedan, Christian & Parsis Laws, a person attains majority at 18 years of age. Under the Juvenile Justice (Care & Protection of children) Act 2000, the age of majority is 18 for both boys & girls. However as per the Child Labour (Prohibition & Regulation) Act, 1986, a 'child' means a person who has not completed his 14 years of age. In Family law the welfare of child with proper protection and care has been the paramount consideration. The children are supreme asset of the nation and for their overall development and growth, it is necessary to provide them with basic necessities irrespective of their sex, caste, colour, religion, creed, wealth or family. Every child has certain civil, social and economic rights which are fundamental and vital.

The International Covenant on Economic, Social and Cultural Rights (ICESCR), 1966; Convention on the Elimination of All Forms of Discrimination against Women (CEDAW), 1979 and Convention on the Rights of the Child (CRC), 1989 are the human rights treaties. The Convention on the Rights of the Child 1989 as ratified by India provides for welfare of children incorporating the full range of human rights for civil, economic, social, cultural, and political rights to children. The Convention has laid down standards in health care; Education and on legal, civil and social services for the protection of children's from all forms of violence (physical and mental), maltreatment and hurt and for protection of their rights. The core principles of this Convention are non-discrimination (Article 2); Devotion to the best interests of the child (Article 3); right to life, survival and development (Article 6) and respect for the views of the child (Article12). The United Nations High Commissioner for Refugees (UNHCR) works with states, national and international partners, and sister agencies to help children of concern. Other organizations working with UNHCR to provide care and protection to children includes the UN Children's Fund (UNICEF), working globally for the child protection from violence, exploitation and abuse; the International Committee of the Red Cross (ICRC), the International Rescue Committee; International Save the Children Alliance; Terre des Hommes; World Vision International; Action for the Rights of Children and the Committee on the Rights of the Child (http://www.unhcr.org/) The World Health Organization (WHO) is a specialised agency of the United Nations that is concerned with global health matters and plays important role in shaping the health research agenda, setting norms and standards, articulating evidence-based policy options, providing technical support to countries and monitoring and assessing health trends.

Right to Health and Care- It is the fundamental and social right of every human being to have the highest standard of health physical and mental, including timely, affordable and proper access to health care facilities read with article 21 of the constitution. The right to health is a right of every body irrespective of caste, culture, gender, religion and economic and social conditions and the state is under duty to :

◆ ensure that children are given opportunities and facilities to develop in a healthy manner and in conditions of freedom and dignity and that childhood and youth are protected against exploitation and against moral and material abandonment. (Article 39(f) of the constitution).

◆ make provision for securing just and humane conditions of work and for maternity relief (Article 42).

◆ make provision of early childhood care and education for all children until they complete the age of six years (Article 45)

◆ raise the level of nutrition and the standard of living and to improve public health, the State shall endeavor to bring about prohibition of the consumption, except for medicinal purposes, of intoxicating drinks and of drugs which are injurious to health (Article 47).

◆ raise the level of nutrition and the standard of living and to improve public health, the State shall endeavor to bring about prohibition of the consumption, except for medicinal purposes, of intoxicating drinks and of drugs which are injurious to health (Article 47).

Right to protection against exploitation- The constitution of India has several provisions that provide for protection of children against exploitation sexual abuse and at work place.

Child trafficking - the trafficking within nation and at transnational level of children, for the purpose of exploitation which includes sexual exploitation and commercial exploitation, forced labour, services, slavery or practices similar to slavery, servitude or the removal of organs, is increasing due to many reasons depending on their physical, social, environmental factor or economical backwardness. Article 21 deals with protection of life and personal liberty and article 23 of the constitution provides for Prohibition of traffic in human beings and other similar forms of forced labour. The *Immoral Traffic (Prevention) Act 1956* abolishes the Commercial Sexual Exploitation and trafficking in women and girls for prostitution as means of living.

Section 370 and 370A of Indian penal code as amended by Criminal Law (Amendment) Act, 2013 deals with trafficking of person and exploitation of trafficked person. Trafficking of minor has been made cognizable and non bailable offence punishable with imprisonment not less than 10 years extendable to life imprisonment with fine.

Child sexual abuse- Child sexual abuse may take the following forms: (a) *sexual harassment i.e.,* uttering words, making sounds or gesture or; exhibiting any body part to children or making a child to do so; Or showing any object in the form of media for pornographic purposes; stalking child directly or through electronic or digital means; or enticing child for pornographic purposes or gives gratification there for.

> **Do you know?**
> Stalking means following a person and contacts, or attempts to contact such person to foster personal interaction repeatedly, despite a clear indication of disinterest by such person. It may include monitoring of the use by a person of the internet, email or any other form of electronic communication or watching or spying on a person in a manner that results in a fear of violence or serious alarm or distress in the mind of such person, or interferes with the mental peace of such person.

(b) *Sexual assault i.e.,* touching of vagina, penis, anus or breast of child or making a child to do so or any other act with sexual intent involving physical contact without penetration.

(c) *penetrative sexual assault-* it is committed by a person by penetration of penis or any object or part of body into the vagina, mouth, urethra or anus of child or by making the child to do so with him or any other person. It also includes manipulation of any part of the body of the child so as to cause such penetration or making the child to do so.

The Indian penal code 1860 as amended in 2013 defines and provides punishment for rape (section 375 and 376); Outraging the modesty of a woman (section 354); Sexual harassment and punishment for sexual harassment. *The Protection of Children from Sexual Offences Act, 2012,* was passed (came into force with effect from 14th November, 2012 along with the Rules framed there under). The act provides for protection of child from sexual assault, sexual harassment and pornography and provides for the establishment of Special Courts for trial of offences under the Act, keeping the best interest of the child as of paramount importance at every stage of the judicial process. Some other important features of the act are:

◆ Child friendly procedures for reporting, recording of evidence, investigation and trial of offences.

◆ The attempt to commit an offence under the act and abetment of the offence (including those who traffick children for sexual purposes) has been also made a punishable offence.

◆ It prescribes stringent punishment graded as per the gravity of the offence, with a maximum term of rigorous imprisonment for life, and fine.

◆ It casts a legal duty upon a person who has knowledge that a child has been sexually abused to report the offence and on such failure, he may be punished with six months imprisonment and/or a fine.

◆ During the investigative process, police should act as child protectors and make urgent arrangements for the care and protection of the child, such as obtaining emergency medical treatment for the child and placing the child in a shelter home.

♦ It stipulates that a case of child sexual abuse must be disposed of within one year from the date the offence is reported.

♦ The National Commission for the Protection of Child Rights (NCPCR) and State Commissions for the Protection of Child Rights (SCPCRs) have been assigned responsibility to monitor the implementation of the Act.

Need for Sexuality education- sexuality education is the process of assisting young people in their physical, social, emotional and moral development as they prepare for adulthood, marriage, parenthood and ageing, as well as their social relationships in the context of family and society. The need to impart appropriate education on sexuality is an important issue that parents and teachers must acknowledge and address if they want to make sure that their children are well adjusted and safe, and will grow up to be mature and balanced individuals. (Sheshadari. S and Rao N, 2012).

Child labour–A child when employed for work in early age, it restricts the fundamental right of children to have education and it may also adversely affects the health and safety of child. Every child has an economic right that includes the right to ensure proper development and protection from exploitation at work.

The International Labour Organisation (ILO) is the first specialised agency of the United Nations founded in 1919 to deal with the labour issues. The International Programme on the Elimination of Child Labour (IPEC) was created in 1992 with the overall goal of the progressive elimination of child labour with immediate priority action for prevention and elimination of the worst forms of child labour.

In India, article 24 of the constitution prohibits employment of children below 14 years of age in factories, mines or other hazardous employment. The Directive Principles of State Policy as enshrined in constitution in article 39 (e) provides that children of tender age should not be abused and that they should not be forced by economic necessity to enter avocations unsuited to their age or strength. Further as discussed above article 39 (f) states that children are given opportunities and facilities to develop in a healthy manner and in conditions of freedom and dignity and that childhood and youth are protected against exploitation and moral and material abandonment. *The Children (Pledging of Labour) Act*, makes any agreement by a parent or guardian to pledge the labour of a child below 15 years of age for payment or benefit other than reasonable wages as illegal and void and such parent or guardian as well as those who employ a child whose labour is pledged is liable for punishment. The Child Labour (Prohibition and Regulation) Act, 1986 prohibits employment of a child below 14 years of age in several kinds of industries, hazardous and non-hazardous (Section 3), the children cannot be employed as domestic workers or servants in Dhaba's (roadside eateries), restaurants, hotels, tea shops or other recreational centres.Any person who employs any child in contravention of the provisions of section 3 of the Act is liable for punishment with imprisonment for a term which shall not be less than three months but which may extend to one year or with fine which shall not be less than ₹ 10,000 but which may extend to ₹ 20,000 or both (Section 14 of the act). *The Goa Children's Act, 2003*, ensures protection for children and the young against exploitation of all kinds and against moral and material abandonment.

Do you know?

Child labour means work that is prohibited for children of certain age groups. It is work performed by children who are under the minimum age legally specified for that kind of work, or work which, because of its detrimental nature or conditions, is considered unacceptable for children and is prohibited.

The child labour under international law may fall under three categories:

♦ The unconditional worst forms of child labour, which are internationally defined as slavery, trafficking, debt bondage and other forms of forced labour, forced recruitment of children for use in armed conflict, prostitution and pornography, and illicit activities.

♦ Labour performed by a child who is under the minimum age specified for that kind of work (as defined by national legislation, in accordance with accepted international standards), and that is thus likely to impede the child's education and full development.

♦ Labour that jeopardizes the physical, mental or moral well-being of a child, either because of its nature or because of the conditions in which it is carried out, known as "hazardous work."

Source: http://www.un.org/

Child marriage–The Child Marriage stunts the growth and development, particularly of the girl child who is the more vulnerable partner. The child marriage may often result in early pregnancy and the complications during child birth and both maternal and infant mortality (both of the mother & child) are common during child birth for young pregnant girls. The child marriage further results in child labour at home and young girls have very little decision making powers. Child marriage makes girls more vulnerable to domestic violence and sexual abuse. It also deprives the girl child of her right to obtain education and live a life of freedom & dignity (see Law Commission report no 205, 2008).

The Hindu Marriage Act, 1955, the Parsi Marriage and Divorce Act, 1936 and the Christian Marriage Act, 1872 all have prescribed the age of marriage as 18 years for girls and 21 years for boys. But the validity of child marriages is not affected by the Hindu Marriage Act, 1955; It is not void or voidable. The Act only prescribes for 15 days simple imprisonment or fine which may extend to ₹ 1,000 or both for such marriages.

Under Muslim law, the marriage can take place at the age of puberty, which is same as the age of majority i.e 15 years, though it could be earlier and the marriage of a child below this age can be contracted with the consent of his/her parent or guardians as the case may be. A minor however has right to repudiate marriage on attaining majority/ puberty but before the age of 18 years provided the marriage is not consummated after attaining the age of puberty under section 2 (vii) of the dissolution of Muslim Marriage act 1939.

The International Convention on the Elimination of All Forms of Discrimination against Women (CEDAW) and Convention on the Rights of the Child provides for eradication of child marriage and makes it obligatory for states to protect children from all form of violence and abuse and neglect.

The Prohibition of Child Marriage Act, 2006 (came into force in Nov 2007) provides for prohibition of solemnisation of child marriages and for matters connected therewith or incidental thereto and has changed the position in regard to child marriage in India. It has made child marriage voidable. Section 3 (1) provides that every child marriage, whether solemnized before or after the commencement of this Act, is voidable at the option of and by the petition to the district court, of the contracting party who was a child at the time of the marriage.The petition can be filed through the guardian or next friend along with the Child Marriage Prohibition Officer [Section 3 (2)] if the petitioner is a minorat the time of filing a petition. However the petition can be filed at any time but before the child filing the petition completes two years of attaining majority [Section 3 (3)] *i.e.,* the girl can file a petition till she becomes 20 years of age and a boy till he becomes 23 years of age. The punishment for solemnising child marriage has been enhanced to rigorous imprisonment of up to 2 years or with a fine up to 1 lakh rupees or both. Further the court can issue an injunction including ex parte interim injunctions against any person including a member of an organisation or an association of persons prohibiting child marriage and any child marriage if solemnised in contravention of an injunction order issued is void ab initio (see sec 14 of the act).

Right to Education

Right to education can be included within the cultural rights of child. The right to education means education with a certain degree of transformative potential, an education of quality and substance. The Universal Declaration of the Human Rights (1948), states that 'education shall be directed to the full development of the human personality and to the strengthening of respect for human rights and fundamental freedom' (Article 26). In India, Article 45 of the Directive Principles of State Policy provides for free and compulsory education for all children until they complete the age of 6 years. Article 46 provides that state shall promote with special care the educational and economic interests of the weaker sections of the people, and, in particular, of the Scheduled Castes and the Scheduled Tribes.

In *Unni Krishnan v. State of Andhra Pradesh (1993 AIR 2178)*, court held that:

"The citizens of this country have a fundamental right to education. The said right, flows from article 21. This right is, however, not an absolute right. Its content and parameters have to be determined in the light of Articles 45 and 41. In other words, every child/citizen of this country has a right to free education until he completes the age of 14 years. Thereafter his right to education is subject to the limits of economic capacity and development of the State."

The Constitution (*Eighty-sixth Amendment*) Act, 2002 inserted Article 21-A in the Constitution of India which provides that the State shall provide free and compulsory education to all children of the age of 6-14 years in such manner as the State may, by law, determine. The fundamental duty is also imposed on parents and guardians of children vide Article 51A (k) that the parent or guardian are under duty to provide opportunities for education to his child or, as the case may be, ward between the age of six and fourteen years. Consequently the Right of Children to free and Compulsory Education (RTE) Act, 2009 was passed that comes in to effect from April 2010.

The act provides for the following:

◆ Right of children to free and compulsory education till completion of elementary education in a neighborhood school and lays obligation on appropriate government to provide the same. For this purpose, no child shall be liable to pay any kind of fee or charges or expenses which may prevent him or her from pursuing and completing elementary education.

◆ The provisions have been made for a non-admitted child to be admitted to an age appropriate class.

◆ The duties and responsibilities of appropriate governments, local authority and parents in providing free and compulsory education, and sharing of financial and other responsibilities between the Central and State Governments have been also specified.

◆ It Provides for 25 per cent reservation for economically disadvantaged communities in admission to Class One in all private schools;

◆ The norms and standards relating inter alia to Pupil Teacher Ratios (PTRs), buildings and infrastructure, school-working days, teacher-working hours are laid down.

◆ It provides for appointment of teachers with the requisite entry and academic qualifications;

◆ It lays down for development of child friendly and child centered learning curriculum.

◆ The act also prohibits physical punishment and mental harassment;

◆ It lays down screening procedures for admission of children; Capitation fee; Private tuition by teachers and running of schools without recognition.

Right to Shelter

Every child shall have the right to shelter/ housing for the acceptable and decent living in a healthy, safe and peaceful environment. Article 25(1) of the Universal Declaration of Human Rights declares that everyone has the right to a standard of living adequate for the health and well-being of himself and his family; It includes food, clothing, housing, medical care and necessary social services. International Covenant on Economic, Social, and Cultural Rights (Article 11.1) provides that the States Parties to the Covenant should recognise the right of everyone to an adequate standard of living for himself and his family, including adequate food, clothing and housing, and to the continuous improvement of living conditions. The Convention on the Rights of the Child (1989), Article 27, lays down that governments should take appropriate measures to assist parents and others responsible for the child to implement the right to an adequate standard of living, particularly with regard to housing. Article 19(1)(e) of the Constitution of India accords fundamental right to residence and settlement in any part of India and right to life has been assured as a basic human right under Article 21 of the Constitution.

In *Shantistar Builders v. Narayan Khimalal Totame, AIR 1990 SC 630,* the Supreme Court observed that:

"The right to life is guaranteed in any civilised society. That would take within its sweep the right to food, the right to clothing, the right to decent environment and a reasonable accommodation to live in. The difference between the need of an animal and a human being for shelter has to be kept in view. For the animal it is the bare protection of the body; For a human being it has to be a suitable accommodation which would allow him to grow in every aspect-physical, mental and intellectual. The Constitution aims at ensuring fuller development of every child. That would be possible only if the child is in a proper home. It is not necessary that every citizen must be ensured of living in a well- built comfortable house but a reasonable home particularly for people in India can even be mud-built thatched house or a mud- built fire-proof accommodation."

In *P. G. Gupta v. State of Gujarat & Ors (1995 SCC, Supl. (2) 182),* court held that the right to residence and settlement is a fundamental right under Article 19(1)(e) and it is a facet of inseparable meaningful right to life under Article 21.

In Chameli Singh v. State of U.P (1996) 2 SCC 549, the right to live in a decent environment has been held to be a component of the right to life and shelter has been held to be home for a human being where he has opportunities to grow physically, mentally, intellectually and spiritually. It has further been held that right to shelter does not mean a mere roof over one's head, but would include all necessary infrastructure which would enable him to live and develop as a human being. Right to shelter would therefore include adequate living space, safe and decent structure, clean and decent surroundings, sufficient light, pure cost free flat being provided to each of them.

State responsibility towards children

The constitution of India imposes on the State a primary responsibility of ensuring that all the needs of children are met and that their basic human rights are fully protected under clause (3) of article 15, clauses (e) and (f) of article 39, articles 45 and 47. In the case of *Sheela Barse v. Secretary, Children's Aid Society 1987 SCR (1) 870*-the Supreme Court held that:

Children are the citizens of the future era. On the proper bringing up of the children and giving them the proper training to turn out to be good citizens depends the future of the country. In recent years, this proposition has been well realised. Every society must, therefore, devote full attention to ensure that children are properly cared for and brought up in a proper atmosphere where they could receive adequate training, education and guidance in order that they may be able to have their rightful place in the society when they grow up. Further Children in Observation Homes should not be made to stay long and as long as they are there, they should be kept occupied and the occupation should be congenial and intended to bring about adaptability in life aimed at bringing about self-confidence and picking of humane virtues. However, for employment in Children's home, the children would not be given any remuneration. In the case *Sanjay Suri & Anr v. Delhi Administration, Delhi & Anr (1988 AIR 414)* he petitioners, a News Editor and a trainee sub-editor, filed writ petitions in the Supreme Court pointing out features of maladministration within the Central Jail at Tihar relating to juvenile under trial prisoners and praying for appropriate directions to the respondents. The Court made several orders with reference to juvenile prisoners and under trials. Under the orders of the Court, the Sessions Judge visited the jail on more than one occasion and made several reports. Some juvenile under trial prisoners were ordered to be released immediately. Some convicted minors were freed on parole (conditional release of a prisoner) for one month. The judgment stressed the need to generate a sense of humanism in jail adminis-tration.

Children in conflict with law- Juvenile Justice System

The word juvenile means relating to young people. The Juvenile Justice Act, 2000, defines "juvenile" or "child" to mean a person who has not completed eighteenth year of age. Further under Protection of Women from Domestic Violence Act,

2005, the child is defined as any person below the age of 18, and includes an adopted step or foster child.

Juvenile delinquency/offending is crime commit-ted by youth less than the statutory age of majority and such crimes are dealt by juvenile courts. Under criminal law no Criminal responsibility can be fixed on a person below 7 years of age or upto 12 years **if the child is found to have not attained the ability to understand the nature and consequences of his/her act under IPC.** Further for purposes of fixing liability for criminal activities like kidnapping, abduction and related offences, age fixed for a child is 16 years for boys & 18 years of girls.

The juvenile justice system as conceived by legislation aims at providing care and protection, treatment, development, and rehabilitation of delin-quent and neglected juveniles who are in conflict with law. There may be various factors that lead to juvenile delinquency *viz.*, low economic status and rejection from peer group; biological and psycho-logical factors; lack of parental guidance and education; peer pressure etc.

The court also observed that "We are anxious to ensure that no child within the meaning of the Children's Act is sent to the jail because otherwise the whole object of the Children's Act of protecting the child from bad influence of jail life would be defeated. It is also a matter of anxiety for us to see that juveniles between the age of 16 to 18 years who are put in custody in the jail are not being kept in separate ward and are allowed to intermingle with adult prisoners because that would also expose them to mal- influences which may prevent their proper rehabilitation...".

A child in need of care and protection as per sec 2(d) of the Juvenile Justice (Care and Protection of Children) Act [JJA], 2000 means a child:

1. who is found without any home or settled place or abode and without any ostensible means of subsistence,

   (a) who is found begging, or who is either a street child or a working child,

2. who resides with a person (whether a guardian of the child or not) and such person-

   i. has threatened to kill or injure the child and there is a reasonable likelihood of the threat being carried out, or

   ii. has killed, abused or neglected some other child or children and there is a reasonable likelihood of the child in question being killed, abused or neglected by that person,

3. who is mentally or physically challenged or ill children or children suffering from terminal diseases or incurable diseases having no one to support or look after,

4. who has a parent or guardian and such parent or guardian is unfit or incapacitated to exercise control over the child,

5. who does not have parent and no one is willing to take care of or whose parents have abandoned 'or surrendered him or who is missing and run away child and whose parents cannot be found after reasonable inquiry,

6. who is being or is likely to be grossly abused, tortured or exploited for the purpose of sexual abuse or illegal acts,

7. who is found vulnerable and is likely to be inducted into drug abuse or trafficking,

8. who is being or is likely to be abused for unconscionable gains,

9. who is victim of any armed conflict, civil commotion or natural calamity;

Salient Features of the JJA

The act provides for constitution of Juvenile Welfare Committees to deal with children in need of care and protection.

As per the Act, "Juvenile in conflict with law" means a juvenile who is alleged to have committed an offence and has not completed eighteenth year of age as on the date of commission of such offence. The Juvenile Justice Board with powers of judicial magistrate is the competent authority to deal with the Juvenile in conflict with the law.

The Act provides that the maximum punishment that can be given to a child in conflict with law before 18 years of age, is 3 years of stay in a rehabilitation home or an observation home. (Section 16(g) of the act).

The Act is a reformative act and aims at rehabilitation through establishment of various kinds of Institutions *viz.*, Children's Home for the reception of child in need of care and protection; Special Homes for the reception of child in conflict with law; Observation Homes for the temporary reception of children during the pendency of any inquiry; After-care Organisations for the purpose of taking care of children discharged from Children's Home or Special Homes.

Family take of Adoption

Adoption is the personal law issue and is recognised under **Hindu Law presently it is governed by Hindu Adoption and Maintenance Act, 1956** and

any adoption made in contravention of the provisions of the act is void and neither create any rights in the adoptive family in favour of any person which he or she could not have acquired except by reason of the adoption, nor destroy the rights of any person in the family of his or her birth (see Section 5 of the Act).

For a valid adoption under Section 6 of the act, following conditions must be complied:

i. the person adopting has the capacity, and also the right, to take in adoption;

ii. the person giving in adoption has the capacity to do so;

iii. the person adopted is capable of being taken in adoption; and

iv. the adoption is made in compliance with the other conditions mentioned in Chapter 2 of the act.

Person capable of taking adoption

Any male Hindu who is of sound mind and is not a minor has the capacity to take a son or a daughter in adoption. Provided that, if he has a wife living, he shall not adopt except with the consent of his wife unless the wife has completely and finally renounced the world or has ceased to be a Hindu or has been declared by a court of competent jurisdiction to be of unsound mind (Section 7). Further any female Hindu, who is (a) of sound mind, (b) not a minor, and (c) not married, or if married, whose marriage has been dissolved or whose husband is dead or has completely and finally renounced the world or has ceased to be a Hindu or has been declared by a court of competent jurisdiction to be of unsound mind, has the capacity to take a son or daughter in adoption. (Section 8).

Persons capable of giving in adoption (Sec. 9)

1. No person except the father or mother or the guardian of a child shall have the capacity to give the child in adoption.

2. Subject to the provisions of sub-section (3) and sub-section (4), the father, if alive, shall alone have the right to give in adoption, but such right shall not be exercised save with the consent of the mother unless the mother has completely and finally renounced the world or has ceased to be a Hindu or has been declared by a court of competent jurisdiction to be of unsound mind.

3. The mother may give the child in adoption if the father is dead or has completely and finally renounced the world or has ceased to be a Hindu or has been declared by a court of competent jurisdiction to be of unsound mind.

4. Where both the father and mother are dead or have completely and finally renounced the world or have abandoned the child or have been declared by a court of competent jurisdiction to be of unsound mind or where the parentage of the child is not known, the guardian of the child may give the child in adoption with the previous permission of the court to any person including the guardian himself.

5. Before granting permission to a guardian to give the child in adoption, the court shall be satisfied that the adoption will be:

♦ for the welfare of the child,

♦ due consideration for the purpose is given to the wishes of the child having regard to the age and understanding of the child,

♦ and that the applicant for permission has not received or agreed to receive and that no person has made or given or agreed to make or give to the applicant any payment or reward in consideration of the adoption except such as the court may sanction.

Do you know?

For the purposes of section 9 as discussed above the expressions "father" and "mother" do not include an adoptive father and an adoptive mother.

Persons capable of being taken in adoption

A persons who may be capable of being taken in adoption (sec 10), if he or she (i) is a Hindu; (ii) has not already been adopted; (iii) has not been married, unless there is a custom or usage applicable to the parties which permits persons who are married being taken in adoption; (iv) has not completed the age of fifteen years, unless there is a Custom or usage applicable to the parties which permits persons who have completed the age of fifteen years being taken in adoption.

Other conditions for a valid adoption (Sec. 11)

In every adoption, the following conditions must be complied with: (i) if any adoption is of a son, the adoptive father or mother by whom the adoption is made must not have a Hindu son, son's son or son's son's son (whether by legitimate blood relationship or by adoption) living at the time of adoption; (ii) if the adoption is of a daughter the adoptive father or mother by whom the adoption is made must not have a Hindu daughter or son's daughter (whether by legitimate blood relationship or by adoption) living at

the time of adoption; (iii) if the adoption is by a male and the person to be adopted is a female, the adoptive father is at least twenty-one years older than the person to be adopted; (iv) if the adoption is by a female and the person to be adopted is a male, the adoptive mother is at least twenty-one years older than the person to be adopted; (v) the same child may not be adopted simultaneously by two or more persons; (vi) the child to be adopted must be actually given and taken in adoption by the parents or guardian concerned or under their authority with intent to transfer the child from the family of its birth or in the case of an abandoned child or a child whose parentage is not known, from the place or family where it has been brought up to the family of its adoption. Provided that the performance of datta homan, shall not be essential to the validity of an adoption.

Effect of adoptions

An adopted child shall be deemed to be the child of his or her adoptive father or mother for all purposes with effect from the date of the adoption and from such date all the ties of the child in the family of his or her birth shall be deemed to be severed and replaced by those created by the adoption in the adoptive family (section 12 of the act). Provided that : (a) the child cannot marry any person whom he or she could not have married if he or she had continued in the family of his or her birth; (b) any property which vested in the adopted child before the adoption shall continue to vest in such person subject to the obligations, if any, attaching to the ownership of such property, including the obligation to maintain relatives in the family of his or her birth; (c) the adopted child shall not divest any person of any estate which vested in him or her before the adoption.

A Valid adoption not to be cancelled by the adoptive father or mother or any other person, nor can the adopted child renounce his or her status as such and return to the family of his or her birth. (section15).

However subject to any agreement to the contrary, an adoption does not deprive the adoptive father or mother of the power to dispose of his or her property by transfer inter-vivos or by will (section 13).

The Juvenile Justice (Care and Protection of Children) Act, 2000 has also incorporated the provision of adoption of child as an alternative to institutional care. Further to strengthen adoption rules and facilitate adoption without any hassles, Government of India under advice of Supreme Court constituted a Central Agency- Central Adoption Resource Agency [CARA] with New Delhi as base to set up guidelines for adoption time to time safeguarding welfare and rights of children while granting adoption or guardianship under Hindu Adoption and Maintenance Act 1956, Guardians and Wards Act 1890 or Juvenile Justice Act of 2000.

Adoption of Children by Foreigner-International adoption

In *Lakshmi Kant Pandey v. Union of India* 1984 AIR 469, the Supreme Court laid down normative and procedural safeguards to be followed while making inter country for ensuring that the child goes into the right family which would provide it warmth and affection of family life and help it to grow and develop physically, emotionally, intellectually and spiritually. The court held that "Every application from a foreigner desiring to adopt a child must be sponsored by a social or child welfare agency recognized or licensed by the government of the country in which the foreigner is resident. No application by a foreigner for taking a child in adoption should be entertained directly by any social or welfare agency in India working in the area of inter-country adoption or by any institution or centre or home to which children are committed by the Juvenile Court... The social or child welfare agency sponsoring the application of the foreigner must also certify that the foreigner seeking to adopt a child is permitted to do so according to the law of his country. These certificates, declarations and documents which must accompany the application of the foreigner for taking a child in adoption, should be duly notarized by a Notary Public whose signature should be duly attested either by an Officer of the Ministry of External Affairs or Justice or Social Welfare of the country of the foreigner or by an Officer of the Indian Embassy or High Commission or Consulate in that country".

With regard to **adoption for Christians, Parsis, and Muslims,** there is no statutory law and a person belonging to these communities can get themselves appointed as guardian under the Guardians and Wards Act, 1890 as discussed previously in this chapter under the head Minor Custody and Guardianship.

Violence against Women

The gender inequality and violence against women persists and is acceptable in various social institutions and is a global phenomenon depending on the social, cultural, political, economical factors and is also based on family structure and relationships. The acts of violence against women may occur either in public or in private life. The violence against women outside the family may occurs in the form of rape, sexual abuse, sexual harassment, sexual assault and intimidation at work, educational institutions and elsewhere, exploitation through trafficking and forced prostitution. The domestic violence happens within the family and includes verbal, physical and psychological violence like insults, humiliation, threats to cause pain, beating battering, sexual abuse of female children in the household, dowry-related violence, forced sex or marital rape, female genital mutilation, intimidation, harassment and economic abuse. In the last many years to curb the violence against women and to provide equal rights to the women has been a matter of legal discourse worldwide. The women's movement and pressure for change across the globe had reflected substantial progress towards gender equality in all spheres of life.

International Legal Framework

The United Nations at international arena is committed to the principle of equality of men and women in their rights, opportunities, responsibilities as well as dignity. The organization started work for the promotion of equal rights for women by constituting the commission on human rights and the commission on the status of women in 1946 and with the adoption of universal declaration of Human rights in 1948, convention on the political rights of women in 1953, convention on the nationality of married women in 1957, Declaration on Elimination of Discrimination against Women,1967 which finally led to adoption of the Convention on the Elimination of All Forms of Discrimination against Women, 1979 (CEDAW). It establishes the norms and standards on discrimination against women, substantive equality, and state obligation and so far 99 countries, including India are signatories to the convention with the commitment to undertake various measures to end discrimination against women in all forms. The convention provides for establishment of a committee on the elimination of discrimination against women. The UN Declaration on Elimination of Violence against Women was adopted in 1993 which defines, what constitutes the 'violence against women' as any gender-based violence acts that result in, or are likely to result in, physical, sexual or psychological harm or suffering to women including threats of such acts, coercion or arbitrary deprivation of liberty whether occurring in public or private life.

In 1996, The UN Special Rapporteur on Violence against Women recommended "A Framework for Model Legislation on Domestic Violence" (UN Model Code), with the objective to serve as a drafting guide to legislatures and organisations committed to provide comprehensive legislation on domestic violence. It defines domestic violence as: all acts of gender-based physical, psychological land sexual abuse by a family member against women in the family, ranging from simple assaults to aggravated physical battery, kidnapping, threats, intimidation, coercion, stalking, humiliating verbal abuse, forcible or unlawful entry, arson, destruction of property, sexual violence, marital rape, dowry or bride-price related violence, female genital mutilation, violence related to exploitation through prostitution, violence against household workers and attempts to commit such acts.

The International Covenant on Economic, Social and Cultural a Rights also contains several provisions particularly important for women. Article 7 recognises her right to fair conditions of work and reflects that women shall not be subjected to sexual harassment at the place of work which may vitiate working environment. UN Development Fund for Women (UNIFEM) is the women's fund at the United Nations has been created that provides financial and technical assistance to innovative programmes and strategies to foster women's empowerment and gender equality.

Law in Indian on Violence against Women

The Indian Constitution in its Preamble, Fundamental Rights, Fundamental Duties and directive Principles provides for gender equality and empowers the State to adopt measures of positive discrimination in favour of women.Article 14 of the Constitution of India guarantees equality before law. Article 15 prohibits discrimination on the grounds of sex. Article 16 states about equality of opportunity for all citizens in matters relating to employment.

The 73rd and 74th Amendments (1993) to the Constitution of India have provided for reservation of seats in the local bodies of Panchayats and Municipalities for women, laying a strong foundation for their participation in decision making at the local levels.

Criminal Law

The Indian Penal Code (IPC) provides penal provisions for certain offences committed against women as given below:

◆ Dowry death (Section 304-B IPC)
◆ punishment for causing miscarriage(Sections 312 to 318)

◆ Assault or criminal force to women to outrage her modesty/molestation (Section 354)
◆ Kidnapping and abduction for specified purpose (Section 363-373 IPC)
◆ Importation of girls up to 21 years of age (Section 366B IPC)
◆ Rape (Section 376 IPC)
◆ Cruelty to women (Section 498-A IPC)
◆ To insult modesty of women/Sexual Harassment (Section 509 IPC)
◆ Eve-Teasing-Obscene acts and songs (Section 294 IPC)

Sections 113(a), 113(b) and 114(c) of Indian evidence act, 1872 provide for presumptions as to abetment of suicide by a married woman within 7 years of marriage, as dowry death of a woman and as to absence of consent of woman for sexual inter-course.

Legislative Initiatives towards Empowerment of Women: There are various women-specific legislations in India with the aim to prevent various forms of discrimination, exploitation, violence and sexual harassment at work place.

◆ The Immoral Traffic (Prevention) Act, 1956
◆ The Dowry Prohibition Act, 1961 (28 of 1961) (Amended in 1986)
◆ The Indecent Representation of Women (Prohibition) Act, 1986
◆ The Commission of Sati (Prevention) Act, 1987 (3 of 1988)
◆ Protection of Women from Domestic Violence Act, 2005
◆ The Sexual Harassment of Women at Workplace (Prevention, Prohibition and Redressal) Act, 2013

Role of judiciary-Judiciary has also played important role in protection of women from violence and gender injustice. In *Bodhisattwa v. Ms. Subhra Chakraborty* (AIR 1996 SC 922), the Supreme Court held that rape is a crime against basic human rights and is also violative of the victim's most cherished of the Fundamental Rights, namely, the Right to Life contained in Article 21. In *Vishakha v. State of Rajasthan* (AIR 1997 SC 301), the Supreme Court considering the inadequacy of legislation on the issue and even assumed the role of legislature to define sexual harassment and laid down instruction for the employers.

The court observed that "in the absence of domestic law occupying the field, to formulate effective measures to check the evil of sexual harassment of working women at all work places, the contents of International Conventions and norms are significant for the purpose of interpretation of the guarantee of gender equality, right to work with human dignity in Articles 14, 15 19(1)(g) and 21 of the Constitution and the safeguards against sexual harassment implicit therein. Any International Convention not inconsistent with the fundamental rights and in harmony with its spirit must be read into these provisions to enlarge the meaning and content thereof, to promote the object of the constitutional guarantee. This is implicit from Article 51(c) and enabling power of the Parliament to enact laws for implementing the International Conventions and norms by virtue of Article 253 read with Entry 14 of the Union List in Seventh Schedule of the Constitution. Article 73 also is relevant. It provides that the executive power of the Union shall extend to the matters with respect to which Parliament has power to make laws. The executive power of the Union is, therefore, available till the parliament enacts to expressly provide measures needed to curb the evil. Thus, the power of this Court under Article 32 for enforcement of the fundamental rights and the executive power of the Union have to meet the challenge to protect the working women from sexual harassment and to make their fundamental rights meaningful. Governance of the society by the rule of law mandates this requirement as a logical concomitant of the constitutional scheme. The exercise performed by the Court in this matter is with this common perception shared with the learned Solicitor General and other members of the Bar who rendered valuable assistance in the performance of this difficult task in public interest. The progress made at each hearing culminated in the formulation of guidelines to which the Union of India gave its consent through the learned Solicitor General, indicating that these should be the guidelines and norms declared by this Court to govern the behaviour of the employers and all others at the work places to curb this social evil".

The following guidelines and norms are prescribed by court lying down the duty of the employer or other responsible persons in work places or other institutions to:

♦ Prevent or deter the commission of acts of sexual harassment

♦ Provide the procedures for the resolution, settlement or prosecution of acts of sexual harassment by taking all steps required.

♦ Establish Complaints Committee headed by women, a special counsellor or other support service, including the maintenance of confidentiality.

♦ Allow employee to raise issues of sexual harassment at workers meeting and in other appropriate forum.

♦ Create awareness of the rights of female employees in this regard.

In *Delhi Domestic Working Women's Forum v. Union of India* (1995, 1 SCC 14), the Supreme Court suggested the broad parameters in assisting the victims of rape. The court laid down that Compensation for victims shall be awarded by the court on conviction of the offender and by the Criminal Injuries Compensation Board whether or not a conviction has taken place. The Board will take into account pain, suffering and shock as well as loss of earnings due to pregnancy and the expenses of child birth if this occurred as a result of the rape.

In *Apparel Export Promotion Council v. A. K. Chopra (AIR 1999 SC 625)*, the Supreme Court opined that the contents of the fundamental rights guaranteed in our Constitution are of sufficient amplitude to encompass all facets of gender equality, including prevention of sexual harassment and abuse and the courts are under a constitutional obligation to protect and preserve those fundamental rights. That sexual harassment of a female at the place of work is incompatible with the dignity and honour of a female and needs to be eliminated and that there can be no compromise with such violations admits of no debate. Further court observed that international instruments on elimination of violence against women casts an obligation on the Indian State to gender sensitise its laws and the Courts are under an obligation to see that the message of the international instruments is not allowed to be drowned.

In *Municipal Corporation of Delhi v. Female Workers (AIR 2000 SC 1274, 1281)*, the Supreme Court held that a just social order could be achieved only when inequalities are obliterated and women, which constitute almost half of the segment of our society, are honoured and treated with dignity.

Protection of Women from Domestic Violence Act, 2005 (PWDVA)- The Act was passed in 2005 with the objective of providing for more effective protection of the rights of women guaranteed under the Constitution who are victims of violence of any kind occurring within the family and for matters connected therewith or incidental thereto. Prior to this act, there was no statutory law to deal specifically with the domestic violence that occurs in the private sphere and the criminal law remedy was available for cruelty against women and there was no comprehensive law providing civil remedies like monetary relief or compensation, cruelty do however form the ground of divorce. The international instruments and legal standards, as discussed above have played important role in protection of women from violence and gender discrimination. The judiciary has also emphasised that while discussing constitutional requirements, court and counsel must never forget the core principle embodied in the International Conventions and Instruments and as far as possible give effect to the principles contained in those international instruments.

Domestic violence as defined under the act (sec 3) - the section states that:

Any act, omission or commission or conduct of the respondent shall constitute domestic violence in case it...

i. harms or injures or endangers the health, safety, life, limb or well-being, whether mental or physical, of the aggrieved person or tends to do so and includes causing physical abuse, sexual abuse, verbal and emotional abuse and economic abuse; or

ii. harasses, harms, injures or endangers the aggrieved person with a view to coerce her or any other person related to her to meet any unlawful demand for any dowry or other property or

iii. has the effect of threatening the aggrieved person or any person related to her by any conduct mentioned in clause (a) or clause (b); Or

iv. Otherwise injures or causes harm, whether physical or mental, to the aggrieved person.

The salient features of PWDVA are as follows:

♦ It is a civil law with the prime objective to provide protection, residence and custody order to aggrieved person, monetary relief and compensation as well as support to the woman (medical facilities; shelter home). The Magistrate can also pass such interim order as he deems just and proper.

♦ An "aggrieved person" *i.e.,* any woman who is, or has been, in a domestic relationship with the respondent and who alleges to have been subjected to any act of domestic violence by the respondent can claim relief under the act.

♦ An aggrieved wife or female living in a relationship in the nature of a marriage can also file a complaint against a relative of the husband or the male partner.

♦ The term 'domestic relationships' has been defined as relationship between two persons who live or have, at any point of time, lived together in a shared household, when they are related by consanguinity, marriage, or through a relationship in the nature of marriage, adoption or are family members living together as a joint family. Thus it broadly includes wives, mothers, sisters, daughters, and live-in-partners.

♦ A police officer, Protection Officer, service provider or Magistrate who has received a complaint of domestic violence is under duty to inform the aggrieved person:

(i) of her right to make an application for obtaining a relief by way of a protection order, an order for monetary relief, a custody order, a residence order, a compensation order or more than one such order under this Act;

ii. of the availability of services of service providers;

iii. of the availability of services of the Protection Officers;

iv. of her right to free legal services under the Legal Services Authorities Act, 1987 (39 of 1987);

v. of her right to file a complaint under section 498A of the Indian Penal Code (45 of 1860), wherever relevant.

♦ Every woman in a domestic relationship have the right to reside in the shared household, whether or not she has any right, title or beneficial interest in the same and shall not be evicted or excluded from the shared household or any part of it by the respondent save in accordance with the procedure established by law.

♦ "Shared household" means a household where the person aggrieved lives or at any stage has lived in a domestic relationship either singly or along with the respondent and includes such a household whether owned or tenanted either jointly by the aggrieved person and the respondent, or owned or tenanted by either of them in respect of which either the aggrieved person or the respondent or both jointly or singly have any right, title, interest or equity and includes such a household which may belong to the joint family of which the respondent is a member, irrespective of whether the respondent or the aggrieved person has any right, title or interest in the shared household.

♦ An aggrieved person or a Protection Officer or any other person on behalf of the aggrieved person may present an application to the Magistrate seeking one or more reliefs under this Act, provided that before passing any order on such application, the Magistrate shall take into consideration any domestic incident report received by him from the Protection Officer or the service provider.

♦ The Magistrate may, at any stage of the proceedings under this Act, direct the respondent or the aggrieved person, either singly or jointly, to undergo counselling with any member of a service provider who possesses such qualifications and experience in counselling as may be prescribed. The Magistrate may also secure assistance of welfare expert as he thinks fit.

♦ Any relief available under the act may be sought for in addition to and along with any other relief that the aggrieved person may seek in any legal proceeding, before a civil court, family court or a criminal court.The relief of a woman under Domestic Violence Act, which is civil in nature, does not stop her from filing a suit under section 498A Indian Penal Code, which is criminal in nature, for cruelty committed within private sphere. Section 498A is both non-bailable and non-compoundable. If any request of compounding the offence under section 498A is brought before the Learned Court, then the judge or magistrate is supposed to decide in the context of compounding.

Concept of Property

The term property means anything owned by a person or entity and includes both movable and immovable property. Corporeal property is the person's right of ownership in a material objects (land, chattels) and incorporeal property is any other proprietary right in leases, securities, and patents, copyright. In *I.C. Golaknath & Ors v. State of Punjab & Anrs* 1967 AIR 1643, 1967 SCR (2) 762, court quoting Noyes (The Institution of Property (1936) p. 436. L3Sup CI/67-11) defined property as " any protected right or bundle of rights (interest or thing) with direct, or indirect regard to any external object (*i.e.,* other than the person himself) which is material or quasi material (*i.e.,* a protected, process) and which the then and there Organisation of Society permits to be either private or public, which is connoted by the legal concepts of occupying, possessing or, using".

In family law, property is of two types : joint family property and separate or self-acquired property. Joint property is one in which two or more persons have joint right, title or interest in a particular property. Under Hindu Mitakshara law joint family property is described as coparcenary property, it may be acquired from three sources:

ancestral property; Acquisition of property with the aid of joint family property by members of the joint family and abandonment of separate claim over any property by member of joint family. Ancestral property refers to any property acquired by the Hindu great grandfather, which then passes undivided down the next three generations up to the present generation of great grandson/ daughter. The joint family property devolves by survivorship and not by succession. Every coparcener has joint interest and joint possession. On the other hand separate property is acquired by many ways like: purchased by an individual from his resources; Small gift made by father out of ancestral movable property; Share on partition; Property held by sole surviving coparcener; Property acquired as gains of special science or learning with the aid of joint family property (see Hindu gains of learning act 1930). The property acquired by gift or will from any person is not ancestral property (see *C. N. Arunachala Mudaliar v. C. A. Muruganatha Mudaliar* 1953 AIR 495). The person is the sole owner of his/her separate property and nobody exercises any right on the same during his lifetime. A person can make a will only of his/her separate property.

Property acquired by female Hindu- Section 14(1) of Hindu succession act provides that any property possessed by a female Hindu, shall be held by her as full owner thereof and not as a limited owner. The "property" includes both movable and immovable property acquired by a female Hindu by inheritance or devise, or at a partition, or in lieu of arrears of maintenance, or by gift from any person, whether a relative or note, before, at or after her marriage, or by her own skill or exertion, or by purchase or by prescription, or in any other manner whatsoever, and also any such property held by her as stridhana. But this did not apply to gift, will or other instrument or the decree, order of a civil court or award which prescribes a restricted estate in such property.

Rights of deceased with regard to the property can be inheritable rights or not inheritable rights. The proprietary rights *i.e.,* rights attached to property like debts are inheritable and remains functional even after the death of the person to whom it belongs and devolves on his legal representatives. The personal rights associated with the deceased are not inheritable and extinguish on his/her death.

Inheritances and Succession

There are two ways of devolution of property *i.e., intestate succession* and *testamentary succession.*

Inheritance is one of the means of acquisition of property. In Intestate Succession, the property devolves according to the law or custom by which the deceased is governed. In testamentary succession, the law empowers a person, to dispose of any property, which is capable of being disposed of by him, by will or other testamentary disposition.

Testamentary succession–The rules relating to testamentary succession among Hindus, Parsis and Christians are contained in the Indian Succession Act, 1925. 'Will' means the legal declaration of the intention of a testator with respect to his property which he desires to be carried into effect after his death. The person making will is called *testator*. A will or any part of a will, the making of which has been caused by fraud or coercion or by such importunity as takes away the free agency of the testator, is void. A will is liable to be revoked or altered by the maker of it at any time when he is competent to dispose of his property by will. Section 59 of Indian Succession Act provides that every person of sound mind not being a minor may dispose of his property by will. Explanation 1 to the section states that a married woman may dispose by will of any property which she could alienate by her own act during her life. Explanation 2 states, persons who are deaf or dumb or blind are not there by incapacitated for making a will if they are able to know what they do by it. Explanation 3 provides that a person who is ordinarily insane may make a will during interval in which he is of sound mind. Explanation 4-No person can make a will while he is in such a state of mind, whether arising from intoxication or from illness or from any other cause that he does not know what he is doing.

Illustrations:

A executes an instrument purporting to be his will, but he does not understand the nature of the instrument, nor the effect of its provisions. This instrument is not a valid will.

A, being very feeble and debilitated, but capable of exercising a judgment as to the proper mode of disposing of his property, makes a will. This is a valid will

---

To execute will (unprivileged), (a) the testator shall sign or shall affix his mark to the will, or it shall be signed by some other person in his presence and by his direction. (b) The signature or mark of the testator, or the signature of the person signing for him, shall be so placed that it shall appear that it was intended thereby to give effect to the writing as a will. (c) The will shall be attested by two or more witnesses, each of whom has seen the testator sign or affix his mark to the will or has seen some other person sign the will, in the presence and by direction of the testator, or has received from the testator a personal acknowledgment of his signature or mark, or of the signature of such other person; and each of the witnesses shall sign the will in the presence of the testator, but it shall not be necessary that more than one witness be present at the same time, and no particular form of attestation shall be necessary.

"Executor" is a person to whom the execution of the last will of a deceased person is, by the testator's appointment, confided. When there is no executor, an administrator is appointed by competent authority to administer the estate of a deceased person. It is important to note that in case of wills made by any Hindu, Buddhist, Sikh or Jain and Parsi dying, after the commencement of the Indian Succession (Amendment) Act, 1962, no right as executor or legatee can be established in any Court of Justice, unless a court of competent jurisdiction in India has granted probate of the will under which the right is claimed, or has granted letters of administration with the will or with a copy of an authenticated copy of the will annexed. "Probate" means the copy of a will certified under the seal of a Court of competent jurisdiction with a grant of administration to the estate of the testator.

In Muslim law, a person disposes off only one third of his property, which is left after the payment of his funeral expenses and his debts by making a will; This is to ensure that lawful heirs are not deprived of their just claims. Any property which is capable of being transferred and which exists at the time of the testator's death, may be disposed off by a will. Every Mohammedan of sound mind and not a minor may dispose of his property by making a valid will. In *Mahomed Altaf All Khan v. Ahmed Burksh* (1876) 25 W.R. 121, it was held that in the Muhammadan Law, no writing is required to make a will valid and no particular form even of verbal declaration is necessary as long as the intention of the testator is sufficiently ascertained. In *Mazhar Husain v. Bodha Bibi* (1898) L.R. 25 I.A. 219 : I.L.R. 21 All. 91 (P.C.), the Privy Council held that a letter operated as a will. An executor under Muslim law is called *wasi*, derived from the term "wasiyyat", meaning a will. A bequest can be revoked either expressly or by implication.

Types of heirs		
Ascendants	**Descendants**	**Collaterals**
Means the ancestors of a person both on the paternal and maternal side.	are the offspring of a person.	are descendants in parallel lines, from a common ancestor or ancestress.
includes father and mother paternal grandfather and paternal grandmother, maternal grandfather and maternal grandmother and their parents.	includes sons and daughter, grandson and granddaughter, great grandson and great granddaughter and so on.	brother, sister; paternal and maternal uncles and aunts and their children how low so ever.
no limit to degree of ascent.	no limit to degree of *descent*.	

Intestate succession–A person who dies without making a will is known as intestate and the persons who are entitled to inherit property after death of intestate are called the heirs. If a Hindu dies intestate *i.e.*, without making a will, then, both separate property as well as joint family property passes on to his heirs in accordance with the Hindu Succession Act, 1956 (the daughter are also coparcener in the property by an amendment in 2005 in the Hindu Succession Act, 1956). The Indian Succession Act, 1925, governs intestate succession of Christians and Parsis.

The Sections 8 to 13 **of the Hindu Succession Act** deal with succession to the property of a Hindu male. **The succession to the property of male Hindu occurs in order (priority) as given below:**

1. **Class I** heirs are preffered and simultaneous heirs-mother, widow, son, daughter, widow of predeceased son and their descendants upto the third generation.

2. **Class II** heirs inherit property only in absence of Class I heirs and include father, brother as well as sister and their children, maternal and paternal uncles and aunts, maternal and paternal grandfather and grandmother etc.

3. **Agnates** - When a person traces his relationship with another related by blood or adoption wholly through males, they are called agnates. The agnates can be descendants, ascendants or collateral. Example: brother, brother's son, son's son, son's son's son.

4. **Cognates** -Whenever in the relationship of a person (blood or adoption) with another, a female intervenes anywhere in line, one is a cognate to another. The cognates can be descendants, ascendants or collateral. Example: sister's son and daughter, daughters' son and daughter.

Here reference to brother or sister does not include reference to brother or sister by utrine blood. In absence of qualified heirs to succeed to property in accordance with the law applicable, property devolves on the government with all the obligations and liabilities to which an heir would have been subject.

Relation by full blood, half blood and uterine blood–The heirs can relate to each other by full blood, half blood or uterine blood. Two persons are related to each other by full blood when they have same father and same mother. When two persons have same father but different mothers, they are related to each other by half blood. Two persons are related to each other by uterine blood, when they have same mother but different fathers

As a general rule the Heirs related to an intestate by full blood shall be preferred to heirs related by half blood, if the nature of the relationship is the same in every other respect. If two or more heirs succeed together to the property of an intestate, they shall take the property (a) per capita (per head) and not per stripes, and (b) as tenants-in common and not as joint tenants. A child who was in the womb at the time of the death of an intestate and who is subsequently born alive have the same right to inherit to the intestate as if he or she had been born before the death of the intestate, and the inheritance shall be deemed to vest in such a case with effect from the date of the death of the intestate. Intestate succession to property of female Hindu is not same as male Hindu and has been dealt in section 15 of Hindu Succession Act, 1956 and has been dealt earlier in this chapter under the heading right of inheritance.

Section 14 : Property of a female Hindu to be her absolute property

In traditional Hindu law, a female Hindu's property were of two kinds; stridhana and women's estate. This Section of the Hindu Succession Act has abolished the division of property belonging to a woman into these two categories. It has converted a woman's estate and stridhana into her full estate. This Section is the continuation of the main object of this Act, namely to grant better rights to women.

Sections 15 and 16

The Act deal with the general rules of succession to the property of a Hindu female dying intestate and the order of succession. It is interesting to note that although there is no such thing as stridhana and woman's estate after the coming into force of this Act, the source of acquisition of a female Hindu's property is still important, as the order of heirs depends upon the source of the property of a Hindu female.

Section 21 : Presumption in case of simultaneous deaths

There may be case when two persons die in an accident or calamity under such circumstances that it is not possible to ascertain which of them died first. In such a situation, presumed the case that both of them died simultaneously or that one of them succeeded the other. There may be controversy regarding success in to the property in such situations becasue of uncertainty as to which survived the other.

Before the enactment of this Section, there was no answer to such questions. The burden of proof was on the party who asserted the affirmative. However this section provides that where two persons died in circumstances rendering it uncertain. Whether either of them and if so which, survived the other, then, for all purposes affecting succession to property, it shall be presumed that younger survived the elder until the contrary is proved.

Rules of intestate succession relating to Christians and Parsis–

they are governed by the Indian Succession Act, 1925. As referred earlier in this chapter, Indian succession act, 1925 recognises three types of heirs; the spouse, the lineal descendants, and the kindred.

Among Christians, the first preference is given to the spouse of the deceased and his lineal descendants and when there are no lineal descendants then property passes onto the spouse of the deceased and those who are kindred. In case there are no lineal descendants or one who is kindred to him, the entire property goes to his or her spouse. In the absence of such spouse, property passes on to lineal descendants or to those who are kindred to him.

Lineal consanguinity - (1) Lineal consanguinity is that which subsists between two persons, one of whom is descended in a direct line from the other, as between a man and his father, grandfather and great-grandfather, and so upwards in the direct ascending line; or between a man and his son, grandson, great-grandson and so downwards in the direct descending line.

(2) Every generation constitutes a degree, either ascending or descending.

(3) A person's father is related to him in the first degree, and so likewise is his son; his grandfather and grandson in the second degree; his great-grandfather and great-grandson in the third degree, and so on.

Kindred or consanguinity-Kindred or consanguinity is the connection or relation of persons descended from the same stock or common ancestor.

In absence of spouse,lineal descendants or kindred to him, property will go to government.

The division of intestate's property among widow, widower, children and Parents in Parsis is dealt in section 51 of the Indian succession Act. The division of share of intestate's property among widow, widower and children has been already studied while dealing with inheritance rights of spouses. The division of shares differs, where a Parsi dies leaving one or both parents in addition to children or widow or widower and children. In such case, the property of which such Parsi dies intestate shall be so divided that the parent or each of the parents shall receive a share equal to half the share of each child.

Rules of intestate succession among Muslims:

There is no codified law for of succession in Muslims and has to be derived from the rules of succession to be found in quran or in traditions as well as pre-Islamic customs as approved by prophet governed by their religious texts. Among Sunnis, heirs are divided into three categories *i.e.*, sharers (Quranic heirs get fixed share of estate of deceased), residuaries (male agnates-descendants, ascendants and collaterals and only four females who are converted from sharer to residuaries), and distant kindred (uterine heirs, covers all other blood relations). Sharers are the most preferred heirs and are allotted their respective shares. The residue if any is then divided to residuaries. In case there are no sharers, the residuaries will succeed to whole inheritance. If there are neither sharers nor residuaries, the inheritance will be divided among such of the distant kindred as are entitled to succeed. The distant kindred are not entitled to succeed so long as there is any heir belonging to the class of sharers or residuaries. But when there is only one sharer *i.e.,* the wife or husband of the deceased and no other sharer or residuary exist, in this case, distant kindred will inherit with the sharer. Here widow will take- share and distant kindred will take- share, if shares is husband of deceased, he will share 1/2 and distant kindred will take other half.

> ### Sharers under Sunni law- twelve
> Male sharers–Husband, father, true grandfather how high so ever and uterine brother.
> (In case, son of deceased is there, then father becomes residuary).
> Female sharers–wife, mother, true grandmother how high so ever, daughter, son's daughter how low so ever, uterine sister, full sister, consanguine sister.

Among Shias, heirs are divided into two categories *i.e.,* (1) heirs by consanguinity-blood relations (Nasab) and (2) heirs by special cause (sabab) which includes heirs by marriage *i.e.,* husband and wife and heirs by special relationship (wala). Heirs by consanguinity are further sub-divided into three classes. Class I includes parents, children and other lineal descendants.Class II includes grandparents, brothers and sisters and their descendants how low so ever. Class III includes paternal and maternal uncles and aunts of the deceased, and of his parents, grandparents how high so ever and their descendants how low so ever. The class I excludes the second and the second class excludes the third but the heirs within class inherit together. The claimants in both the categories *i.e.,* heirs by consanguinity and heirs by marriage succeed together, if there are heirs of both the categories. To determine share, the heirs are divided in two classes sharers and residuaries. There is no class of distant kindred.

> ### Sharers under Shia law- nine
> Husband, wife, father, mother, daughter, uterine brother, uterine sister, full sister, consanguine sister.

LET US SUM UP

⇨ The term family has been derived from Latin word 'familia'. It is as a major social institution, a group of persons created by consanguinity (by birth), by affinity (marriage), or adoption. A family can be Nuclear- conjugal family; Matrifocal and Joint or the extended families.

⇨ In India Separate personal laws govern Hindus, Muslims, Christians and followers of other religions. The Hindu law is applicable to Hindus, Sikhs, Jains , Buddhists and to any other person who is not a Muslim, Christian, Parsi or Jew by religion.

⇨ The Parsis and Christians have codified law but the law of marriage and divorce of Jews and Muslims are not codified in India and they are governed by their religious laws.

⇨ The Mitakshara and Dayabhaga are the two major schools of Hindu personal laws that have been followed in medieval India. The major difference between two schools was related to inheritance. Under Mitakshara School, the ownership of property starts from the birth and the sons have equal rights along with the father in the ancestral property even during the life time of the father. It provides for inheritance through survivorship where living males can inherit property. On the other hand Dayabagha School provides for inheritance by the way of succession where the heirs of deceased can inherit property.

⇨ The Muslims follows their personal laws called Muslim Law or Mohammedan Law based on Quran (divine law), Sunna (hadith), Sahabah, Ijmaand Qiyas. The two major denominations of Islam are Sunni and Shia's. Both of them though share common religious beliefs but differ on interpretation of Hadith and sharia law. In India the majority of Muslims are Sunni's.

⇨ In the Mughal Era, the Hindus and Muslims were largely governed by their own personal laws and customs. In the beginning of British period also personal laws of the communities were followed. The courts in British era had relied on the translated texts on digests and manuals and gradually the precedents were developed and followed by the courts and judges, the whole court system was rationalized abolishing the native law officers (pandits and kazis) attached to the courts. The family laws pertaining to various religious communities: Hindus Christians, Parsis were also codified by legislation during British period.

⇨ The Constitution of India provides for freedom of conscience and the right to profess practice and propagate religion to all persons and freedom to manage religious affairs and lays down for justice, liberty, equality, and fraternity assuring the dignity to all. But the Part III of the Constitution (fundamental rights) does not touch upon the personal laws of the parties as held in *Krishna Singh vs Mathura Ahir* (1980 AIR 707). However the attempts have been made by government to have secular family law in India such as the Section 125 of the Criminal Procedure Code; Child Marriage Restraint Act, 1929; Dowry Prohibition Act, 1961; Special Marriage Act, 1974; The Immoral Traffic (Prevention) Act 1986, the Indecent Representation of Women (Prohibition) Act 1986, the Commission of Sati Act 1987; the Medical Termination of Pregnancy Act, 1971, the Prenatal Diagnostic Techniques (Regulation and Prevention of Misuse) Act 2002; the Maternity Benefit Act, 1961 and the Protection of Women from Domestic Violence Act 2005.

➪ In Hindu laws some reforms have been introduced by codification of Hindu Marriage Act (1955), Hindu succession Act (1956), Hindu Minority and Guardianship Act (1956), and Hindu Adoptions and Maintenance Act (1956) and also through various amendments introduced from time to time. The reforms have been also introduced in other laws governing Christians and Parsis through other legislations like Indian Divorce (Amendment Act) 2001; Indian Succession Amendment Act 2002; Marriage Laws (Amendment) Act 2001; The Indian Divorce act 1869 (as amended by acts 49 and 51 of 2001). The Muslim Women (Protection of Rights & Divorce) Act, 1986 was passed to provide Muslim women right to Divorce on certain grounds but comparatively, the Muslim Personal Law has not been reformed much and by and large has remained unchanged.

➪ The Family Courts Act 1984 was enacted to establish the family courts (subordinate to the High Court) as special courts due to pressure from various Women's associations, welfare organisations and individuals to provide a forum that can resolve family disputes without resorting to adversarial system of trial with the aim to promote conciliation and secure speedy settlement of disputes relating to marriage and family affairs.

➪ The Rajasthan and Karnataka were the first two states to set up family courts. The act was implemented in Delhi only in 2009 with presently six family courts in function. The Family courts deals with the following suits and proceedings between the parties to a marriage :

   i. For decree of nullity of marriage, restitution of conjugal rights, judicial separation or dissolution of marriage.

   ii. For a declaration as to the validity of a marriage or as to the matrimonial status of any person.

   iii. With respect to the property of the parties or of either of them.

   iv. For an order or injunction in circumstances arising out of a martial relationship;

   v. For a declaration as to the legitimacy of any person.

   vi. For maintenance.

   vii. In relation to the guardianship of the person or the custody of, or access to, any minor.

➪ The role of the lawyers has been limited to legal experts or 'amicus curiae' with the aim to encourage conciliation and prevent corruption, manipulation, long and bitter court litigation and excessive litigation costs and the party before a Family Court is not entitled as of right to be represented by a legal practitioner as opposed to the practice of the other courts in an adversarial system of adjudication.

➪ However there is need to remove existing disparity in practice followed by different states in relation to appointment of the counselors, their role, qualifications and remuneration; to clearly define the role and task of counselors and to train them with gender-sensitivity, as essential for fair and just reconciliation and settlement processes.

➪ Marriage is a social institution and a legal union. It provides the status of husband and wife to the couples; confer legitimacy on children born after marriage; create rights to maintenance and inheritance of property on husband, wife and children. If either spouse deserts or withdraws from the society of the other spouse without any reasonable cause, the aggrieved party can approach court for the relief of restitution of conjugal rights. The marriage is dissolved either by the death of either of the spouse or either by divorce through court which results in termina-tion of a marital union and status of being husband and wife, and ceases the right of inheritance and cohabitation of spouses.

➪ Marriages are solemnised in every religion by performance of certain ceremonies which may differ from religion to religion and are considered valid subject to certain conditions required to be fulfilled by the parties to the marriage. The Hindu, Christian and Parsis law all recognises the monogamy form of marriage, the age for marriage is 21 years for the bridegroom and 18 years for the bride, parties should not be within the degrees of prohibited relationship and are of sound mind and capable of giving valid consent. Muslim law recognises polygamy and for a valid marriage, both the parties to marriage should be of sound mind and had obtained puberty (generally presumption is 15 years but it can be earlier), marriage (nikah) is solemnised generally with recitation of certain verses from Quran but no religious ceremony is essential.

⇨ In general there are two bars or impediments to marriage, absolute or relative. If absolute bar exists, Marriage is void or void ab initio *i.e.*, does not exist from the very beginning (null) and when relative bar exists, a marriage is voidable *i.e.*, the marriage is perfectly a valid marriage unless avoided. The sunni sect under Muslim law classifies marriage into three categories valid (sahih); void (batil) and irregular/fasid (which is capable of becoming valid marriage by remedying the prohibition). But the Shia sect do not recognise the distinction between irregular and void marriage and the marriage which are irregular under sunni are void under shia law. The Parsi and Christian law does not recognise any distinction between void and voidable marriages and the statutory law provides only some grounds where marriage may be declared as null and void or dissolved.

⇨ Marriage imposes certain marital rights and obligations on both the spouses like right of Husband and wife to society and comfort of each other called conjugal rights, rights of maintenance and inheritance, right on matrimonial property, custody and guardianship of children.

⇨ Conjugal right includes enjoyment of association or alliance, sympathy, confidence and an emotional and physical intimate relationship between spouses. Section 9 of Hindu Marriage Act, Section 22 of the Special Marriage Act, 1954; Section 32 of the Indian Divorce Act, 1869 (Christians); Section 36 of the Parsi Marriage and Divorce Act, 1936 respectively provides decree for restitution of conjugal rights to the aggrieved party.

⇨ The marriage confers on husband an obligation to provide wife means of support or livelihood out of his earnings and even the divorced women have right to maintenance under section 125 of the Code of Criminal Procedure code, a secular law.The special marriage act and the statutory law governing Hindu, Christian and Parsis provides for alimony-pendent lite and permanent alimony and maintenance rights to both spouses.

The Hindu wife has also the right to claim maintenance under Hindu Adoptions and Maintenance Act (HA & MA) which is independent of the right to maintenance by both the Hindu spouses under section 24 of HMA.

⇨ Any property or gifts (stridhan) given to wife by her parents and in-laws and by relatives and friends, is the absolute property of women under Hindu law.

⇨ The Muslim Women (Protection of Rights on Divorce) Act, 1986 lays down under that Mahr or other properties of Muslim woman is to be given to her at the time of divorce, however a Muslim woman is not entitled to dower if separation takes place without consummation of marriage. The act also provides that reasonable and fair provision and maintenance is to be made and paid to Muslim divorced women within *the iddat* period by her former husband. In case where a Magistrate is satisfied that a divorced woman has not re- married and is not able to maintain herself after the iddat period, he may make an order directing such of her relatives as would be entitled to inherit her property on her death according to Muslim law to pay such reasonable and fair maintenance to her as he may determine fit and proper and in case she has no relatives as mentioned or such relatives or any one of them have not enough means to pay the maintenance, court can order state Waqf Board to pay maintenance.

⇨ There are different laws of succession governing persons belonging to different religions. The rules relating to devolution of property of a Hindu male or female intestate *i.e.*, dying without making a will is prescribed in the Hindu Succession Act, 1956. Under the Act, both husband and wife are included in the category of class I heirs (who are entitled to inherit property after the death of intestate) and are also called preferential heirs and simultaneous heirs but for the purpose of succession the property of Hindu female, source of the property matters. In case a female dying intestate has obtained property: by inheritance or any other sources, property will firstly devolves on husband as simultaneous heir [Section 15 (1)].

⇨ Inherited any property from her father or mother, it shall devolve to son, daughter, son and daughter of predeceased son or daughter. In this category husband is not included. In absence of such heirs, the property will devolve on heirs of father [Section15 (2) (a)].

- Inherited any property from her husband or from her father-in-law shall devolve, in the absence of any son or daughter of the deceased (including the children of any pre-deceased son or daughter) upon the heirs of the husband [Section 15 (2) (b)].

- The Christians and Parsi's are governed by Indian succession act, 1925 that recognises three types of heirs; the spouse, the lineal descendants, and the kindred. in case of Christians, where intestate has left a widow and (a) any lineal descendants- widow will get 1/3 of his property and the remaining 2/3 shall go to his lineal descendants; (b) has no lineal descendant, but has left persons who are of kindred to him- widow will get 1/2 of his property and the other half goes to those who are kindred to him; (c) none who are of kindred to him, the whole of his property shall belong to his widow.A husband surviving his wife has the same rights in respect of her property, if she dies intestate, as a widow has in respect of her husband's property, if he dies intestate.

- The property of which a Parsi dies intestate shall be divided in the case - (a) where such Parsi dies leaving a widow or widower and children- all have equal shares; (b) where such Parsi dies leaving children, but no widow or widower- among the children in equal shares.

- Muslim law, do not recognise distinction between ancestral or self acquired property and the right of an heir comes in to existence on death of ancestor. The primary heirs under muslin law are Father, mother, son, daughter, Husband and wife. On the death of wife, the share of husband is 1/4 of the property when there is a child or son's child, how low so ever; but he takes when there is no child or son's. In case of the death of the husband, the share of the wife is 1/8 when there is a child or son's child, how low so ever ; but when there are no such children, then her share becomes 1/4. The Muslim cannot dispose off more than 1/3 of his property by a will.

- The law relating to custody and guardianship in Hindus is governed by Hindu Marriage Act *1956* and the Hindu Minority and Guardianship Act 1956 (HM&GA*);* Indian Majority Act, 1875 and Guardians and Wards Act, 1890. the father, and after him, the mother is the natural guardian of a Hindu minor boy or an unmarried girl, though the custody of a child up to the age of five years ordinarily lies with the mother;in case of an illegitimate boy or an illegitimate unmarried girl, the mother, and after her, the father is the natural guardian;Husband is the guardian in the case of a married girl. The guardian can be testamentary and can also be appointed by court.The Muslims, do not have codified law for custody and guardianship. The father is recognised as the sole guardian of the person and property of the minor children (legitimate) and mother is not recognized as a guardian, natural or otherwise, even after the death of the father.

- A marriage is dissolved either by the death of either of the spouse or either by divorce through court and results in termination of a marital union and status of being Husband and wife, it ceases right of inheritance and cohabitation. The Hindu Marriage Act, 1955, governs divorce among Hindus. The Parsi Marriage and Divorce Act, 1936 governs the divorce among Parsis. The Indian Divorce Act, 1869, governs divorce among Christians and provides for grounds of divorce based on fault/guilty grounds *viz*; adultery, cruelty, bigamy, desertion, conversion etc and also recognises divorce by mutual consent. Muslims, do not have a codified law for marriage and divorce and are governed by their religious texts but the dissolution of Muslim marriage act, 1939 lays down grounds under which women can obtain decree of dissolution of marriage.

- Under the Hindu, Mohammedan, Christian & Parsi Laws and the Juvenile Justice (Care & Protection of children) Act 2000, the age of majority is 18 years for both boys and girls. The Indian Majority Act, 1875, defines a minor as a person who is below 18 years of age and in case where a minor is under superintendence of the Courts of Wards, the age of majority is 21 years.

- The Convention on the Rights of the Child 1989 as ratified by India provides for welfare of children incorporating the full range of human rights for civil, economic, social, cultural, and political rights to children. The core principles of this convention are non-discrimination; devotion to the best interests of the child; right to life, survival and development and respect for the views of the child. The right to health and care; the right to protection from abuse, neglect, exploitation (sexual, at work); right to education; right to expression and information and right to shelter and nutrition are the basic rights of children.

- The protection, development and welfare of children have always been the focus area of the government. The Applied Nutrition Programme (ANP) was introduced in Orissa in 1963 and was later extended to Tamil Nadu and Uttar Pradesh with the objectives of promoting production of protective food such as vegetables and fruits and to ensure their consumption by pregnant and nursing mothers and children. Balwadi Nutrition Programme (BNP) was introduced in 1970-71 for providing supple-mentary food to children. The National Policy for children was adopted in 1974 with a view to provide adequate services to children, both before and after birth and through the period of growth to ensure their full physical, mental and social development. The government in 2007 to 2012 targeted to implement a nation-wide mid-day meals scheme in schools and improving the implementation of the Integrated Child Development Scheme(ICDS) launched in 1975.

⇨ The Preamble, article 21 and articles 38 and 39, 42,45 and 47 of the Constitution provides for right to health. Article 21 further deals with protection of life and personal liberty and article 23 of the constitution provides for Prohibition of traffic in human beings and other similar forms of forced labour. The *Immoral Traffic (Prevention) Act 1956* abolishes the Commercial Sexual Exploitation and trafficking in women and girls for prostitution as means of living. Section 370 and 370A of Indian penal code as amended by Criminal Law (Amendment) Act, 2013 deals with trafficking of person and exploitation of trafficked person. Trafficking of minor has been made cognizable and non bailable offence punishable with impri-sonment not less than 10 years extendable to life imprisonment with fine. The Protection of Children from Sexual Offences Act, 2012, provi-des for protection of child from sexual assault, sexual harassment and pornography and provi-des for the establishment of Special Courts for trial of offences.

⇨ Article 24 of the constitution prohibits employ-ment of children below 14 years of age in facto-ries, mines or other hazardous employment. The Directive Principles of State Policy as enshrined in constitution in article 39(e) and article 39 (f) provides that children of tender age should not be abused and be given opportunities and facilities to develop in a healthy manner in conditions of freedom and dignity. The Child Labour (Prohi-bition and Regulation) Act, 1986 prohibits emp-loyment of a child below 14 years of age in several kinds of industries, hazardous and non-hazardous,the children cannot be employed as domestic workers or servants in Dhaba's (road-side eateries), restaurants, hotels, tea shops or other recreational centres.

⇨ The Child Marriage stunts the growth and development, particularly of the girl child making them vulnerable to domestic violence and sexual abuse. The Prohibition of Child Marriage Act, 2006 provides for prohibition of solemnisation of child marriages and for matters connected therewith or incidental thereto and has changed the position in regard to child marriage in India by making such child marriage voidable.

⇨ The education and information plays an impor-tant role in the development of children and determines their social participation and identity. The right to information means seeking informa-tion of facts or knowledge and also includes expression, ideals and emotions and is the part of the right to freedom of speech and expression guaranteed by Article 19(1) (a) of the constitution of India. Article 45 of the Directive Principles of State Policy provides for free and compulsory education for all children until they complete the age of 6 years. Article 46 provides that state shall promote with special care the educational and economic interests of the weaker sections of the people, and, in particular, of the Scheduled Castes and the Scheduled Tribes. The Constitution (*Eighty-sixth Amendment*) Act, 2002 inserted Article 21-A in the Constitution of India makes it fundamental right of all children of the age of 6-14 years in such manner as the State may, by law, determine. Consequently the Right of Children to free and Compulsory Education (RTE) Act, 2009 was passed. The right to residence and settlement is also a fundamental right under Article 19(1)(e) and it is a facet of inseparable meaningful right to life under Article 21.

⇨ The Juvenile Justice (care and protection of children) act, 2000 deals with juveniles in conflict with law and children in need of care and pro-tection aiming at rehabilitation through establish-ment of various kinds of Institutions like Children's Home for the child in need of care and protection, Special Homes for the child in conflict with law, Observation Homes for the temporary reception of children during the pendency of any inquiry and After-care Organizations for the purpose of taking care of children discharged from Children's Home or Special Homes.

⇨ Adoption is the personal law issue and the adoption in Hindu's is governed by Hindu Adoption and Maintenance Act, 1956 and any adoption made in contravention of the provisions of the act is void. An adopted is deemed to be the child of his or her adoptive father or mother for all purposes with effect from the date of the adoption and from such date all the ties of the child in the family of his or her birth is deemed to be severed and replaced by those created by the adoption in the adoptive family. The Juvenile Justice (Care and Protection of Children Act, 2000) has also incorporated the provision of adoption of child as an alternative to institutional care.

⇨ Domestic violence includes any act, omission or commission or conduct of the respondent that (a) harms or injures or endangers the health, safety, life, limb or well-being, whether mental or physical, of the aggrieved person or tends to do so and includes causing physical abuse, sexual abuse, verbal and emotional abuse and economic abuse; b) harasses, harms, injures or endangers the aggrieved person with a view to coerce her or any other person related to her to meet any unlawful demand for any dowry or other property or (c) has the effect of threatening the aggrieved person or any person related to her by any conduct mentioned in clause (a) or clause (b); or (d) otherwise injures or causes harm, whether physical or mental, to the aggrieved person.

⇨ The Protection of Women from Domestic Violence Act, 2005 (PWDVA) was passed with the objective of providing more effective protection of the rights of women guaranteed under the Constitution who are victims of violence of any kind occurring within the family and for matters connected therewith or incidental thereto. Under the act wives, mothers, sisters, daughters, and live-in-partners who are in domestic relationship can file application for relief (protection, residence and custody order, monetary relief or compensation).

⇨ property is any protected right or bundle of rights (interest or thing) with direct, or indirect regard to any external object (*i.e.* other than the person himself) which is material or quasi material (*i.e.*, a protected, process) and which the then and there Organisation of Society permits to be either private or public, which is connoted by the legal concepts of occupying, possessing or, using.

⇨ Joint property is one in which two or more persons have joint right, title or interest in a particular property. The joint family property devolves by survivorship and not by succession. Every coparcener has joint interest and joint possession. Ancestral property refers to any property acquired by the Hindu great grandfather, which then passes undivided down the next three generations up to the present generation of great grandson/daughter.

⇨ A person can acquire separate property by purchase from his own resources, gift made, share on partition, property held by sole surviving coparcener, property acquired as gains of special science or learning with the aid of joint family property. The person is the sole owner of his/her separate property and nobody exercises any right on the same during his lifetime.

⇨ A person can make a will only of his/her separate property. Any property acquired by Hindu female is her absolute property.

⇨ There are two ways of devolution of property *i.e.*, *intestate succession* and *testamentary succession*. In Intestate Succession, the property devolves according to the law or custom by which the deceased is governed. In testamentary succession, the law empowers a person, to dispose of any property, which is capable of being disposed of by him, by will or other testamentary disposition.

⇨ The Hindus, Parsis and Christians making testamentary disposition or will are governed by Indian Succession Act, 1925. Mohammedan of sound mind and not a minor can dispose of 1/3 of his property by making will. 'Will' means the legal declaration of the intention of a testator with respect to his property which he desires to be carried into effect after his death. The person making will is called *testator*.

⇨ No right as executor or legatee can be established in any Court of Justice, unless a court of competent jurisdiction in India has granted probate of the will under which the right is claimed, or has granted letters of administration with the will or with a copy of an authenticated copy of the will annexed, in case of wills made by any Hindu, Buddhist, Sikh or Jain and Parsi dying, after the commencement of the Indian Succession (Amendment) Act, 1962.

⇨ Probate is the copy of a will certified under the seal of a Court of competent jurisdiction with a grant of administration to the estate of the testator.

⇨ In case Hindu dies intestate then, both separate property as well as joint family property passes on to his heirs in accordance with the Hindu Succession Act, 1956 The Indian Succession Act, 1925, governs intestate succession of Christians and Parsis. Muslims do not have rules of succession the rules of succession are derived from quran, traditions and their religious texts. Sunnis recgnises heirs into three categories *i.e.,* sharers, residuaries and distant kindred. Sharers are the most preferred heirs and are allotted their respective shares. The residue if any is then divided to residuaries. The distant kindred are not entitled to succeed so long as there is any heir belonging to the class of sharers or residuaries.

⇨ Among Shias, heirs are divided into two categories *i.e.,* (1) heirs by consanguinity- blood relations (Nasab) and (2) heirs by special cause (sabab) which includes heirs by marriage i.e. husband and wife and heirs by special relationship (wala). Heirs by consanguinity are further sub-divided into three classes: Class I, Class II and Class III. To determine share, the heirs are categorized as sharers and residuaries and there is no class of distant kindred.

Terminal Questions

Define family. Discuss the family law that govern Hindus and Muslims in the medieval India.

1. Discuss the administration and development of Hindu and Muslim personal laws in British-India.

2. "Attempt at securing secular family laws to all the diverse religious communities in India is a continuous debate". Examine with the help of case laws.

3. Write a note on the following:
   (a) Family law and Gender equality
   (b) statutory Laws governing different communities in India

4. Discuss the salient features of family courts act.

5. What Suits and proceedings/ subject-matters fall within the jurisdiction of the family courts?

6. Explain in brief:
   (a) Need for family courts
   (b) Role of counselors and gender sensitivity

7. Define marriage and describe briefly various form of marriage.

8. Differentiate between void and voidable marriage.

9. What are the conditions for valid marriage under Hindu law?

10. Enlist the ground of nullity of marriage under Parsis and Christian law.

11. Discuss absolute bars to marriage under Hindu and Muslim law.

12. Comparatively analyze the grounds of divorce available to the Hindu, Parsis and Christian, husband and wife under law in India.

13. Differentiate between joint family property and separate property.

14. Define will. Who are the persons capable of making will?

15. Explain the rules relating to intestate succession under Hindu Law.

16. Discuss the law relating to protection of women from domestic violence in India?

17. Define the following:

I. Conjugal Rights	II. Stridhan
III. Guardian	IV. Foster mother
V. Consanguinity	VI. Agnates
VII. Cognates	VIII. Kindred

●●

Project on Unit 2

PROJECT 1

M.C. MEHTA *VS* KAMAL NATH

Fact

An article was published in the Indian Express stating that a private company "Span Motels Pvt. Ltd." had built a motel on the bank of the River Beas on a land. The land was leased by the Indian Government to the respondent in 1981. Respondent's family was the owner of the above said private company. Span Motels had also encroached upon an additional area of land adjoining this leasehold area and constructed embankments around 1993 at its own expense. This adjacent area was later leased out to Span Motels when Respondent was the Minister in 1994. The motel used earthmovers and bulldozers to turn the course of the River Beas, create a new channel and divert the river's flow. The course of the river was diverted to save the motel from future floods. River Beas witnessed massive floods in 1995. The Supreme Court took notice of the news articles and asked Central Pollution Board to inspect the matter and submit the report. The Central Pollution Control Board submitted report that after the passage of 1995 flood, the respondent's company took additional steps to protect their property. The left side channel (the main channel), which had become less active, has been dredged by blasting big boulders and increasing its capacity. The mouth of the natural relief/spill channel has been blocked by construction of wire crate and dumping of boulders. The area has almost been levelled. Respondent's company has not consulted any Flood Control Expert as it appeared from the way of construction of the wire crate. No proper revetment was done while crating. Any kind of Construction to block the natural flow of water is illegal. The river was in a highly unstable regime after 1995 massive floods. No new construction and no economic activity should be allowed in this flood prone area except flood protection measures.

Issue

The foremost issue was whether respondent had any role in the private company that own Span motel. Secondly, it was important to know whether respondent's private company made construction on river banks to as flood protection measure or not. Thirdly, whether the above said property covered under public trust doctrine so that no private company can misused the natural resources and harm the ecological balance.

Conclusion

Public Trust Doctrine means certain resources like air, sea, waters and the forests have such a great importance to the people as a whole that it would be wholly unjustified to make them a subject of private ownership. The doctrine enjoins upon the government to protect the resources for the enjoyment of the general public rather than to permit use for private ownership or commercial purposes. River Beas, being a young and dynamic river, if water velocity is not sufficient to carry the boulders, those are deposited in the channel often blocking the flow of water. Under such circumstances the river stream changes its course, remaining within the valley but swinging from one bank to the other. The area being ecologically fragile and full of scenic beauty should not have been permitted to be converted into private ownership and for commercial gains. The public has a right to expect certain lands and natural areas to retain their natural characteristic. Moreover, in Vellore Citizens Welfare Forum *vs* Union of India and Indian Council for Enviro-Legal Action *vs* Union of

India, it was settled by this Court that one who pollutes the environment must pay to reverse the damage caused by his acts.

Judgment

It was held that the Respondent had interest in the above mentioned private company as many family members were member of that private company. The constructions made by Respondent's company were not to protect themselves from flood as they started constructions even before government's order. Since the Indian legal system is based on English Common Law, it includes the public trust doctrine as part of its jurisprudence. The State is the trustee of all natural resources which are by nature meant for public use and enjoyment. The Supreme Court of India decided that prior approval for the additional leasehold land, given in 1994, was quashed. The government was ordered to take over the area and restore it to its original condition.

Respondent's private company was ordered to pay compensation to restore the environment. Respondent's company was also asked to remove various constructions on the bank of the River Beas. Respondent's company was also required to show why a pollution fine in addition should not be imposed, pursuant to the polluter pays principle. In addition, the motel was prohibited from discharging untreated effluents into the river.

Probable Viva Questions

1. What do you understand by public trust doctrine?

2. Is right to clean and healthy environment a fundamental right ?

3. Explain in short the report submitted by Central Pollution Control Board ?

4. What is polluter pays principle ?

5. What was the judgment in the case of M.C Mehta *vs* Kamal Nath ?

❏❏

PROJECT 2

HUSSAINARA KHATOON & OTHERS *VS* HOME SECRETARY, STATE OF BIHAR

Fact

Habeas Corpus writ petition was filed before the Supreme Court for releasing large number of trial prisoners who were locked in the prisons of Bihar for a very long time. An alarmingly large number of men and women, including children, were behind prison bars for years awaiting trial in courts of law. The offences with which some of them were charged were trivial. That means even if proved the maximum punishment they would get was for few months, perhaps a year or two. Yet some were locked in jail for more than three years and some are locked behind the bars for almost ten years without proper trial. By depriving them fair trial, the question arose where the fundamental rights of those prisoners were deprived.

Issue

The main issue was whether the fundamental rights of the under trial prisoners were violated by keeping them in prison for long time without proper trial.

Conclusion

Fair trial and fair investigation are important human rights. Under Article 21 of Indian Constitution, fair trial and fair investigation are the fundamental rights. That means no person can be deprived of fair trial. Fair trial includes speedy trial. A person cannot be locked behind the bars on ground of absence of trial and administrative inability. Under Article 14 equality before the law and equal protection of law is also fundamental right. Article 39A also emphasises that free legal service is an inalienable element of 'reasonable, fair and just' procedure for without it a person suffering from economic or other disabilities would be deprived of the opportunity for securing justice. Thus if any person is poor and is not in position to appoint lawyers, the State should ensure that lawyers are provided to such poor person.

Judgment

The Court held that the procedure under which a person may be deprived of his life or liberty should be 'reasonable fair and just.' Free legal services to the poor and the needy is an essential element of any 'reasonable fair and just' procedure. A prisoner who is to seek his liberation through the court's process should have legal services available to him. The right to free legal service is therefore, clearly an essential ingredient of 'reasonable, fair and just' procedure for a person accused of, an offence. It is a fundamental right guaranteed by Article 21 of the Constitution. This is a constitutional right of every accused person who is unable to engage a lawyer and secure legal services, on account of reasons such as poverty, indigence or incommunicado situation, the State is under a mandate to provide a lawyer to such accused person. The State cannot avoid its constitutional obligation to provide speedy trial to the accused by pleading financial or administrative inability. The State is under a constitutional mandate to ensure speedy trial and whatever is necessary for this purpose has to be done by the State.

Probable Viva Questions

1. Explain the facts of the Hussainara Khatoon vs Home Secretary case.

2. What do you understand by 'reasonable, fair and just' procedure?

3. What do you understand by speedy trial ?

4. Is free legal service a fundamental right ? Explain in the context of Constitutional provisions.

5. What was the judgment in the Hussainara Khatoon *vs* Home Secretary case ?

❑❑

PROJECT 3

MANEKA GANDHI *VS* UNION OF INDIA

Fact

Petitioner was a known journalist. The authorities on July 4th 1977 issued a notice of impoundment of the passport to the petitioner citing reasons as in the interest of general public. As soon as the petitioner got the notice of such impound she reverted back to the authorities asking for specific detailed reasons as to why her passport shall be impounded. The authorities however, answered that the reasons were not to be specified in the interest of the general public. The petitioner approached Supreme Court under Article 32 of the Constitution for the enforcement of fundamental right mentioned under article 14 against the arbitrary action of the authorities. The petition was further amended and enforcement of article 21 *i.e.,* Protection of Life & Personal Liberty, article 19(1)(a) *i.e.,* Right to freedom of speech & article 19(1)(g) *i.e.,* Right to freedom of Movement was sought for.

Issue

The most important issue of this case was that the whether the authorities in impounding passport of the petitioner had violated petitioner's fundamental rights like right of personal liberty and right to freedom of speech and movement. Secondly, whether there is any nexus between article 14, 19 and 21.

Conclusion

The procedure established by law need necessarily be just, fair and reasonable. It was held in Satwant Singh case that right to travel abroad is well within the ambit of article 21. Without proper reason, impounding passport of the petitioner is unreasonable and unjust. Thus the fundamental right guaranteed by article 21, of right to liberty, is violated in this case. Moreover article 14, 19 and 21 are interconnected. Everyone should get equality before the law and equal protection of law. Principle of Natural Justice is not separated and exclusive to the Constitution. The respondent contended before the court that the passport was impounded because the petitioner was required to appear before some committee's for enquiry. The Court reject has rejected.

Judgment

The Court in Maneka Gandhi case adopted the dissenting view of Justice Fazal Ali in A.K. Gopalan v. State of Madras. The court held that the while the procedure established by law should be reasonable, just and fair it shall be free from any unreasonableness and arbitrariness. The court held that though the phrase used in article 21 is "procedure established by law" instead of "due process of law" however, the procedure must be free from arbitrariness and irrationality. The court overruled Gopalan case by stating that there is a unique relationship between the provisions of article 14, 19 & 21 and every law must pass the tests of the said provisions. Earlier in Gopalan the majority held that these provisions in itself are mutually exclusive. Therefore, to correct its earlier mistake the court held that these provisions are not mutually exclusive and dependent on each other. The right to travel abroad as held in Satwant Singh is within the scope of guarantees mentioned under article 21. The rights discussed under 19(1)(a) & 19(1)(g) are not confined to the territorial limits of India.

Probable Viva Questions

1. What do you understand by right to liberty ?
2. What do you understand by Procedure Established by Law ?
3. Do you think right to travel outside is a fundamental right covered under article 21 ?
4. Is there any nexus between article 14, 19 and 21 of the Constitution of India ?
5. What was the judgment in the case of Maneka Gandhi *vs* Union of India ?

❏❏

Bibliography

Chapter 1
Theory and Nature of Political Institutions

References and suggested readings

- Aldar John. *Constitutional and Administrative Law.* 6th Ed. Palgrave Macmillan. New York.
- Divya J Moses. "Encroaching the Boundaries of the Doctrine of Separation of Powers". 20 June, 2010. 10 Oct, 2013 <http://www.lawyersclubindia.com>
- Hamilton, Alexander; Madison, James; and Jay, John. *The Federalist.* Edited by Jacob E. Cooke. Middletown, Conn: Wesleyan University Press. 1961.
- Herman Finer. *The Theory and Practice of Modern Government.* Methuen. New York. 1962.
- J. W. Garner. *Political science and Government.* Word press. Calcutta.1952.
- L. S. Rathore, S. A. H. Haqqui. *Political Theory and Organizations.* Eastern Book Company. Lukhnow. 2003.
- Leonard. *Totalitarianism.* The pall Mall Press. London. 1972.
- M.J.C. Vile. *Constitutionalism and the Separation of Powers.* 2nd ed. Indianapolis. Liberty Fund. 1998. Chapter: *FOUR:Montesquieu.. 21 Oct 2013*<http://oll.libertyfund.org/ >
- Marsilius of Padua. *The Defender of Peace.* New York. 1956. trans. with an intro by Alan Gewirth.vol. 1, p. 43.
- Mittal D.P. *NaturalJustice Judicial Review & Administrative Law.* Taxman Allied Services (P.) Ltd. New Delhi.
- O.P. Gauba. *An Introduction of Political Theory.* Macmillan India Limited. New Delhi. 1981.
- P.J. Fitzgeralad. *Salmond on jurisprudence,BookI.*N.M.TripathiPvt Ltd.1966.
- R.M. MacIver. *The Modern State.* Oxford University Press. London. 1962.
- Richard Benwell and Oonagh Gay. "The Separation of Powers –house of common library". 15 August 2013<http://w w w. publications.parliament.uk>.
- Ruth Bader Ginsburg. "Judicial Independence: The Situation of the U.S. Federal Judiciary". 85 *NEB. L. REV.* 2011. < http://digitalcommons.unl.edu>.
- Sathe S.P. *Administrative Law.* 7th Ed. Lexis Nexis. Butterworths. New Delhi.
- Stéphane Beaulac. The Social Power of Bodin's 'Sovereignty' and International Law. *Melbourne Journal of International Law* .Vol 4.
- Takwani C.K. *Lectures on Administrative Law.* 4th Ed. Eastern Law Company. Lucknow.
- Wade and Phillips. 1960
- William Blackstone. *Commentaries on the Laws of England, Book 1: The Rights of Persons, Chapter 2of the Parliament.* (1765-1769).
- William Blackstone. *The English Constitution.* 7th ed. 1984.
- David Thomson (1939). "Review of Alfred Cobban 'Dictatorship: Its History and Theory". *Philosophy.* Volume 14 . Issue 56. October 1939. pp 493-493. The Royal Institute of Philosophy.
- Contrat Social," Bk. III, Ch. 1. Cited in Harold J. Laski. *Authority in the Modern State.* Yale University Press, 1919.Batoche Books. Kitchener, 2000
- Savigny, "System des romischenRechts," vol. I, p. 22.
- Schäffle, Albert.*Bau und Leben des sozialenKörpers* [structure and life of the social body].4 vol. 1875–78. rev. ed. 1896.
- Thomas Hobbes. *Leviathan.* 1651.
- Herbert Spencer.*Principles of Sociology.* Vol.1.New York D. Appleton.1897
- Barry E. Carter & Philip R. Trimble. *International law.* 3 ed.Boston. Little brown. 1999
- Garner, James Wilford. *Introduction to Political Science a Treatise on the Origin, Nature, Functions, and Organization, of the State.* 1910. Reprint. London: Forgotten Books, 2013. 40-1. Print.
- John Mitchelle.*City of Revelation, On the Proportions and Symbolic Numbers on the Cosmic Temple.* page 61, (ISBN – 0-345-23607-6).1972

Websites:

- http://india.gov.in/
- http://indiacode.nic.in/
- http://jurisonline.in/
- http://legalservicesindia.com
- http://oll.libertyfund.org/
- http://www.annenbergclassroom.org/
- http://www.britannia.com/
- http://www.civilserviceindia.com/
- http://www.constitution.org/
- http://www.hardnewsmedia.com
- http://www.india-in-your-home.com
- http://www.parliamentofindia.nic.in/
- http://www.preservearticles.com
- http://www.pucl.org/
- http://www.whitehouse.gov/
- https://www.indiankanoon.org
- https://www.parliament.nsw.gov.au

Chapter 2
Nature and Sources of Law

References and suggested readings:

- Sewell and Debrett, *The Institutes of Hindu Law: or, The Ordinances of Manu.* Calcutta. 1796.
- Locke, John. *Two Treatises of Government.* Ed. Peter Laslett. Cambridge. Cambridge University Press. 1988, 137.
- Catherine MacKinnon *Are Women Human?: And Other International Dialogues.* Cambridge: Harvard Univ. Press, 2006
- "India, being A Common Law Country". 2010. < http://Supremecourtofindia.Nic>
- "Brief   History of Law in India. 2010. <http://www. Barcouncilof india.Org/> .

◆ "Research Guide: Customary Law in India". *Law Library of Congress.* July 2013.<Http:// www.law.gov>

◆ "The Pure Theory as Ideal Type: Defending Kelsen on the basis of Weberian Methodology". Yale University, School of Law.<Http://www.thefreelibrary.com>.

◆ AIR Manual, 31-33,157, 179-180.

◆ *American Realist School of Jurisprudence.* 2012.< http://newindialaw>

◆ Aristotle. On *Rhetoric.* G. A. Kennedy, Trans. Oxford, UK: Oxford University Press. . 1991.

◆ Aristotle. *The Politics.* Trans. E. Barker. (1946) Bk. I. 1252 D.

◆ Austin, John. "The province of jurisprudence determined and the uses of the study of jurisprudence". London. Weidenfeld and Nicolson. 1954.

◆ Austin, John. *Lectures on Jurisprudence and the Philosophy of Positive Law.* St. Clair Shores, MI: Scholarly Press, 1977.

◆ Austin, John. *The Province of Jurisprudence Determined.*Cambridge: Cambridge University Press, 1995.

◆ Black's Law Dictionary. 8th Edition. p. 918.

◆ British History: Middle Ages. "Common Law - Henry Ii and the Birth of a State." *BBC.* 2010. <Http://www.bbc.co.uk>.

◆ Cicero. The *Republic (De Republica).* C.W. Keyes, Trans. and Ed. Loeb Classical Library: London. 1928.

◆ Cardozo, Benjamin.*The Growth of the Law.* Yale University press: New Haven. 1924 : 52.

◆ D.H. Chaudari. *The Hindu Marriage Act 1955.* 3rd ed. 1966: 61.

◆ Davis, F. James. "Law as a type of social contract". *Society and the Law: New Meanings for an Old Profession.* The free press of Glencoe. New York.1962 : 43.

◆ *Delegated legislation.* Oxford dictionary of politics.

◆ Diamond. "The Work of the Law Commission". *Law Teacher.* 10 (1976): 11 at II: Kirby. "Law Reform: Why". ?" *50 Austl. LJ.* 1976: 460.

◆ Finnis, John. "The Truth in Legal Positivism," in Robert P. George, *The Autonomy of Law.* Oxford: Clarendon Press, 1996: 195 214; *Natural Law and Natural Rights.* Oxford: Clarendon Press, 1980: 33,290,351.

◆ Friedman, Lawrance. *American Law: An Introduction.* W.W. Norton and Company. New York. 1984:6.

◆ Friedmann, Wolfgang. *Legal Theory.* Third Indian Reprint. 2003: 95

◆ G.M. Paton. *A Textbook of Jurisprudence.* 3rd ed. pp. 180-181

◆ Gray. *The Nature and Source of the Law.* 2nd Ed. New York, Macmillan. 1924: 84

◆ H.J. Abraham. *The Judicial Process.* 1968: 223

◆ H.L.A. Hart. "Book Review of the Morality of Law". *Harvard Law Review.* 78 (1965): 1281; "Positivism and the Separation of Law and Morals." *Harvard Law Review.* 71 (1958): 593; *Essays on Bentham.* Oxford: Clarendon Press. 1982; *The Concept of Law.* Second Edition. Oxford: India, paper back 2002:91.Originally published 1961 : 26

◆ H.S. Gour's. *Hindu Code.* Volume 1, Fifth Edition.

◆ *Halsbury's Laws of England.* 4th Edn. Vol 44, pp. 981-84.

◆ Hoebel, E. Adamson. *The law of Primitive man, a study of Comparative Legal Dynamics.* Cambridge: Harvard University Press. 1954 : 26, 28,292.

◆ Hobbes, Thomas. Leviathan, Pt. I. Chap 13;

◆ Hobbes, Thomas "Leviathan". The Great Legal Philosophers. Ed. Clarance Morris. Philadelphia. Pennsylvania: University of Pennsylvania Press, 1971. 109-133.

◆ Holmes, Oliver. "The Path of Law". *Harvard Law Review.* 10th march.1897:461

◆ Holland. *The Elements of Jurisprudence.* 13th edn. Indian economy reprint. Universal Law publishing. 2007. Originally published, 1880.

◆ Jacob, Herbert. *Justice in America, courts, lawyers, and the judicial process.* 4th Ed. Boston. Little, Brown. 1984.

◆ Jeremy Bentham. *A Fragment of Government.* Cambridge: Cambridge University Press, 1988; *Of Laws in General.* London: Athlone Press, 1970; *The Principles of Morals and Legislation.* New York: Hafner Press, 1948.

◆ Jeremy M. Miller. "Law's Empire". *Campbell. Rev.* 9 (1986): 203.

◆ Jerome Frank. *Law and the modern mind.* 1930: 46.

◆ K. Olivercrona. *Law as Fact.* 2nd edn. London.1971:51-156; *Legal Language and Reality, from, essays on Honour of Pound.* Newman.edn.1962:151.

◆ Kaul A. K. *A text book of Jurisprudence.* Satyam Law International. New Delhi. 2009

◆ Kenneth Einar Himma. "Natural Law". 2001. *Internet Encyclopedia of Philosophy.* 10th Oct. 2013<http://www.iep.utm.edu/>

◆ Kurup Apoorv. "Tribal Law in India – How Decentralized Administration is Extinguishing Tribal Rights and Why Autonomous Tribal Governments Are Better". *7 Indigenous L.J.* (2008): 71- 95.

◆ Leon Duguit. *Encyclopaedia of State and Law.*<http://www.Law>.

◆ Llewellyn. "The normative, the legal and the law-jobs: the problem of juristic method". *49 Yale LJ.* 1940: 1355.

◆ Locke. *Of Civil Government.* BK, III, CH. IX, sec. 123.

◆ Lon L. Fuller. *The Morality of Law.* Revised Edition. New Haven: Yale University Press, 1964.

◆ Lon L. Fuller. The Case of the Speluncean Explorers in the Supreme Court of Newgarth, 4300. *Harvard law review.* vol. 62. No 4. February 1949. The Harvard Law Review Association. Cambridge, Mass., U.S.A.

◆ Lundstedt. *Legal Thinking Revisited.* Stockholm. 1956.

◆ Malinowski. *Crime and Custom in Savage Society.* Patterson NJ: Littlefield. 1959, originally published in 1926:55

◆ M.P. Jain & S.N. Jain *Principles of Administrative Law.* Lexis Nexis: Butterworth's. Wadhawa Nagpur. 2010.

◆ Mukherjea, J., op. cit., 1951 S.C.R. 747 (973). 670 Practice and Procedure of Parliament.

◆ P. J. Fitzgerald. *Salmond on Jurisprudence,* 1966, 12th Ed. Indian Economy Reprint. Universal Law Publishing Co. Pvt Ltd. New Delhi. 2009.

◆ Price, David E. "Who Makes the Law? Creativity and Power in Senate Committees". Cambridge, MA: Schenkman. 1972.

◆ Raz. *The concept of a legal system.* Oxford, 1970: 1-3

◆ R. Dworkin. *Law's Empire.* Cambridge. Harvard University Press, 1986: 45-73.

◆ R. Cross. *The House of Lords and the Rules of Precedent: Law, Morality and Society.*1977.

◆ R. Dworkin. *Taking Rights Seriously.*(1977: 24-26); Second Indian Reprint. Universal Book Co. Chapters 14 and 15. 1999.

◆ *Recognition of Aboriginal Customary Laws* (ALRC Report 31). 1986. Last modified on 19 July 2012. http://www.alrc.gov.au/-

◆ Roscoe Pound. *Jurisprudence III.* part 5, 83

◆ Ross. E. Adamson. *Social Control.* Macmillan. New York. 1922:106.

◆ Salmond, John. *Jurisprudence.* 9th edition, London, Sweet and Maxwell Limited. 1937: 2010.

◆ Savigny. *System.i.p.*22,35,168.

◆ Sat. Br. 14.4, 2.23; Br. Ar. Up. R, 4, I4, cited Tagore Lect. I880, p. 136.

◆ Tariq Ahmad. Top of Form

◆ *The report of the committee of minister's powers.* pp. 51-53.

◆ Thomas Aquinas. *On Law, Morality and Politics.* Indianapolis: Hackett Publishing Co., 1988; *Summa Theologica, Part I-II (Pars Prima Secundae).* The Complete American Edition. European Graduate School Egs. 1997:20; *Summa Theologiae: A Concise Translation_.* T. Mcdermott, Trans. Allen, Tx: Christian Classics. 1991.

◆ Towseef Ahmad. "Legislation as a source of law: raison d'etre". 2013.

◆ Vago Steven. *Law and Society.* 2nd Ed. Prentice Hall. Englewood Cliffs. New Jersey. 1988:9-11.

- William Blackstone. *Commentaries on the Law of England*. Chicago: The University of Chicago Press, 1979.
- William Ebenstein. "The Pure Theory; the Basic Norm of Law".2004-2007.

Case law:
- Ahmad Khan *v.* Channi Bibi(1925), 52 IA 379, 3834
- Ajai Verma *v.* Vijai Kumari (1939) 41 BOMLR 700).
- Bhimashya & Ors. *v.* Smt. Janabi @ Janawwa, (2006) 13 SCC 627
- Delhi Laws Act, A.I.R. 1951 S.C.
- Devi Das Gopal Krishan *v.* State of Punjab (A.I.R. 1967 S.C. 1895 -1901)
- Dr. Surajmani Stella Kujur *v.* DurgaCharan Hansdah (AIR 2001 SC 938).
- Effuah Amissah *v.* Effuah Krabah (AIR 1936 P.C. 147)
- Gwalior Rayon Mills Mfg. (Wvg.) Co. Ltd. *v.* Assistant Commissioner of Sales Tax, (A.I.R. 1974S. C)
- Hari Shankar Bagla *v.* State of Madhya Pradesh (1955 S.C.R. 380 SC)
- Hitendra Vishnu Thakur and Ors. etc. ect. *v.* State of Maharashtra and Ors. (1994) 4 SCC 602.
- *Krishna Kumar v. UOI 1990 (4) SCC 207 at 226-27*
- Laxmibai (Dead) Thru Lr'S. & Anr *v.* Bhagwanthbuva (Dead) Thru Lr'S. 2013
- M.C. Mehta *v.* Union of India and Ors. (8 SCC. 1996. 462)
- M/s. Tata Iron and Steel Co. Ltd. *v.* Workmen of M/s. Tata Iron and Steel Co. Ltd., (A.I.R. 1972 S.C. 1917)
- Maharashtra State Board *v.* Paritosh Bhupesh Kumar Shethetc (1985 SCR (1) 29.)
- Mookka Kone *v.* Ammakutti Ammal (AIR 1928 Mad 299 (FB))
- Municipal Corporation of Delhi *v.* Birla Cotton Spinning and Weaving Mills, Delhi, (A.I.R. 1968 S.C. 1232)
- Paul Wilson & Co. A/S *v.* Partenreederei Hannah Blumenthal (1983) 1 AC 854 (873).
- Raj Narain Singh *v.* Chairman, Patna Administration Committee (1955 S.C.R. 290 SC)
- Edward Mills Co. *v.* State of Ajmer (1955 S.C.R. 735 SC).
- Rylands *v.* Fletcher (1868), L.R. 3 H.L. 330.
- Salekh Chand (Dead) thr. Lrs. *v.* Satya Gupta & Ors. (2008) 13 SCC 119.
- Smt. Ass Kaur (Deceased) By L.Rs *v.* Kartar Singh (Dead) By L.Rs. & Ors (AIR 2007 2369-para 9,10,11)
- T. SaraswatiAmmal *v.* Jagadambal & Anr. (AIR 1953 SC 201)
- Ujagar Singh *v.* Mst. Jeo (AIR 1959 SC 1041)
- R.B.S.S. Munnalal and Others *v.* S.S. Rajkumar and Others [AIR 1962 SC 1493
- Siromani *v.* Hemkumar & Ors. (AIR 1968 SC 1299)
- *Vishaka v.* State of Rajasthan (1997) 6 SCC 241.
- Walworth *v.* Holt, 4 My. And Cr. 635 3 Table Talk, tit. 'Equity.'
- *Paul Wilson & Co. A/S v. Partenreederei Hannah Blumenthal*, (1983) 1 AC 854 (873)
- *Krishna Kumar v. UOI 1990 (4) SCC 207 at 226-27.*
- Union of India and Others *v.* Dhanwanti Devi and Others [(1996) 6 SCC 44]
- *M.C. Mehta v. Union of India 1988 AIR 1115*

Websites:
- http://www.lawweb.in/2013/06/
- http://www preservearticles.com
- http://www.mightylaws.in
- http://www.britannica.com
- http://upscportal.com/
- http://www.legalserviceindia.com
- http://www.lawnotes.in/natural_Law
- http://www.dailykashmirimages.com/
- http://www.ebc-india.com
- http://indiankanoon.org/
- http://www.indiacourts.in
- http://ncm.nic.in/ncm_manual.pdf.

Annexure A

REPORTS SUBMITTED BY LAW COMMISSION OF INDIA AFTER INDEPENDENCE (1955-2012)

First Law Commission – **Chairman–Mr. M. C. Setalvad (1955-1958)**

1	Liability of the State in Torts.	1956
2	Parliamentary Legislation relating to Sales Tax.	1956
3	Limitation Act, 1908	1956
4	On the proposal that High Courts should sit in Benches at different places in a State.	1956
5	British Statutes applicable to India.	1957
6	Registration Act, 1908	1957
7	Partnership Act, 1932	1957
8	Sale of Goods Act, 1930	1958
9	Specific Relief Act, 1877	1958
10	Law of Acquisition and Requisitioning of Land.	1958
11	Negotiable Instruments Act, 1881	1958
12	Income Tax Act, 1922	1958
13	Contract Act, 1872	1958
14	Reform of Judicial Administration.	1958

Second Law Commission–Chairman–Mr. Justice T. L. Venkatrama Aiyyar (1958-1961)

15	Law relating to Marriage and Divorce amongst Christians in India.	1960
16	Official Trustees Act, 1913.	1960
17	Report on Trusts Act, 1882.	1961
18	Converts' Marriage Dissolution Act, 1866.	1961
19	The Administrator-General's Act, 1913.	1961
20	The Law of Hire-Purchase	1961
21	Marine Insurance	1961
22	Christian Marriage and Matrimonial Causes Bill, 1961	1961

Third Law Commission–Chairman–Mr. Justice J. L. Kapur (1961-1964)

23	Law of Foreign Marriages.	1962
24	The Commission of Inquiry Act, 1952	1962
25	Evidence of Officers about forged stamps, currency notes, etc. Section 509-A Cr.P.C. as proposed.	1963
26	Insolvency Laws	1964
27	The Code of Civil Procedure, 1908.	1964
28	The Indian Oaths Act, 1873.	1964

Fourth Law Commission–Chairman–Mr. Justice J. L. Kapur (1964-1968)

29	Proposal to include certain Social and Economic Offences in the Indian Penal Code	1966
30	Section 5 of the Central Sales Tax Act, 1956, taxation by the States of Sales in the course of import.	1967
31	Section 30 (2) of the Indian Registration Act, 1908-Extension to Delhi.	1967
32	Section 9 of the Code of Criminal Procedure, 1898-Appointment of Sessions Judges, Additional Session Judges and Assistant Sessions Judges.	1967
33	Section 44, Code of Criminal Procedure, 1898.	1967
34	Indian Registration Act, 1908.	1967
35	Capital Punishment.	1967
36	Sections 497, 498 and 499 of the Code of Criminal Procedure, 1898-Grant of bail with condition.	1967
37	The Code of Criminal Procedure, 1898 (Sections 1 to 176).	1967
38	Indian Post Office Act, 1898.	1968

Fifth Law Commission–Chairman–Mr. K. V. K. Sundaram (1968-1971)

39	Punishment of imprisonment for life under the Indian Penal Code.	1968
40	Law relating to attendance of Prisoners in Courts.	1969
41	The Code of Criminal Procedure, 1898.	1969
42	Indian Penal Code.	1971
43	Offences against the National Security.	1971
44	The Appellate jurisdiction of the Supreme Court in Civil Matters.	1971

Sixth Law Commission–Chairman–Mr. Justice Dr. P. B. Gajendragadkar (1971-1974)

45	Civil Appeals to the Supreme Court on a Certificate of Fitness.	1971
46	The Constitution (Twenty-fifth Amendment) Bill, 1971.	1971
47	The Trial and Punishment of Social and Economic Offences.	1972
48	Some questions under the Code of Criminal Procedure Bill, 1970.	1972
49	The Proposal for inclusion of agricultural income in the total income for the purpose of determining the rate of tax under the Income-tax Act, 1961.	1972
50	The Proposal to include persons connected with Public examination within the definition of "Public Servant" in the Indian Penal Code.	1972
51	Compensation for injuries caused by automobiles in hit-and-run cases.	1972
52	Estate Duty on Property acquired after death.	1972
53	Effect of the Pensions Act, 1871 on the right to sue for pensions of retired members of the public services.	1972
54	The Code of Civil Procedure, 1908.	1973
55	Rate of interest after decree and interest on costs under sections 34 and 35, of the Code of Civil Procedure, 1908.	1973
56	Statutory Provisions as to Notice of suit other than section 80, Civil Procedure Code.	1973
57	Benami Transactions.	1973
58	Structure and Jurisdiction of the Higher Judiciary.	1974
59	Hindu Marriage Act, 1955 and Special Marriage Act, 1954.	1974
60	The General Clauses Act, 1897.	1974
61	Certain problems connected with power of the States to levy a tax on the sale of goods and with the Central Sales Tax Act, 1956.	1974

Seventh Law Commission–Chairman–Mr. Justice Dr. P. B. Gajendragadkar (1974-1977)

62	Workmen's Compensation Act, 1923.	1974
63	The Interest Act, 1839.	1975
64	The Suppression of Immoral Traffic in Women and Girls Act, 1956.	1975
65	Recognition of Foreign Divorces	1976
66	Married Women's Property Act, 1874.	1976
67	The Indian Stamp Act, 1899.	1977
68	The Powers of Attorney Act, 1882	1977
69	The Indian Evidence Act, 1872.	1977
70	The Transfer of Property Act, 1882.	1977

Eighth Law Commission–Chairman–Mr. Justice H. R. Khanna (1977-1979)

71	The Hindu Marriage Act, 1955- Irretrievable breakdown of marriage as a ground of divorce.	1978
72	Restriction on practice after being a permanent Judge, Article 220 of the Constitution.	1978

73 Criminal liability for failure by Husband to pay maintenance or permanent alimony granted to the wife By the court under certain enactments or rules of law.   1978

74 Proposal to amend the Indian Evidence Act, 1872 so as to render Admissible certain statements made by witnesses before Commission of Inquiry and other statutory authorities.   1978

75 Disciplinary Jurisdiction under the Advocates Act, 1961.   1978

76 Arbitration Act, 1940.   1978

77 Delay and arrears in trial courts.   1979

78 Congestion of under trial prisoners in jails.   1979

79 Delay and Arrears in High Courts and other Appellate Courts.   1979

80 Method of Appointment of Judges.   1979

Ninth Law Commission--Chairman–Mr. Justice P. V. Dixit (1979-1980)

81 Hindu Widows Re-marriage Act, 1856.   1979

82 Effect of nomination under section 39, Insurance Act, 1938.   1980

83 The Guardians and Wards Act, 1890 and certain provisions of the Hindu Minority and Guardianship Act, 1956.   1980

84 Rape and allied offences-some questions of substantive law, procedure and evidence.   1980

85 Claims for compensation under Chapter 8 of the Motor Vehicles Act, 1939.   1980

86 The Partition Act, 1893.   1980

87 Identification of Prisoners Act, 1920.   1980

Tenth Law Commission–Chairman–Mr. Justice K. K. Mathew (1981-1985)

88 Governmental Privilege in Evidence: Sections 123-124 and 162, Indian Evidence Act, 1872 and Articles 74 and 163 of the Constitution.   1983

89 The Limitation Act, 1963.   1983

90 The Grounds of Divorce amongst Christians in India: section 10, of the Indian Divorce Act, 1869.   1983

91 Dowry deaths and law reform: Amending the Hindu Marriage Act, 1955, the Indian Penal Code, 1860 and the Indian Evidence Act, 1872.   1983

92 Damages in applications for Judicial Review Recommendations for legislation.   1983

93 Disclosure of sources of information by mass media.   1983

94 Evidence obtained illegally or improperly: proposed section 166A, Indian Evidence Act, 1872.   1983

95 Constitutional Division within the Supreme Court- A proposal for.   1984

96 Repeal of certain obsolete Central Acts.   1984

97 Section 28, Indian Contract Act, 1872: prescriptive clauses in contracts.   1984

98 Sections 24 to 26, Hindu Marriage Act, 1955: Orders for interim maintenance and orders for the maintenance of children in matrimonial proceedings.   1984

99 Oral and written arguments in the Higher courts.   1984

100 Litigation by and against the Government: some recommendations for reform.   1984

101 Freedom of Speech and Expression under Article 19 of the Constitution: recommendation to extend it to Indian Corporations.   1984

102 Section 122(1) of the Code of Criminal Procedure, 1973: imprisonment for breach of bond for keeping the peace with sureties.   1984

103 Unfair Terms in Contract.   1984

104 The Judicial Officers' Protection Act, 1850.   1984

105 Quality Control and Inspection of consumer goods.   1984

106 Section 103A, Motor Vehicles Act, 1939: effect of Transfer of a Motor Vehicle on Insurance.   1984

107 Law of Citizenship.   1984

108 Promissory Estoppel.   1984

109 Obscene and Indecent advertisements and displays: sections 292-293, Indian Penal Code.   1985

110 The Indian Succession Act, 1925.   1985

111 The Fatal Accidents Act, 1855.   1985

112 Section 45 of the Insurance Act, 1938.   1985

113 Injuries in Police Custody- Suggested section 114B, Evidence Act.   1985

Eleventh Law Commission–Chairman–Mr. Justice D. A. Desai (1985-1988)

114 Gram Nyayalaya.   1986

115 Tax Courts.   1986

116 Formation of an All India Judicial Service.   1986

117 Training of Judicial Officers.   1986

118 Method of appointment to subordinate courts/ subordinate judiciary.   1986

119 Access to Exclusive Forum for Victims of Motor Accidents under Motor Vehicles Act, 1939.   1987

120 Manpower Planning in Judiciary: A Blueprint   1987

121 A New Forum for Judicial Appointments.   1987

122 Forum for National Uniformity in Labour Adjudication.   1987

123 Decentralisation of Administration of Justice : Disputes Involving Centres of Higher Education.   1988

171 The Biodiversity Bill, 2000   2000
172 Review of Rape Laws   2000
173 Prevention of Terrorism Bill, 2000   2000
174 Property Rights of Women: Proposed Reforms Under the Hindu Law   2000

Sixteenth Law Commission–Chairman–Mr. Justice B. P. Jeevan Reddy (2000-2001)

and Mr. Justice M. Jagannadha Rao (2002-2003)

175 The Foreigners (Amendment) Bill, 2000   2000
176 The Arbitration and conciliation (Amendment) Bill, 2002   2001
177 Law Relating to Arrest   2001
178 Recommendations for amending various enactments, both civil and criminal   2001
179 Public Interest Disclosure and Protection of Informers   2001
180 Article 20 (3) of the Constitution of India and Right to Silence   2002
181 Amendment to Section 106 of the Transfer of Property Act, 1882   2002
182 Amendment of Section 6 of the Land Acquisition Act, 1894.   2002
183 A Continuum on the General Clauses Act, 1897 with special reference to the admissibility and codification of external aids to   2002
     interpretation of statutes.
184 Legal Education & Professional Training and Proposals for amendments to the Advocates Act, 1961 and the University Grants   2002
     Commission Act, 1956.
185 Review of the Indian Evidence Act, 1872.   2003

Seventeenth Law Commission–Chairman–Mr. Justice M. Jagannadha Rao (2003-2006)

186 Proposal to Constitute Environment Courts   2003
187 Mode of Execution of Death Sentence and Incidental Matters   2003
188 The Proposals for Constitution of Hi-Tech Fast - Track Commercial Divisions in High Courts.   2003
189 Revision of Court Fees Structure   2004
190 The Revision of the Insurance Act, 1938 and the Insurance Regulatory and Development Authority Act, 1999   2004
191 Regulation of Funds collected for Calamity Relief.   2004
192 Prevention of vexatious litigation.   2005
193 Transnational Litigation, Conflict of Laws, Law of Limitation.   2005
194 Verification of Stamp Duties and registration of Arbitral Awards.   2005
195 The Judges (Inquiry) Bill, 2005   2006
196 Medical Treatment to Terminally Ill Patients (Protection of Patients and Medical Practitioners)   2006
197 Public Prosecutor's Appointments.   2006
198 Witness Identity Protection and Witness Protection Programmes   2006
199 Unfair (Procedural and Substancive) Terms in Contracts   2006
200 Trial by Media: Free Speech v. Fair Trial Under Criminal Procedure (Amendments to the Contempt of Court Act, 1971)   2006
201 Medical Treatment after Accidents and During Emergency Medical Condition and Women in Labour   2006

Eighteenth Law Commission–Chairman–Dr. Justice A. R. Lakshmanan (2007-2009)

202 Proposal to Amend Section 304-B of the Indian Penal Code   2007
203 Section 438 of the Code of Criminal Procedure, 1973 as Amended by the Code of Criminal Procedure (Amendment) Act, 2005   2007
     (Anticipatory Bail)
204 Proposal to Amend the Hindu Succession Act, 1956 as amended by Act 39 of 2005.   2008
205 Proposal to Amend the Prohibition of Child Marriage Act, 2006 and other allied laws.   2008
206 Proposal for enactment of new Coroners Act applicable to the whole of India   2008
207 Proposal to amend Section 15 of the Hindu Succession Act, 1956 in case a female dies intestate leaving her self acquired property   2008
     with no heirs.
208 Proposal for amendment of Explanation to Section 6 of the Hindu Succession Act, 1956 to include oral partition and family   2008
     arrangement in the definition of "partition"
209 Proposal for omission of Section 213 from the Indian Succession Act, 1925   2008
210 Humanization and Decriminalization of Attempt to Suicide.   2008
211 Laws on Registration of Marriage and Divorce –A Proposal for Consolidation and Reform.   2008
212 Laws of Civil Marriages in India – A Proposal to Resolve Certain Conflicts   2008
213 Fast Track Magisterial Courts for Dishonoured Cheque Cases   2008
214 Proposal for reconsideration of Judges cases I, II and III - SP GUPTA v. UOI   2008
215 L . Chandra Kumar be revisited by Larger bench of Supreme Court of India   2008
216 Non-Feasibility of Introduction of Hindi as Compulsory Language in the Supreme Court of India   2008
217 Irretrievable Breakdown of Marriage - Another Ground for Divorce.   2009
218 Need to accede to the Hague Convention on the Civil Aspects of International Child Abduction (1980).   2009
219 Need for Family Law Legislations for Non-resident Indians.   2009
220 Need to fix Maximum Chargeable Court-fees in Subordinate Civil Courts.   2009

Nineteenth Law Commission–Chairman–Mr. Justice P. V. Reddi, 2009-2012)

Twentieth Law Commission–Chairman–Mr. Justice D. K. Jain (25.01.2013 - 05.10.2013)

Source: http://www.lawcommissionofindia.nic.in/

Chapter 3
Historical Evolution of Indian Legal System

References and suggested readings:

◆ "Evolution of Law: A short history of Indian legal Theory". <http://www.legalindia.in>

◆ "Hierarchy of Courts". <http://www.hrdiap.gov.in>.

◆ D.D. Basu. *Commentary on Constitution of India.* 8th ed.Lexis Nexis. Butterworth Wadhwa, Nagpur.2011.

◆ Dayanand, Navoneel. "Overview of Legal Systems in the Asia-Pacific Region: India" *Overview of Legal Systems in the Asia-Pacific Region (2004).* Paper 1.

◆ Cornell Law Library. 2004. <http://scholarship.law.cornell.edu/>

◆ Dhavan S.S. "The Indian Judicial System: A Historical Survey". http://www.allahabadhighcourt.in/event/TheIndianJudicialSystem_SSDhavan.pdf.

◆ Ibn Battuta's.*Travels in Asia and Africa.* George Routledge. London 1929:194

◆ John F. Riddick. *The History of British India: A Chronology.*

◆ KamakhiyaNarainTiwary. "Modern Indian Legal System and Principles- Ancient Indian Antecedents". *Think India Quarterly Journal.*Vol 15.

◆ *KautilyaArthashastra.* Translated by R. Shamasastry, Bangalore Government Press 1915.

◆ M.P. Singh. *Outlines of Indian Legal & Constitutional History.* 8th ed. Universal Law Publishing Co. New Delhi. 2010.

◆ *Modern History Sourcebook: India: Regulating Act, 1773* http://www.fordham.edu/halsall/mod/1773indiaact.asp

◆ Muhammad Basheer Ahmad. *The Administration of Justice in Medieval India:A Study in Outline of the Judicial System Under the Sultans and the Badshahs of Delhi Based Mainly Upon Cases Decided by Medieval Courts in India Between 1206-1750 A.D.* The Aligarh Historical Research Institute. The Aligarh University, 1941, Law Journal Press, Allahabad.

◆ Muller, Max(ed). *Brihaspatismriti.* 33 (1906):387.

◆ *Readings in the sociology of the professions.* Edited by sheokumarlal. Gyan Publishing House (September 8, 1988).

◆ Constituent assembly debates (proceedings)-(9th December, 1946 to 24th January, 1950.) <(http://parliamentofindia.nic.in>.

◆ Sharma B.K. *Introduction to the Constitution of India.* 3rd ed. Prentice hall of India. New Delhi. 2005

◆ *The Laws of Manu.* Translated by George Buchler. Sacred Books of the East, Volume 25.

◆ U. B. Singh .*Administrative System in India: Vedic Age to 1947.* APH, 1998

◆ Varadachariar,S. *The Hindu Judicial System.* Lucknow University. Lucknow. 1964:88.

◆ Shivaraj S. Huchhanavar.*The Legal system in ancient India.* 2012. <http://www.legalservicesindia. com>

◆ Justice Markandey Katju. "Ancient Indian Jurisprudence". Speech delivered on 27.11.2010 at Banaras Hindu University, Varanasi.

◆ *Summary on Kautilya's Arthashastra: Its Contemporary Relevance.* Indian Merchants' Chamber. (2004)

- Mirat I, p. (133, 168, 307, 321, 335) and Mirat Supp., 145,149,150
- Ain I, Blochman, page 270
- Ain II, Jarrett, pp. 43, 45, 47, 49
- Storia I, p. 68.
- Dr. R. K. Lahri . "What are Puranas? Are they Myths?". <http://www.boloji.com/>
- Sri Swami Sivananda. *All about Hinduism*. A Divine Life Society Publication. Uttar Pradesh: India. 6th ed 1997. Originally published in 1947.
- J. Donald Walters.*The Hindu Way of Awakening: Its Revelations, Its Symbols – An Essential View of Religion*. Jaico Publishing House. 1999.
- Friedlmeier, Chakkarath, Schwarz. *Culture and Human Development*. Psychology Press. 2005.
- Kriyananda, Swami. *The Hindu Way of Awakening*. Crystal Clarity Publishers. 1998
- Rama, Swami. *Perennial Psychology of Bhagavad Gita*. Himalayan Institute Press. 1985.
- Sen, R.K. and Basu, R.L. *Economics in Arthasastra*. New Delhi: Deep & Deep Publications. 2006
- **Dyanesh Kumar**. "The two highest officials of Central Administration were the 'Vakil' and the 'Wazir' (India)". 5 Aug. 2014.<http://www.preservearticles.com>
- BM Gandhi.*VD Kulshestra's Landmarks in Indian Legal and Constitutional History*. 10th Edition. 2012.

- *John Keay India : A History*
- *New York : Grove Press Books. 2000.*

Websites:
- *http://www.legalindia.in*
- *http://www .lawmin.nic.in/*
- *http://www.hrdiap.gov.in*
- *http://parliamentofind*ia.nic.in
- www.barcouncilofindia.org
- http://www.indianetzone.com/
- http://nammachennai.in/a
- http://www.boddunan.com
- http://dialogue.hubpages.com/
- http://lex-warrier.in/
- http://www.indohistory.com
- http://www.boloji.com/
- http://scholarship.law.cornell.edu/
- http://archive.org/
- http://supremecourtofindia.nic.in/
- http://indianscriptures.50webs.com
- www.dlshq.org/
- http://www.gktoday.in/government-of-india-act-1935/
- http://parliamentofindia.nic.in/ls/debates/facts.htm

Chapter 4
Civil and Criminal Courts and Process

References and suggested readings:

- Ashutosh. *Rights of Accused*. Universal Law Publishing Co. Pvt. Ltd. New Delhi. 2009
- C.K. Takwani. *Civil Procedure*. 7 ed. Eastern Book Co. 1997.
- *Central Administrative Tribunal (CAT)*. 20th may, 2014 <http://cgat.gov.in>
- *Central Govt. Industrial Tribunal cum Labour Courts*. Ministry of labour and employment, government of India.22nd June, 2014 <http://labour.nic.in>
- Dr. Hans Gross. Criminal investigation. 5th ed. Universal Law Publishing Co. Pvt.Ltd. New Delhi. 2002.
- D.D. Basu. *Shorter Constitution of India*. 13th ed. Wadhwa and Co. Publishers. Agra. 2004.
- Justice A. P. Subba. "Historical Perspective of the Sikkim Judiciary". 24th May, 2014 <http://www.highcourtofsikkim.nic.in/hc_profile.htm>.Lucknow. 2008.
- Madan Lal Sharma. "The role and function of prosecution in Criminal justice". *Resource material series no. 53*. 2nd June, 2014 <*http://www.unafei.or.jp*>
- Om Prakash. "Constitutional Remedies". *Orissa Review*. Jan 2007.
- Pillai, *K. N. Chandrasekhara. R. v. Kelkar's Criminal Procedure*. Eastern Book Company.
- Singh, M. P. *v. N. Shukla's Constitution of India*. Eastern Book Company. Lucknow. 2012.
- Takwani, *C. K. Civil Procedure*. Eastern Book Company. Lucknow. 2009.

Websites:
- < *http://www.unafei.or.jp*>
- <http://cgat.gov.in>
- <http://indiankanoon.org>
- <http://labour.nic.in>
- <http://www.helplinelaw.com/docs/>
- <http://www.silf.org.in>

- <http://www.lawzonline.com/>
- <http://www.keralaw.com/judgments>
- <http://www.advocatekhoj.com/>
- *District Courts* of India - Indian Courts. <http://indiancourts.nic.in/districtcourt.html>
- Gauhati High Court.<http://ghconline.gov.in/>
- High Court of Bombay .<http://bombayhighcourt.nic.in/ history. php#>
- High Court of Calcutta. <http://calcuttahighcourt.nic.in/ history .htm>
- High Court of Jammu & Kashmir. <http://jkhighcourt.nic.in/ history.html>
- High Court of Kerala. <http://highcourtofkerala.nic.in/ history. html>
- High Court of Punjab and Haryana. <http://highcourtchd.gov.in/>
- Judgement- supreme court of India. <supremecourtofindia.nic.in/ outtoday/wr68.pdf>
- Jurisdiction-Delhi High Court. < http://highcourt.nic.in/.../ Court Rules>
- Madras High Court. <http://www.hcmadras.tn.nic.in/>
- State-high-courts-of India. <http://www.preservearticles.com>
- The High Court of Judicature at Patna.< http://patnahighcourt. bih.nic.in/>
- Case status: disposed and pending cases-case status. Supreme Court of India. http:// courtnic.nic.in/ courtnicsc.asp
- All India Reporters, 2012, 2011, 2010, 2009. All India Reporter Pvt. Ltd. Wadhwa Publishers. Nagpur. <>

Acts :
- Civil procedure code, 1908
- Criminal procedure code 1973 with latest amendments.
- Evidence act, 1872
- Indian penal code, 1860
- The Police Act, 1861

Chapter 5
Family Justice System

References and suggested readings:

◆ Applied Nutrition Programme. National Institute Of Health and Family Welfare. http:// Nihfw.Nic.In/.

◆ Banerjee, Gooroodass. *Tagore Law Lectures: the Hindu law of marriage and stridhan.* Thackers edition.1879.

◆ Derrett.*Religion, Law and State in India.*Faber and Faber.1968pp. 274-320.

◆ DiFonzo, James Herbie. "Customized Marriage". Indiana Law Journal: 75: 3(2000) http://www. repository.law.indiana.edu/

◆ Dr. Savita Bhakhry. "Children in India and their Rights". National Human Rights Commission.2006.

◆ Ernest Havemann Marlene Lehtinen. *Marriage & Families New Problems,New Opportunities.*Prentice Hall, Englewood cliffs, New Jersey.1986.

◆ Ethel Klein, Jacquelyn Campbell, Estasoler Marrisa Ghez. *Ending domestic violence Changing Public Perceptions/Halting the epidemic.* Sage Publications. 1997.

◆ Five Year Plans. Planning Commission Government of India. Http://planningcommission.nic.in/

◆ Flavia. *Family Law.* Vol. 2. New Delhi: Oxford UP. 2011.

◆ Mark Galanter. "The Displacement of Traditional Law in Modern India".*Journal of social issues. 24:4(1968)*

◆ Herma Hill Kay. "A Family Court. The California Proposal". *56 Cal. L. Rev. 1205. 1969.* http:// scholarship.law.berkeley.edu/.

◆ Hyde V. Hyde and Woodmansee.[L.R.] 1 P. & D. 130. http://www.uniset.ca/

◆ Johannes JŸtting and Christian Morrisson. "Culture, Gender and Growth". *Policy Insights.* 15. OECD. 2005.

◆ Kapadia, K. M. *Marriage and family in India.* Calcutta, India: Oxford University Press. 1982.

◆ Law commission of India. "Proposal to amend the prohibition of child marriage act, 2006 and other allied laws". Report no. 205. Government of India. February 2008.

◆ Marc Galanter and jayanth Krishnan. "Religious Conflict a Comparison of India and Israel". *Religion and Personal Law in Secular India: A Call to Judgment.* Edited by Gerald James Larson. Indiana University Press. Bloomington and Indianapolis.2001.

◆ Molly Kalafut. Marriage History around the World.2005. http://molly.kalafut.org/

◆ Paras Deewan. *Hindu law.* Orient Publishing Company. 2007.

◆ Reeta Sonawat. "Understanding Families in India: A Reflection of Societal Changes". *Psicologia: Teoria e Pesquisa Mai-Ago 2001, Vol. 17 n. 2, pp. 177-186.*

◆ Sheshadari. S and Rao .N. *Parenting the art and science of nurturing.* Byword Books Private Limited. 2012.

◆ Sriram, R. Family studies in India: Appraisal and new directions. 1993. In T. S. Saraswati & B. Kaur (Eds.). *Human development and family studies in India: An agenda for research and policy* New Delhi, India: Sage Publishers. 122-128.

◆ Tahir Mahmood. *The Muslim Law of India.* 3rd Edition. LexisNexis. Butterworths. 2002.

◆ Williams, Rina Verna.Postcolonial Politics and Personal Laws: Colonial Legal legacies and the Indian State. New York: Oxford University Press. 2006.

◆ Skinner v Orde and others (North-West Provinces) [1871] UKPC 66 (20 December 1871). The Judicial Committee of the Privy Council decisions.Http://www.bailii.org/uk/cases/UKPC/1871/1871_66.html.

◆ H.K.saharay. *Family law in India.* Eastern Law House.kolkata.2011.

◆ Aquil Ahmad. Mohammedan law.21st edn. Edited by I.A.Khan. Law publishers. 2004.

◆ Jaising, Indira, and Monica Sakhrani. *Law of Domestic Violence: A User's Manual for Women.* New Delhi: Universal Law Pub., 2007.

Websites:

◆ http://mhrd.gov.in/rte

◆ http://ncw.nic.in/

◆ http://wcd.nic.in/.

◆ http://www.ilo.org/

◆ http://www.who.int/.

◆ http://doj.gov.in/s

◆ http://islam.about.com/

◆ http://www.criticaltwenties.in/

◆ http://districtcourtsnamchi.nic.in/

◆ http://delhifamilycourts.gov.in/history.html

◆ http://www.archive.india.gov in/

◆ http://www.wisegeek.com/

◆ http://www.advocatekhoj.com/library/bareacts/parsimarriage/schedule.phyp

◆ http://www.legalindia.in/

◆ http://www.infoplease.com/

◆ http://indiacode.nic.in/

◆ http://www.indiankanoon.org/

◆ http://www.businessgyan.com/b/hindu_ancestral_property

◆ http://wrcaselaw.wordpress.com

◆ www.religionfacts.com/islam/sects/**shia**.htm

◆ http://www.al-islam.org/inquiries

◆ http://www.delhi.gov.in

◆ http://pib.nic.in/newsite